A SOUTH DIVIDED

A SOUTH

PORTRAITS OF DISSENT IN THE CONFEDERACY

DIVIDED

DAVID C. DOWNING

David C Downing

CUMBERLAND HOUSE

NASHVILLE, TENNESSEE

A SOUTH DIVIDED
PUBLISHED BY CUMBERLAND HOUSE PUBLISHING
431 Harding Industrial Dr.
Nashville, Tennessee 37211

Cover design by Gore Studio, Inc., Nashville, Tennessee

Library of Congress Cataloging-in-Publication Data
Downing, David C.
   A South divided : portraits of dissent in the Confederacy / David C. Downing.
       p. cm.
   Includes bibliographical references.
   ISBN-13: 978-1-58182-587-9 (hardcover : alk. paper)
   ISBN-10: 1-58182-587-0 (hardcover : alk. paper)
   1. Dissenters—Confederate States of America—History. 2. Dissenters—United States—History—Civil War, 1861–1865. 3. Confederate States of America—Politics and government. 4. Confederate States of America—Social conditions. 5. Political culture—Confederate States of America. 6. United States Army—Southern unionists. 7. Unionists (United States Civil War) 8. United States—History—Civil War, 1861–1865—Social aspects. 9. United States—History—Civil War, 1861–1865—Participation, African American. I. Title.
E487.D64 2007
973.7'17—dc22   2006100135

Printed in the United States of America

1 2 3 4 5 6 7 8 9 10—10 09 08 07

For my brothers
Jon, Jim, Joe, and Don

CONTENTS

ACKNOWLEDGMENTS

I WOULD like to express my gratitude first to the many local and regional historians who assisted my on-site research for this project during the summer of 2003. I am especially indebted to Deborah Wright, an archivist at the Avery Research Institute at the College of Charleston; to Benjamin Campbell of Richmond, Virginia; to the members of the Savannah Historical Society; to Michael C. Hardy of Crossmore, North Carolina; to Professor Allen W. Ellis of Northern Kentucky University; and to my uncle, Donald Downing, for supplying me with archival materials on the guerrilla war in northeastern Missouri.

I would also like to express my thanks to acquisitions editor Stacie Bauerle and editor Ed Curtis at Cumberland House and to my agent, Giles Anderson, for their efficiency and professionalism in seeing this project through the publication process. Thank you as well to the research librarians at Elizabethtown College and Gettysburg College and to my resourceful student assistants, Leslie Stillings, Allyson Dawson, and Lauren Defont.

I am grateful to a number of scholars in American history for their helpful suggestions and corrections on working drafts of A South Divided. Thanks especially to David Brown and Thomas Winpenny at Elizabethtown College and to John Fea at Messiah College. Thank you as well to my colleagues in the English department, Carmine Sarracino and Kevin Scott, and to other consulting readers, including Jerry Graham, Judy Morley, and Camille Bzdek.

I am fortunate to have an informal Civil War roundtable among members of my family, and I am thankful for suggestions from my wife, Crystal, and my brothers Jim and Joe. I am especially grateful to my twin brother, Don, for providing additional research materials as well as in-depth editorial advice. Don's assistance was especially valuable in providing narrative shape and descriptive detail for chapter 7, "'The Wolf Has Come': The Battle for Indian Territory."

INTRODUCTION

I N HIS MEMOIR OF the Civil War, Gen. Grenville Dodge mentions, almost casually, that the headquarters escort during William T. Sherman's March to the Sea was the "First Alabama Cavalry, U.S.A."[1] First Alabama Cavalry, *U.S.A.?* At first glance, it looks like misprint. How could a regiment of Alabamians, one thousand strong, be riding in a place of honor with one of the Union's most formidable armies? Were there that many soldiers in Alabama willing to help cut a broad path of destruction through their sister state of Georgia? Willing, if need be, to fight against fellow Alabamians?

The answer is yes. During the war there were more than two thousand troopers from the Deep South who served in the First Alabama Cavalry (USA). These were among the more than one hundred thousand white Southerners who served in the Federal army and navy during the Civil War.[2]

Overall, the Confederate war effort was a showcase of solidarity, boldness, and determination. In physical resources, the seceding states were at a severe disadvantage. They had less than half the population of those remaining in the Union, one-sixth the financial reserves, and one-ninth the industrial capacity. But what the Confederates lacked in material might, they made up for in spirit. Visiting Louisiana in 1861, Bostonian George Ticknor was deeply impressed by the fierce resolve he saw all around him: "There is no division among the people here. There is but one mind, one heart, one action. . . . Every night the men are drilling. Young and old, professional men and laborers, lawyers, doctors, and even the ministers are all drilling. The ladies hold fairs, make clothes for the army, and animate the men by appeals to their chivalry and their patriotism to resist the enemy to the death. What is seen in New Orleans pervades the whole South. Never were a people more united or more determined."[3]

At about the same time, another Northerner in Louisiana, William Tecumseh Sherman, had a very different reaction to the onrush of war. Serving as superintendent of the Louisiana State Military Academy, the Ohio-born

Sherman warned one of his colleagues, a Virginian: "You people of the South don't know what you are doing. This country will be drenched in blood, and God only knows how it will end. It is folly, madness, a crime against civilization! You people speak so lightly of war; you don't know what you're talking about. War is a terrible thing! You mistake, too, the people of the North. They are a peaceable people but an earnest people, and they will fight, too. They are not going to let this country be destroyed without a mighty effort to save it."[4]

Ticknor and Sherman were both partly right and partly wrong. Ticknor was certainly correct about the dedication and unflinching will that characterized the Confederacy's struggle for independence. But he was too quick to generalize from New Orleans to the whole South. Sherman would later prove himself an expert on war as a "terrible thing." But he seemed unaware at the time how many Northerners would have preferred to stay peaceable rather than fight for the Union.

Despite the early outpouring of patriotic fervor in North and South, both sides would have to deal with dissidents throughout the war. Lincoln had to contend with guerrillas in Kentucky and Missouri, with violent mobs in Baltimore and draft riots in New York City, with "Copperheads" and Peace Democrats. At one time or another, the federal government censored or suppressed three hundred opposition newspapers in Northern states.[5] In the summer of 1864, war-weariness in the North was so widespread that Lincoln wrote a private memorandum, countersigned by members of his cabinet, in which he predicted his own defeat in the upcoming election. (That was before the fall of Atlanta, perhaps the last great turning point in the war before Appomattox.)

The Confederacy too had its dissenters. When South Carolina first threatened to secede, James Petigru, a prominent Charleston attorney, complained that the state was "too small to be a republic, and too large to be an insane asylum."[6] Petigru remained an outspoken Unionist throughout the war. And in the Confederate capital, Richmond, one of the wealthiest women in town, Elizabeth Van Lew, operated an extensive spy network for the Federal army and helped support the largest prison breakout of the war: the escape of more than a hundred Union officers from Libby Prison.

Apart from individuals like these, there were whole segments of society and large sections of the country that presented major problems for Confederate leaders. Most obvious, of course, was the black population of the South, comprising three and a half million of the South's nine million residents. Throughout the war, there were fears of a slave insurrection. But, for the most part, blacks did not take up arms directly against their masters; rather they took to their feet. By war's end, more than a half million African Americans had crossed into Federal lines. Of these, more than two hundred thousand would eventually serve in the Union army and navy.[7]

And then there were the mountaineers. From western Virginia to north Alabama, the mountains were so full of Union sympathizers that Appalachia would eventually be seen as a wedge driven deep into the heart of the Confederacy. Indeed, about three-quarters of the white Southerners who fought in Union blue were from the upcountry, small farmers without slaves who had little in common with patrician planters from the cotton-growing regions.[8]

The mountain folk who did not go north but stayed home proved to be almost as troublesome to the Confederacy. In northwestern Virginia, Unionists seceded from the secessionists and carved out a new state. East Tennessee tried to do likewise and had to be occupied as "enemy territory" by Southern forces. North Carolina had a secret society of ten thousand men called the Heroes of America, while Alabama suffered depredations by Unionist guerrillas who called themselves the "Prowling Brigades" and "Destroying Angels."[9]

A South Divided is an account of Southern dissidents in the American Civil War. The term *dissident* is used here in its broadest sense, referring not only to one who expresses vocal opposition but to anyone who refuses to consent by word or action (or nonaction). The term *dissident* avoids the obvious pitfalls of a value-laden term such as *traitor*. It is also preferable to other ambiguous terms such as *loyalist*, *disloyalist*, or *Unionist*. As discussed in the conclusion of this book, there are ongoing debates, sometimes heated, about the causes of the war, its consequences, or even what it should be called. A related issue is how to label Southerners who did not support the Confederacy. At the time they were called traitors, tories, deserters, and mossbacks. Since then they have been called "disloyalists" in one classic Southern study, "Lincoln's Loyalists" in a more recent book published in the North.[9] Obviously, the word *loyal* does not stand alone. It always gives rise to the question, loyal to whom or what? A Southerner who is loyal to the Union is disloyal to the Confederacy and vice versa.

Another term for Southern dissidents in the Civil War is *Unionist*, meant by some as a compliment, by others as an insult. The term often had broad connotations: anyone who clung to the Union and rejected the claims of the Confederacy. Sometimes it referred specifically to Northerners living in the South, such as the "Union Circle" in Georgia, "Secret Yankees" such as Cyrena Stone, a Vermonter who resided in Atlanta throughout the war.[10] But the term *Unionist* isn't broad enough to include the whole spectrum of Southern dissent. Slaves who ran away from their masters were not trying to support the Union; they were trying to get free. And deserters who left their posts, trekking back to their own neighborhoods, cared little about preserving the Union; they wanted to preserve their homes and families. While other dissenters might deliver speeches or print pamphlets, runaway slaves, draft evaders, and deserters all dissented with their feet.

In the past quarter century, there has been an upsurge of interest in Southern dissenters during the Civil War, a fascination evinced in both scholarly and popular works. Some of these books, such as William W. Freehling's *The South vs. the South* (2001), offer excellent analytic investigations of Southern diversity before and during the war. Other books, such as Martin Crawford's *Ashe County's Civil War* (2001), present thorough, in-depth portraits of the war as experienced by a particular group or community. *A South Divided* attempts to provide a panoramic overview of Southern dissent (broadly defined), focusing on particular individuals whose stories are as unique as human fingerprints, yet who also embody different strands of what has been called the "Other South."[11]

The British man of letters Thomas Carlyle once declared that "history is the essence of innumerable biographies." The history of Southern dissenters in the Civil War can be described in terms of broad demographics, but it can also be explored in terms of fascinating individual stories. Some dissidents were Unionists by principle, some were merely isolationists who could have echoed Jefferson Davis's famous plea, "All we ask is to be left alone." Some were high-minded and bold, risking their lives and fortunes for the cause they believed in. Others were little more than outlaws, plunderers, and highwaymen posing as Unionist partisans.

The pattern of Southern dissent is a complex one, involving every state of the Confederacy and every year of the war. The following chapters have been organized in a roughly chronological order, with many different states becoming, in their turn, arenas for internecine conflict. Thus West Virginia is discussed early in the book, since the Unionists in the trans-Allegheny began trying to break away from the Old Dominion in the first summer of the war. Other trends, such as Confederate desertions after Gettysburg and Vicksburg or the use of Southern blacks as Federal soldiers, became increasingly significant as the war progressed, so they are taken up later in the book. An individual such as Elizabeth Van Lew is most closely associated with events in the last year of the war, so her story is recounted in the final chapter. Though many of these chapters are interrelated, they can also be read separately as narratives about individuals or representative groups.

Some of the following chapters trace stories of lasting historical significance; others discuss individuals whose lives have left only a faint imprint on the archival record. The collective action of hundreds of thousands of black Southerners assuredly affected the course of the war; so too did the actions of tens of thousands of whites in the Southern mountains. The life of Mississippi deserter Jasper Collins or Virginia seamstress Rebecca Wright just as certainly had very little impact on the war's final outcome. And yet their stories are a part of the American story, part of the seamless fabric of our history.

A SOUTH DIVIDED

1

A CLASH OF VALUES IN THE ANTEBELLUM SOUTH

THE OCCASION WAS A formal state banquet in memory of Thomas Jefferson. After the prepared speeches, there was a call for voluntary toasts. The president of the United States stood to his full height and raised his glass, a signal that all should stand. Then he glared hard at a distinguished gentleman from South Carolina and resolutely offered the toast: "Our Union: it must be preserved." The Carolinian was taken aback, and his hand trembled so that a bit of wine spilled out of his glass. When the others resumed their seats, he remained standing and offered a toast of his own: "The Union: next to our liberties, most dear."[1]

This scene did not take place on the eve of the Civil War, nor were the two speakers from the North and South, respectively. This tense exchange occurred on April 13, 1830, a full generation before the war. And the two speakers were both Southerners and both slaveholders. It was President Andrew Jackson of Tennessee who toasted the Union and Vice President John C. Calhoun who replied that the liberties of the states were even more dear.

Jackson and Calhoun became outright enemies in the years that followed their famous toasts. In 1832, Calhoun became the first U.S. vice president to resign from office, preferring to serve instead as a senator from his home state of South Carolina. Calhoun was the architect of the doctrine of nullification, or as he called it, "state interpretation." In 1828, Congress had passed a high tariff on imported goods, which protected fledgling Northern industries from foreign competition but strained an already depressed agricultural economy in South Carolina. The new national tariff was enacted under the "general welfare" clause of the Constitution, but it seemed to Calhoun to serve only Northern welfare.

John C. Calhoun

Called the "Tariff of Abominations" in the South, the new law also raised the question of whether a federal government strong enough to enforce protective tariffs would have the power to regulate domestic institutions such as slavery. While still vice president, Calhoun secretly wrote a closely reasoned essay called "The South Carolina Exposition and Protest," explaining that the federal government was based on a compact among the states and asserting that a state could nullify any federal laws it considered unconstitutional. If other states disagreed, they could amend the Constitution according to a two-thirds majority in both houses of Congress, followed by ratification by three-quarters of the states.

The term *nullification* did not become widespread until the early 1830s, but the issue behind it was as old as the republic itself. Most people associate Unionism with the North and states' rights with the South. But the competing claims of national and state sovereignty varied from generation to generation, depending upon regional interests. The colonies were originally incorporated under the Articles of Confederation and Perpetual Union, passed by the Second Continental Congress in 1777 and ratified in 1781. But the Union referred to hardly existed beyond that heading. Article 1 of the document calls the United States of America a "Confederacy," and article 2 declares that "each state retains its sovereignty, freedom, and independence, and every power, jurisdiction, and right" that has not been expressly delegated to the United States.

In his original draft of the Articles, John Dickinson, a lawyer from Pennsylvania, had written, "[The] Colonies unite themselves so as never to be divided by any Act whatever."[2] That language sounded too rigid to other delegates who had recently passed the Declaration of Independence, and Dickinson's phrasing was quickly revised—almost to the point of being reversed. As amended and ratified, the Articles call the confederation "a firm league of friendship" among the states. Under the Articles, individual states issued their own currencies, enacted tariffs and duties for goods passing over state lines, and made their own treaties with Indian tribes within their borders. There was no national executive, and the national assembly sometimes went for months without the quorum it needed to conduct any business.[3]

When the new constitution was passed in 1787 "in order to form a more perfect Union," the phrasing was not merely ornamental but a reference to the all-too-evident flaws in the Articles of Confederation. The new constitution was silent on the issue of secession, leaving some to assume that the national government was formed by a voluntary compact among states, while others considered it an inviolable contract created by the people of the United States themselves. Ultimately, this question would not be settled by arguments but by armies.

Andrew Jackson

In general, the doctrine of states' rights reasserts itself whenever one section of the country finds itself at odds with the actions of the federal government. In 1798, under the Federalist administration of John Adams, the states of Kentucky and Virginia passed resolutions, penned by Thomas Jefferson and James Madison respectively, that the federal government should confine itself to powers granted it expressly in the Constitution. Under the presidencies of Jefferson (1801–9) and Madison (1809–17), the roles were reversed. Northern merchants strenuously objected to the Embargo Act of 1807, which outlawed trade with belligerents in the Napoleonic Wars, mainly France and Britain. During the War of 1812, derisively called "Mr. Madison's War" in the North, twenty-six representatives from the New England states met in Hartford, Connecticut, in December 1814 to discuss their grievances, mainly the disruption of trade caused by what they considered a needless war. Though the delegates met in secret, it became widely known that they had discussed (and ultimately rejected) a proposal for seceding from the Union. The War of 1812 came to an end before members of the Hartford Convention could formally present their complaints to the national authorities in Washington. Instead of undermining the Union, the Federalists who met at Hartford succeeded only in undermining their own party. Their talk of secession sounded to many like little less than treason. The Federalist Party fared poorly in the elections of 1816, and it went out of existence a few years later.

Perhaps South Carolinians in the next decade should have attended more fully to the fate of the Federalists after the War of 1812. Whatever its constitutional merits, the doctrine of nullification, as enunciated by Calhoun and others, was vigorously condemned in both North and South. President Andrew Jackson, who was born in South Carolina, declared that "nullification leads directly to civil war and bloodshed and deserves the execration of every friend of the Country."[4] Jackson equated nullification with treason and angrily declared to a congressman from South Carolina, "If one drop of blood be shed there in defiance of the laws of the United States, I will hang the first man of them I can get my hands on to the first tree I can find."[5] Jackson singled out Calhoun specifically as a worthy candidate for the hangman's noose.[6]

Though less violent in their rhetoric, the legislatures of South Carolina's sister states in the South were equally firm in denouncing nullification. Virginia declared that its own Resolutions of 1798 did not sanction the proceedings in South Carolina. North Carolina declared state nullification to be "revolutionary in its character, subversive of the Constitution of the United States and [leading] to a dissolution of the Union." From Georgia came even more severe censure: "We abhor the doctrine of Nullification as neither peaceful, nor a constitutional remedy, but, on the contrary, as tending to civil commotion and disunion." The Alabama legislature condemned nullification as "unsound in theory and dangerous in practice," something that could only incite "anarchy and civil discord, and finally to the dissolution of the Union." Mississippi's assembly added that nullification was in "direct conflict with the welfare, safety and independence of every State in the Union; and to no one of them would its consequences be more deeply disastrous, more ruinous than to the State of Mississippi."[7]

Yet it was one thing to speak out against South Carolina's doctrine of nullification and quite another thing to stamp it out by force. After South Carolina issued its ordinance nullifying the Tariff of 1832 in November of that year, Jackson responded the next month with a special proclamation declaring nullification to be unconstitutional and "incompatible with the existence of the Union."[8] In January 1833, he introduced the Force Bill to Congress, authorizing the president to use the Federal army and navy to uphold Federal laws. The president's views on nullification were endorsed in most of the Northern states, as well as the slave states of Maryland and Delaware and the western counties of Virginia.[9] But in most Southern states, the cries of denunciation were turned away from the nullifiers toward those who would attempt to refute the doctrine by military force. A newspaper reporter in Virginia wrote that a distinguished gentleman from that state had told him, "The Executive can never march troops against South Carolina, through eastern Virginia, *but over our dead bodies*."[10] In Georgia, North Carolina, and Alabama, there were widespread reports of volunteers coming forward, offering to assist in the defense of South Carolina. Daniel Webster, the eminent senator from Massachusetts, feared that things were nearing a flash point, that parties on both sides were expecting "a decision by the sword."[11]

Eventually, the nullification crisis was overcome by compromise, that political expedient that sometimes resolves a conflict and sometimes merely postpones it. While one Southerner, John C. Calhoun, proposed to nullify Federal law, and another Southerner, Andrew Jackson, threatened to enforce the nation's laws with muskets and bayonets, it fell to a third Southerner, Henry Clay of Kentucky, to steer a compromise through Congress. Under Clay's guidance, the national tariffs were gradually reduced, allowing both sides to save face. The nullification crisis passed, though in retrospect, it seems a kind of dress rehearsal for the Civil War. South Carolina had defied the national authority, and the Federal executive had responded with the threat of military action. Other Southern states showed that they did not want to see the Union undermined, but neither did they want to see it preserved by force.

The fact that, in the nullification crisis, both extremes and the middle were all represented by prominent Southerners illustrates well the diversity of the South in the antebellum years. The influential historian William W. Freehling argues that there were really three Souths before the Civil War— the Deep South, the Middle South, and the Border South.[12] The Deep South states (Alabama, Florida, Georgia, Louisiana, Mississippi, South Carolina, and Texas) depended most heavily on slave labor for their export crops— rice and indigo in South Carolina, sugar in Louisiana, and of course, a cotton belt running from the Sea Islands of South Carolina all the way to east Texas. In the Deep South before the war, nearly half the population was black. In the Middle South states (Arkansas, North Carolina, Tennessee, and Virginia) about a third of the population consisted of slaves, and these were concentrated most heavily in tobacco-growing regions such as eastern Virginia and western Tennessee. In the states of the Border South (Delaware, Kentucky, Maryland, and Missouri), about one-eighth of the population was enslaved. In the years just before the Civil War, only 1.5 percent of blacks in the Deep South were free. In the Middle South this figure rose to 7 percent and in the Border South to 21 percent.[13] In Maryland, there were almost as many free blacks as there were slaves; in Delaware there were two thousand slaves in the whole state, less than 3 percent of the total population.[14]

Freehling sees three Souths roughly divided by latitude—upper, middle, and lower. But one could just as easily talk about two Souths distinguished by altitude. Wherever there were mountains, from western Virginia to northern Arkansas, the soil and topography did not favor plantations, which meant fewer slaves and slaveholders and a greater attachment to the Union—or else a fierce desire to be left alone by outsiders.

SOUTHERN CRITICS OF SLAVERY

SOON AFTER his election in November 1860, Abraham Lincoln wrote a private letter to Alexander H.Stephens of Georgia, later to become vice president of the Confederacy. Lincoln tried to reassure his longtime acquaintance that, as president-elect of the United States, he had no intention of interfering with slavery in the Southern states. "I suppose, though," he concluded, "this does not meet the case. You think slavery is *right*, and ought to be extended; while we think it is *wrong* and ought to be restricted. That I suppose is the rub. It certainly is the only substantial difference between us."[15] In contrasting *you* with *we*, Lincoln seems to have in mind the South and the North. But if this is so, then he greatly oversimplified the case. There were many in the North, including men like Ulysses S. Grant and William T. Sherman, later to become Lincoln's most trusted generals, who expressed few qualms about the institution of slavery. And there were individuals throughout the South who thought slavery was immoral or impractical or both.

In his classic study *The Other South* (1974), Carl Degler effectively demonstrates that a minority in the antebellum South—whether pro-Union or antislavery—was not nearly as silent as is often supposed. During debates over the Missouri Compromise of 1820, for example, Congressman Robert Reid of Georgia called slavery "an unnatural state, a dark cloud which obscures half the luster of our free institutions." (Having said that, Reid added that slavery was an inherited evil that could not be abolished, only regulated and partially reformed.[16]) In the same year Elihu Embree, a native Tennessean, called slaveholders "monsters in human shape." Joseph

Doddridge, a minister in western Virginia, complained about the circular reasoning used to defend the bondage of blacks: "We debase them to the condition of brutes and then use their debasement as an argument for perpetuating their slavery." Robert J. Breckinridge of Kentucky published a book in 1830 describing slavery as "an ulcer eating its way into the very heart of the state." In 1847, Henry Ruffner, the president of Washington College (now Washington and Lee), who was himself a slave owner, published a pamphlet arguing that slave labor was economically unsound, noting that the Northern free-labor states, even with their poorer soils and harsher climates, had far more robust economies than Southern slave states. Kentuckian Cassius Clay offered a similar critique of slavery on economic grounds throughout the 1850s, as did North Carolinian Hinton Rowan Helper. As these and many other examples supplied by Degler show, the antislavery voices in the prewar South may have been small in number, but they were too persistent and too vocal to be ignored.

SARAH AND ANGELINA GRIMKÉ:
THE UNLIKELIEST ABOLITIONISTS

IN BOTH the North and the South, critics of slavery in the generation before the Civil War offered a number of possible remedies, often in combination: gradual freeing of slaves over a period of decades; compensated emancipation; relocation of blacks to Africa. The most radical solution, and the most violently unpopular, was abolition: the immediate and uncompensated liberation of all those held in bondage. Abolitionists were usually found in the North, and they were often notorious, either for the fierceness of their rhetoric, such as William Lloyd Garrison, or for the fierceness of their deeds, such as the fanatical John Brown. Among those associated with the abolition movement before the war, the two most unlikely yet most influential were Sarah and Angelina Grimké of South Carolina.

Sarah Grimké was born in 1792, the sixth child and second daughter of John and Mary Grimké of Charleston. John Faucheraud Grimké, of Huguenot ancestry, belonged to the city's elite. He was a Revolutionary War veteran and a wealthy slaveholding planter who also practiced law and eventually became the presiding justice for the supreme court of the state. As part of one of Charleston's leading families, Sarah grew up surrounded by a large retinue of household slaves, including a cook, butler, nursemaids,

Sarah Grimké

chambermaids, coachmen, stable boys, and personal servants. Though she took the usual lessons in reading, writing, music, drawing, and needlework, Sarah showed more zest for the subjects intended for her brothers: mathematics, geography, history, and natural science. When she asked to study Latin and law with her older brother Thomas, her father said no—though he is said to have remarked that, if Sarah had been born a boy, she would have become one of the most distinguished jurists in the country.[17]

In later years, Sarah recalled an incident from childhood that she felt marked her for life. At the age of four, she accidentally walked into a room where one of the slave women was being whipped. Sarah was so astonished and horrified she ran out of the house in tears and disappeared down the street. After half an hour, she was found at one of the Charleston wharves, pleading with a sea captain to take her away to some land where such scenes didn't take place. After that, Sarah often cried when she heard that a slave was going to be punished, and she went to her room to pray that God might intervene. Among other slave-owning families in Charleston, Sarah witnessed even more brutal punishments. In one nearby house, a young mixed-blood woman who kept running away was whipped until she bled, then fitted with a three-pronged iron collar. Finally, her front tooth was pulled out so she could be easily identified if she ran away again. The most gruesome incident of all came when Sarah was traveling by coach in the low country outside Charleston: she saw a human head on a pole, the remains of a slave from a nearby plantation who had run away once too often, set there as a warning to others.[18]

Sarah's sister Angelina was born in 1805, the fourteenth and last child of John and Mary Grimké. Sarah was thirteen years older than Angelina, and she asked to be named godmother at the christening. In many respects, Sarah played the part of mother for Angelina in the years that followed. Perhaps because of the special bond between the two sisters, Angelina later recalled childhood traumas similar to Sarah's. When she was old enough to go to school, Angelina began attending Charleston Seminary, established to educate children from the leading families in the city.

One day, Angelina watched curiously when a little slave boy was told to cross the room and open a window. She couldn't understand his stiff, awkward gait—like an old man's—until he passed in front of her. She saw that his back and legs were striped with scars, as well as fresh lacerations still oozing blood. Angelina fainted at the sight, and she cried uncontrollably later when she tried to tell Sarah what she had seen.

Angelina Grimké

A great change in the Grimké sisters' lives came in June 1819, when their father, then in his sixties, fell seriously ill and was told he should seek treatment from medical specialists in Philadelphia. Sarah was then twenty-six, strong-willed, independent-minded, with no prospects for marriage, nor seeking any. It was decided that she should accompany her father on the voyage north, the first time she had ever traveled outside her home state. Sarah spent two months consulting doctors and nursing her father. But nothing could be done, and he died later that summer in Pennsylvania, buried in a simple graveside service far from home.

During her time in Philadelphia and on the voyage back to South Carolina, Sarah became acquainted with the Society of Friends, or Quakers, who stressed simplicity of dress and speech, peacemaking, and the equality of men and women. Though some Quakers had been slave traders or slave owners in colonial days, they were generally outspoken opponents of what was called "the peculiar institution." As early as 1688, a Quaker congregation in Germantown, Pennsylvania, had published a circular condemning slavery. The Society of Friends formed an abolition society in 1775 and prohibited their members from owning slaves the following year. They also organized boycotts against goods produced by slave labor.

Already appalled by slavery, Sarah studied what Quaker literature she could find and began attending the meetings of Friends in Charleston, only a handful of people who met for silent worship, relying on what they called their "inner light." Having lived outside slave society for a summer, Sarah spent two years trying to readjust to her native Charleston, concluding eventually that she simply couldn't go home again. In 1821, she sailed once more for Philadelphia, afterward returning to South Carolina only for brief visits.

None of this went unnoticed by Angelina Grimké, thirteen years younger. When she was twenty-two, her older sister made one of her rare visits to Charleston, largely on a mission to "save" her sister and goddaughter.[19] Angelina responded, agreeing with most of what Sarah had to say. The younger sister stopped attending the family's Episcopal church, which held that slaveholding itself was not wrong, only the abuse of slaves. She briefly tried Presbyterianism, then began attending Quaker meetings in Charleston the following year. Unfortunately, by that time, the congregation had dwindled to two old men who were not on speaking terms because one was a slaveholder and the other was not. In 1829, Angelina, aged twenty-four, sailed to Philadelphia to join her sister; she never again saw her native city. She was accepted into the same Meeting (church) as her sister, and both were active in teaching and volunteer work.

The Grimké sisters would probably have lived out the rest of their lives in quiet obscurity had it not been for a letter to the editor. Angelina began attending abolitionists' lectures and reading their literature, eventually joining the Philadelphia Female Anti-Slavery Society in May 1835. That summer she saw more and more stories in the newspaper about abolitionists throughout the North being mobbed and beaten. William Lloyd Garrison, the editor of the abolitionist newspaper, the *Liberator*, which he had founded four years earlier, was paraded around the streets of Boston with a noose around his neck. Amos Phelps was severely injured after being struck with a brick while lecturing against slavery in Farmington, Connecticut. Charles Stuart was beaten by a mob in New York. Other antislavery speakers were shouted down, pelted with rotten eggs, tarred and feathered, or publicly whipped.[20]

In August 1835, Angelina decided to write a letter of encouragement to Garrison. She did not submit it for publication nor did she give permission for her name to be used. But she expressed her heartiest support and pleaded that abolitionists should "be prepared to meet a martyr's doom" rather than give up their principles. "The ground upon which you stand is holy ground," she continued, "never—never surrender it. If you surrender it, the hope of the slave is extinguished, and the chains of his servitude will be strengthened a hundred fold." Noting that the first Christian martyr, the deacon Stephen, was stoned by a mob, Angelina argued that those who believe in the "cause of bleeding humanity" should be willing to follow his example: "If persecution is the means which God has ordained for the accomplishment of this great end, EMANCIPATION; then, in dependence upon him for strength to bear it, I feel as if I could say, LET IT COME; for it is my deep, solemn, deliberate conviction that *this is a cause worth dying for*. . . . Yes! LET IT COME—let *us* suffer, rather than insurrections should arise."[21]

Garrison was so taken by Angelina's letter that he published it in its entirety in the *Liberator*, including her name. Besides its unusual emphasis on martyrdom rather than militarism, the letter stood out because of its author. Angelina's father and older brother Thomas (both deceased by then) had been nationally known jurists, and here was a member of the Charleston Grimkés speaking out eloquently in support of the antislavery cause. Those same Charleston Grimkés were, of course, horrified to hear about the letter. In Philadelphia, Angelina's Quaker circle also strongly disapproved. In the 1830s, the Society of Friends in Pennsylvania were rent by their own divisions: city Quakers vs. country Quakers; those accepting the Christian doctrine of the Trinity vs. those who did not; those who supported abolition vs. those who thought Friends should back away from causes that incited violence. Sometimes the greatest challenge for peacemaking congregations is to find peace among themselves.

But Angelina stood her ground. Though she had not given permission for the letter to be printed, she did not recant. At first, even her older sister Sarah disapproved, complaining that she had brought shame upon them among their closest friends. But Angelina (replying by letter from Shrewsbury, New Jersey, where she was staying for a brief visit) gently admonished her sister for accepting the judgment of their friends as "an infallible criterion," instead of seeking the approval of a Higher Judge. She recalled the experiences that had brought them both to live among the Philadelphia Quakers in the first place: "Thou knowest what I have passed through on the subject of slavery; thou knowest I am an exile from the home of my birth because of slavery." Explaining the circumstances of her writing the letter, Angelina ended with two quotations from Scripture—"Judge not by appearance, but judge righteous judgment" and "Judge nothing before the time." She signed the letter, "thy afflicted sister, A. E. G."[22]

Apparently, the time had come for the younger sister to teach the older, for Sarah soon joined Angelina against others in the congregation who felt that Quaker women should steer clear of controversy. In fact, the two sisters agreed to resist racism wherever they found it, North or South. In the meetinghouse of their own congregation of Friends in Philadelphia, there was a "colored bench" set aside for black members. Not long after Angelina's letter appeared in the *Liberator*, the two sisters made a point of sitting with black worshipers on the bench.

In the late 1830s, both Grimké sisters began to distance themselves from their secluded Quaker circle in Philadelphia and openly embraced the cause of abolition that was gaining momentum in the North. The year after her letter was published in the *Liberator*, Angelina published, under her own name, a pamphlet called *An Appeal to the Christian Women of the South*, arguing at length that the Bible and Christian tradition did not support chattel slavery. Referring to herself as a Southerner and a "sympathizing friend," she pleaded with Southern women to take the lead on this issue if men would not. Though it was probably the most influential tract ever published by a female abolitionist, Angelina's pamphlet did not appeal to Christian women of the South, and it was publicly burned in Charleston. Later that same year (1836), Sarah Grimké wrote an equally inflammatory tract, *An Epistle to the Clergy of the Southern States*, mixing biblical texts with historical examples to show that American slavery was both unjust and unrighteous.

Having entered the fray, the Grimkés pursued the cause of abolition with an energy and force surprising for two sisters raised in a tradition of Southern gentility and living among Quakers who stressed quietude. Becoming members and then leaders of the American Anti-Slavery Society (founded in 1833), the Grimkés undertook a strenuous six-month tour of New England, speaking at nearly ninety meetings in more than sixty different cities and towns. Wherever they went, the Grimkés were celebrated by some, execrated by others. Angelina was especially effective as a public speaker, her frail figure and plain dress belying the dynamism and eloquence of her orations, which sometimes lasted two hours. Sometimes called "Devilina," she was controversial not only for her abolitionist views but also for speaking to "mixed" audiences, black and white, women and men.[23] At one meeting in Pennsylvania Hall in Philadelphia, she continued to speak over the shouts and curses of angry protesters outside. Her audience began to murmur and stir restlessly when stones were heard rattling off the windows. But she went on speaking in even tones, condemning mob violence even as bricks crashed through the windows, raining down on the floor amid shards of broken glass.

In 1839, the two sisters provided much of the material for abolitionist preacher Theodore Weld's *American Slavery as It Is*, combining their own eyewitness accounts of seeing slaves flogged, tortured, or starved with the testimony of others about the wretched conditions endured by blacks in the South. The book sold one hundred thousand copies in its first year and was widely distributed in Great Britain. It was also used by Harriet Beecher Stowe in her even more sensational and best-selling book, *Uncle Tom's Cabin* (1852).

In the 1840s, the Grimké sisters began to recede from public view. Angelina married Theodore Weld in 1838 and bore three children in the next six years. Her health had always been delicate, and in her middle years she was less able to travel and speak to large audiences. Settling first in New Jersey, then later in Massachusetts, the Welds, accompanied by Sarah Grimké, spent their later years focusing more on education. The schools they founded, both in New Jersey and Massachusetts, were unusual at the time in that they featured coeducational classes and encouraged women in traditionally male sports, such as diving or rowing. The Grimkés also became increasingly active on behalf of woman's rights, both sisters circulating petitions for female suffrage and both casting ballots in local elections in 1870 (which did not count, of course, since women would not gain the right to vote in America for another half century).

Sarah Grimké died in Massachusetts in 1873 at the age of eighty-one. Angelina followed her in 1879, dying at age seventy-four. For most of their adult lives, the two sisters were estranged from their many siblings and cousins in Charleston. The two relatives with whom they remained close in later years were Archibald Henry Grimké and Francis James Grimké. These were their two mixed-blood nephews, educated at Lincoln College, Pennsylvania, about thirty miles west of the neighborhood in Philadelphia where Sarah and Angelina first began what they considered their "Northern exile."

SOUTHERN VOICES FOR COMPENSATED EMANCIPATION

THE GRIMKÉ sisters were among very few Southerners before the war who advocated abolition. In 1827, Benjamin Lundy, the Quaker editor of a newspaper called *Genius of Emancipation* published in Tennessee, estimated that there were about five thousand abolitionists in the South.[24] The New Jersey–born Lundy was an abolitionist himself, so his estimate may be inflated. Even so, that number would represent about only one-fifth of 1 percent of white Southerners at that time. Although those favoring outright abolition were few indeed, there were greater numbers of Southerners willing to discuss less drastic and economically disruptive measures. Virginians George Washington and Thomas Jefferson and Tennessean Andrew Jackson all considered schemes for paying off slave owners and returning blacks to Africa.[25] Kentuckian Henry Clay offered the most concrete proposal, arguing in 1827 that the Federal government could return fifty thousand American slaves to Africa every year at an annual cost of about one million dollars.[26] Of course, no such public plan was ever adopted, but there was a unique private experiment that achieved surprising success on a small scale. This singular program of compensated emancipation was not paid for by the government but by slaves themselves. And their sponsor was not an opponent of slavery but a prosperous slaveholder: John McDonogh of Louisiana.

McDonogh was born in Baltimore in 1779, the son of a successful merchant of Scots-Irish descent. At the age of twenty-one, he traveled to New Orleans on business and decided to settle there permanently. He was a shrewd entrepreneur and a hard worker, sometimes putting in eighteen-hour days. By his midtwenties, McDonogh had already accumulated a small fortune when he began buying vast tracts of land carved out of the 1803 Louisiana Purchase. Within a few years, his land holdings were said to encircle New Orleans, and he owned one tract that ran continuously for fifty miles along the banks of the Mississippi.

Before he was thirty, McDonogh was already one of the wealthiest men in the South. And he lived like it. He owned a splendid, well-furnished mansion in the most fashionable district of New Orleans. He dressed in the latest Regency styles and threw extravagant dinner parties and soirees, taking pride in his pure-bred horses and well-stocked wine cellar. As one of the city's preeminent bachelors, McDonogh sought the hand of one of its most eligible belles, the beautiful sixteen-year-old daughter of Don Pedro Almonastre, a Spanish courtier who had made a fortune of his own in the New World. Initially, McDonogh's suit was welcomed, and he began building a vast manor house, which he called his "castle," on his estate across the Mississippi from New Orleans. He had already completed two wings of the structure and purchased the very best furniture money could buy, including individual mirrors valued at five hundred dollars, when he abruptly received word from the Almonastre family that the engagement had been called off. The grandee's elegant daughter had been promised instead to the son of a Spanish count, a better social match for the high-born heiress than an untitled American, regardless of his wealth.

McDonogh was devastated. He sold his mansion in the city and moved permanently to his plantation across the river. Ending construction on his castle, he took up residence in three rooms of one completed wing and crated up all the priceless furnishings. (These sat neglected for decades. When he died in 1850, having never married, the whole lot sold for only $350.) For nearly forty years, McDonogh lived on his plantation with his slaves, only crossing the river to New Orleans to do business. Reverting to the strict Scottish Presbyterianism in which he had been raised, he worked hard, lived simply, and quoted the Bible and Ben Franklin on the virtues of sobriety, honesty, and industry. He entertained no one at his estate, called McDonoghville, and he spoke to no one in the city, except on business matters. When he came to New Orleans, he walked alone, holding himself aloof, continuing to dress in dandyish Regency clothes that were every year more threadbare and out of fashion. Though he had been considered handsome, even dashing, in his youth, McDonogh in later years had a somewhat gaunt, angular look, with a shock of white hair, a furrowed brow, and a down-turned mouth that gave him a stern, censorious appearance.

FROM WILLIAM H. SEYMOUR, *THE STORY OF ALGIERS* [LA] (1896)

John McDonogh

One of the few occasions anyone saw the elder John McDonogh interact with someone else, apart from business, occurred on a busy street in New Orleans. A little girl saw the aging gentleman standing silent and alone, and she went up and offered him a few flowers she had picked. He blushed, accepted the bouquet, then turned his head to hide the tears brimming in his eyes and trickling down his cheeks. When he died in 1850, McDonogh bequeathed $1.5 million for the education of poor children in New Orleans and Baltimore. One of the provisions of his will was that boys and girls from the schools established in his name should plant flowers on his grave and water them regularly.

McDonogh's transformation from bon vivant to recluse was like something out of a novel, a Great Gatsby turned into a Silas Marner. Yet for all this, McDonogh continued to prosper. Apart from the mysteries he kept locked away in his heart, there was also a mystery about his slaves. They rose and started work earlier than anyone else, and they often kept working after dark, sometimes till midnight. Yet they did not have white overseers and were not driven by the lash. They were comfortably housed, well clothed and fed, and allowed to keep their own garden plots and farm animals. And they seemed to have unfeigned respect and affection for their master. When one of McDonogh's slave gangs worked a construction project in the city, a neighbor watched for several days and marveled at their hard work and efficiency, even with no white overseer present. The neighbor was particularly impressed by the skill and energy of a bricklayer named James. The neighbor offered McDonogh a fair price for the worker, was refused, and then doubled his offer. But the eccentric old planter explained that while he sometimes bought slaves, he never sold them.

The curiosity of McDonogh's neighbors turned into concern when two of his longtime slaves were seen leaving for Liberia, the colony in western Africa established for freed slaves from America. McDonogh's former slaves left with new suits of clothes, farming tools, and letters of recommendation. When McDonogh was asked to explain, he replied cryptically that he had given them their freedom as "an act of simple honesty alone."[27] Perhaps sensing that this was not answer enough, McDonogh followed up with a long letter in July 1842 to the *New Orleans Commercial Bulletin* explaining how it came about that two of his slaves had been set free and sent abroad.

It had all begun twenty years earlier, he recounted, when he noticed his slaves, who worked for him six days a week, were doing their own chores on Sundays, which he considered a violation of the Sabbath. He agreed to give them Saturday afternoons off, so long as they kept Sundays as a day of rest and worship. (He built them a church on his plantation for this purpose, sometimes delivering Sabbath sermons himself.) Noticing that the slaves worked much more diligently on their own time, he decided three years later to try an experiment. He told his slaves that he would pay them for work they did for him on Saturday afternoons, 62½ cents for men and 50 cents for women. Instead of giving them cash, he would keep track of their work credits and allow them to buy back "slave time" from him. After a certain amount of time, they would accumulate enough credits to buy their entire Saturdays as free-labor days. If they chose to continue working, they could eventually buy back more days of slave time. After fifteen years of working extra time, both Saturdays and early or late hours on weekdays, they would have paid off their full market value, and he would certify that they had purchased their own freedom.

McDonogh called in each slave every six months or so to review their accounts and show them what progress they had made. He trained some of his slaves to be overseers, clerks, and bill collectors, and he saw to it that everyone learned farming or a trade. He insisted that his freed slaves remove themselves to Liberia, because he did not believe that whites and blacks could live together in harmony as free peoples. But he made arrangements to provide land for them in their new home, and he sent two to be educated in the North, at his expense, so that his freed slaves in Liberia would have the benefit of a trained physician and a pastor.

To those who might object that all of a slave's time belongs to the slave's master, so he need not keep a record of a slave's overtime, McDonogh replied not in terms of legalities but in terms of psychology: "Without hope, a certain something in the future to look forward to and aspire to, man would be nothing. Deprive him of the aspiring faculty of the soul, and he would grovel in the dust as a brute."[28] McDonogh added that his plan benefited owners as much as slaves. Besides the fact that this system would cost owners no money, McDonogh asked if every "humane master" would not enjoy a great deal of satisfaction "knowing that he was surrounded by friends, on whose faithfulness and fidelity he and his family could rely, under every possible contingency?"[29] He observed that, even though his slaves had already been a "well-disposed and orderly people" before his agreement with them, they exhibited an entirely new level of energy and efficiency once they knew they were gradually working their own way out of bondage. He added a personal note, saying that the sixteen years since he began the experiment had been among the happiest of his life, knowing that he was "surrounded by those who looked upon me in the light of a friend and father."[30]

One can never be too sure about a master's perception of how he is viewed by his slaves. But in McDonogh's case, his observations seemed borne out by those of others. When his former slaves took ship for Liberia, they openly expressed their affection for him and wrote him from Liberia, addressing him as "Dear Father and Friend" and closing "From your faithful servant and son" or "Your friend and servant till death."[31]

McDonogh never seemed to question the basic morality of slavery, and he himself noted there was no particular generosity in requiring slaves to work overtime for fifteen years in order to obtain their freedom. Though he was certainly no radical, his experiment, which allowed eighty slaves to purchase their own freedom, contains a certain implied critique of any system that denied human beings a sense of hope or dignity. When he died in 1850, leaving the bulk of his estate to establish free schools for the poor, the few whites who attended his funeral stood stony-faced while the large crowd of blacks assembled there let the tears fall freely to express their sense of loss.[32]

OUT OF ONE SOUTH, MANY

McDONOGH RECOMMENDED his experiment to other slave owners and even to Congress, adding an important caveat that such a plan would require integrity and goodwill on the part of masters as well as sincere concern for the welfare of their slaves. But McDonogh was one of a kind, and his plan never went any further than the program for compensated emancipation proposed by Henry Clay back in 1827. Clay was not destined to be known as the Great Compensator but rather as the Great Compromiser, mainly because of his central role in the Missouri Compromise of 1820, his moderating influence in the nullification crisis of 1832, and his series of proposals collectively known as the Compromise of 1850, which temporarily soothed antagonisms between North and South.

In the 1850s, though, the escalation of tension outpaced the efforts of the compromisers, drowning out moderate voices in both North and South. There was the publication of Harriet Beecher Stowe's *Uncle Tom's Cabin* in

For almost forty years, the issue of slavery occupied all branches of government. While compromises eased tensions on several occasions, they did not resolve the underlying problem.

LIBRARY OF CONGRESS

1852, inflaming both sides with its sensational portrayal of slave suffering and slave-owner cruelty. Then came the Kansas-Nebraska Act in 1854, an experiment in popular sovereignty in the territories that would ignite virtual civil war among proslavery and antislavery forces in the region. In 1857, the Dred Scott decision of the U.S. Supreme Court outraged many Northerners with its pronouncement that slaves, as property, had no legal rights and its ruling that the Missouri Compromise of 1820 had been unconstitutional in outlawing slavery in the Northern territories. Then came John Brown's infamous raid on Harpers Ferry in 1859, an attempt to foment a slave rebellion in a part of Virginia where there were hardly any slaves. The final drum taps in a long roll calling both sides to battle were Lincoln's election in November 1860 and South Carolina's ordinance of secession the following month.

The contrast in what William Freehling calls the three Souths can be clearly seen in their pattern of secession in 1861. The other Deep South states all followed South Carolina out of the Union within three months of the election, before the "Black Republican" even took office in March. The Middle South states did not secede until after the surrender of Fort Sumter in April and Lincoln's call for seventy-five thousand volunteers to suppress "combinations too powerful to be suppressed by the ordinary course of judicial proceedings." However much they may have disapproved of breaking up the Union, the majorities in the Middle South were even more disturbed by the idea of maintaining the Union by force. Though it took several months for the pattern to become clear, it would turn out that all four Border South states (Delaware, Kentucky, Maryland, and Missouri) would remain in the Union. That section of Virginia that bordered the North, the

John Brown's 1859 raid on Harpers Ferry sent waves of anxiety throughout the South. With the rise of the Republican Party and its perceived abolitionist stance, the South weighed separation from the Union as its only option.

LIBRARY OF CONGRESS

trans-Allegheny region, also chose to remain in the Union, entering in the middle of the war as the new state of West Virginia.

Apart from the broad geographical divisions one can see on a map, there were thousands of individuals to be taken into account: yeoman farmers in the sandy, wiregrass regions of central Mississippi where cotton would not grow; wealthy Louisiana planters who felt the institution of slavery would be better preserved by the rule of law within the Union than by the vagaries of war outside it; and Quakers and Mennonites in the Shenandoah Valley who objected to the use of force, regardless of the principles involved. The antebellum South (like the North) was a complex mosaic of competing interests and ideals, a diversity that would become all too evident when the exigencies of war made it imperative for all to declare their allegiance—and to act upon it.

2

CROSSOVER SOLDIERS AND THEIR BATTLES

During the Revolutionary War, George Washington tried without success to get a company of New Jersey militiamen to swear allegiance to the United States. They steadfastly refused, insisting, "New Jersey is our country."[1] Things hadn't changed all that much in the next century, when Southerners undertook what they considered a second war for national independence. Once it became clear which states would join the Confederacy and which ones would stay in the Union, the vast majority of men, North and South, went with their states.

There were, however, a significant number of what might be called *crossover soldiers*, Northerners who fought for the South and Southerners who fought for the North. Samuel Cooper, who began the war as the highest-ranking officer in the Confederate army and its inspector general, was born and raised in New Jersey. John C. Pemberton from Pennsylvania spent twenty-four years in a U.S. Army uniform before the war. But his closest friends during his West Point days were all Southerners, and he married a woman from Virginia. After the fall of Sumter, he was offered the rank of colonel in the Federal army, but he resigned instead and accepted a commission from Jefferson Davis as a lieutenant colonel. Winning rapid promotions, Pemberton was a lieutenant general by the time he was assigned to command the all-important defenses at Vicksburg, overlooking the Mississippi. When the city surrendered to Ulysses S. Grant in July 1863, Pemberton, the "Yankee," was widely blamed for the defeat. Though he was even accused of treason, Pemberton remained faithful to the Confederate cause, ending the war as a colonel of artillery in the Rebel army.

Others crossed over the other way. Lincoln's first general in chief of the army, Winfield Scott, was a Virginian, despised in his home state not only for joining the foe but for leading it. Though his Anaconda Plan for isolating the South by controlling the Mississippi and blockading Confederate ports was ridiculed early in the war, it turned out to be an important part of the formula that led to eventual victory. Another well-known Southerner in the Federal army was John Gibbon, who led one of the fiercest fighting units in the eastern theater, the Iron Brigade. Gibbon was a North Carolinian whose three brothers all fought for the Confederacy.

One of the most surprising crossovers of the Civil War was a naval officer, Charles Steedman of South Carolina. When Commander Steedman announced his intention to remain in the Federal navy in 1861, he received a stinging letter from his brother James, a wealthy planter who lived near Charleston. James wrote that there was still time for Charles to prove his loyalty to his people: "I felt that my blood was cold in my veins . . . my brother a traitor to his mother country . . . where lie the bones of his father, mother, and many dear relatives."[2] James added that a true Southerner could never allow "Northern principles to contaminate his pure soul," concluding that "we all expect you to do your duty to your God, your State, and Truth." Charles replied with as much grim resolution as his brother: "I am as I have always been, a Union man—I know no North or South . . . all that I know is my duty to flag & country which I have served for the last 30 years." Charles Steedman continued to do his duty as he saw it, rising to the rank of captain by the end of the war and participating in the Union navy's attacks on his home city of Charleston.

The problem of choosing sides was by far most painful for men from the Border States. It is a tale often told that Robert E. Lee was offered command of all the Union armies and that he spent an agonizing night at his home in Arlington, Virginia, pacing the floor and praying, before famously announcing that he had no desire to draw his sword—save in defense of his native state. Given the brilliant career that followed, it is hard to believe in retrospect that Lee could have actually had such a divided mind on the subject. But at the time, it seemed to his sons that the family would cast its lot with the Union. William H. F. "Rooney" Lee told friends that the people had lost their senses and were making a terrible mistake. His older brother, Custis, proposed that the family estate at Arlington be fortified as a Federal outpost. But when Robert E. Lee followed his state out of the Union, Rooney and Custis followed their father, both eventually becoming generals in the Confederate army.[3]

Though the Lee family, except for one of Robert's nephews, all fought for the Confederacy, other Border State families were literally divided brother against brother. Senator John J. Crittenden of Kentucky, who sponsored the famous Crittenden Compromise in an eleventh-hour attempt to preserve the Union, had two sons who became Civil War generals but fought on opposite sides. Both had disappointing careers. The eldest son, Thomas, led a Federal corps that was routed at Chickamauga in September 1863; the younger son, George, was arrested for dereliction of duty after losing a battle in his home state, and he eventually resigned his commission in the Confederate army.

More distinguished were the Terrell brothers of Virginia. Older brother James sided with his state and led a Confederate regiment in most of the major battles in the eastern theater, including First and Second Bull Run, Fredericksburg, the Wilderness, and Spotsylvania. He rose to the rank of brigadier general, falling in battle outside Richmond, an hour's ride from his home. Younger brother William joined the Union army and fought out west, earning praise for his valor at Shiloh. Like his brother, William rose to the rank of brigadier, and like his brother, he was killed in battle. He fell in Perryville, Kentucky (1862), more than five hundred miles from home. Later their bereaved father buried his sons side by side under a headstone that read: "Here lie my two sons. Only God knows which was right."[4]

DAVID GLASGOW FARRAGUT

IN ONE unusual case, the Civil War united two brothers who might have been expected to fight on opposite sides. David Glasgow Farragut was originally christened *James* Glasgow Farragut, named after James Glasgow, a family friend and high state official in North Carolina. Farragut's mother was a North Carolinian, though the Farraguts lived in east Tennessee when he was born in 1801. Moving to New Orleans when James was six, the Farraguts became very close to another family, the Porters. When Mrs. Farragut died of yellow fever in 1808, Commo. David Porter took in James Glasgow as a foster son, the young man later changing his name to David in honor of his guardian.

Farragut became a midshipman in the U.S. Navy at the age of nine and survived his first sea battle, during the War of 1812, at the age of twelve. He was thirteen years old when his foster brother, David Dixon Porter, was

LIBRARY OF CONGRESS

David G. Farragut

born in Pennsylvania. Though both men spent most of their adult lives at sea, Porter considered himself a Northerner, while Farragut married and settled in Norfolk, identifying himself before the war as a Virginian. But Farragut had been stationed in Charleston Harbor during the Nullification Crisis of 1831, and he tended to associate nullification and secession with the Deep South elite, not with the common people. Perhaps like Charles Steedman, Porter's many years abroad made him think of himself first as an American, not a Southerner. So, despite strong family ties in New Orleans and Norfolk, Farragut left Virginia the day after it seceded, heading north for service in the Federal navy.

Farragut's most trying test of allegiance came late in December 1861. The Federal secretary of the navy, Gideon Welles, had been impressed by Farragut's boldness during the Mexican War (1846–48) and was further impressed by how speedily the Farraguts departed from Virginia after that state left the Union. But would the Southern-born captain be willing to command naval forces attacking Confederate seaports where he still had strong bonds of family and friendship? Welles sent Farragut's foster brother, David Porter, to find out.

Though the two men had not seen each other in ten years, Porter went to Farragut's lodgings in Brooklyn, found the sixty-year-old Farragut to be every bit as robust and energetic as he had been in his prime. Porter started the conversation by bringing up their fellow naval officers who had resigned to join the Confederacy. "Those damned fellows will catch it yet!" muttered Farragut, which Porter considered a good answer to his opening question. He then raised the topic of Farragut's leading a naval expedition against a major Southern port. His foster brother showed a great deal of interest till Porter hinted the port he had in mind was Norfolk. Farragut balked at the idea of attacking his own home city, where his wife's family still lived. As they discussed at length the anguish of choosing between one's country and one's friends and kindred, Farragut became increasingly agitated. Finally, he jumped out of his chair and exclaimed to Porter, "I will take the command! Only don't you trifle with me!"[5]

Of course, the actual expedition Porter had in mind was against New Orleans, with Farragut in overall command and himself in charge of the mortar flotilla. Porter's nineteen mortar boats turned out to be of little use in the campaign, and it was Farragut's running twenty-four wooden warships past Forts Jackson and St. Philip, guarding the southern approaches to the Crescent City, that led to its capture in April 1862. That spring, Porter's fraternal regard for his foster brother seemed tinged with a good measure of sibling rivalry.

David D. Porter

Farragut had questioned the need for mortars all along, while Porter was sending dispatches to Washington suggesting that Farragut might be too old for the job, that his mind tended to wander from the task at hand.

By the end of the war, there would be plenty of chances for both brothers to distinguish themselves. David Porter proved especially effective working with William T. Sherman to capture Fort Hindman, Arkansas, in January 1863 and working with Gen. Alfred Terry to capture Fort Fisher, North Carolina, in January 1865. Ironically, the two most celebrated victories of the war for David Farragut, the Southerner, came against commanders who had left Union states to join the Confederacy. Commanding the defenses at New Orleans was Mansfield Lovell, who had been the deputy commissioner of streets in New York City just before the war. And Farragut's principal adversary in the battle of Mobile Bay (August 1864) was Franklin Buchanan of Maryland, captain of the ironclad ram *Tennessee*. In 1866, David G. Farragut was the first person ever awarded the rank of full admiral in the U.S. Navy. Four years later, his foster brother David D. Porter became the second person to achieve that rank.

GEORGE H. THOMAS

THE UNION army, like its navy, took one of its very best commanders from the South. George Henry Thomas of Virginia may well deserve the title "the most underrated general of the Civil War." He never lost a battle in which he was in overall command, and when he was involved in a Union defeat, it was often because his superior officers did not heed his advice. Thomas was

born in 1816, the son of John Thomas, a
slaveholding physician and farmer who lived
in Southampton County, in the southeastern
corner of the state.

The most memorable event in George
Thomas's early years was the Nat Turner rebellion, which occurred in Southampton
County when George was fifteen years old.
Nat Turner was a slave in the nearby Travis
household, outwardly docile and compliant,
but with apocalyptic visions of a great war of
black liberation. On the night of August 21,

George H. Thomas

1831, Turner slaughtered the Travis family in their beds. Then he and about
sixty followers, mostly field hands from surrounding farms, spent a night
and a day going from homestead to homestead, massacring all they found
within their reach, including women and children. Word of the bloody uprising quickly spread, and most of the rebels were shot or captured before
the state militia could arrive. Turner himself hid in the woods for six weeks,
but he was eventually caught and hanged. All told, about seventy whites
had been killed in Nat Turner's rebellion, and probably even more blacks,
both his followers and other slaves caught up in a backlash of bloody
reprisals. Turner's insurrection never threatened to ignite a widespread slave
revolt, but it generated waves of anxiety throughout the South. In Virginia,
Thomas Jefferson's grandson, T. J. Randolph, initiated a prolonged debate in
the House of Delegates, arguing that slaves should gradually be freed and
then deported to Africa.

In local tradition, fifteen-year-old George Thomas proved his mettle
during the Turner revolt, helping to evacuate his family, then riding to warn
neighbors of the impending danger. William Tecumseh Sherman, Thomas's
first-year roommate at West Point, once said that George was given his commission to the military academy as a reward for his bravery during the Nat
Turner scare. Sherman's recollection has never been verified, so it is not
clear whether this tale is based in fact or folklore.[6]

Throughout his life, George Thomas was known for his careful prepara-
tion. So it was very much in character that he left his home in Virginia for
West Point several weeks early in the summer of 1836 in order to brush up
on his studies before the fall term began. He need not have worried, for he

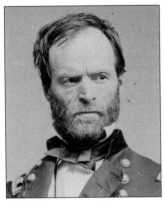

William Tecumseh Sherman

was a capable student and an accomplished rider. Thomas, at age twenty, was older than most others in his freshman class, and at nearly six feet, he was also taller. With his steady, self-possessed demeanor, George was called "Old Tom" or "George Washington" by his classmates. He graduated twelfth in the class of 1840; his friend "Cump" Sherman graduated sixth.

Upon leaving the military academy, Thomas received a commission as a second lieutenant in the artillery. He distinguished himself in the Seminole War of 1844 and was promoted to first lieutenant, earning brevet promotions to captain and then major during the Mexican War. (A brevet rank is honorary, awarded for gallant or meritorious service, and does not carry the authority or compensation of the actual rank.)

In 1851, Thomas returned to West Point as an instructor, teaching cavalry tactics to Philip H. Sheridan of Ohio and J. E. B. "Jeb" Stuart of Virginia and training John Bell Hood of Texas in the manual of artillery. While on the faculty at the academy, Thomas married Frances Kellogg of Troy, New York. In 1855, George Thomas was promoted to the rank of major in the regular army and assigned to the elite Second Cavalry, led by Col. Albert Sidney Johnston and Lt. Col. Robert E. Lee. Thomas received his most serious battlefield wound fighting Indians, not Confederates. In 1860, during a skirmish with Comanches on the Texas frontier, he was shot in the chin with an arrow, an injury that took almost a year to heal fully.

When Lincoln was elected president in November 1860, Thomas was a forty-four-year-old major of cavalry, serving in Texas under seventy-year-old Gen. David Twiggs. By this time Thomas had become a stocky, imposing figure with wavy black hair and a full beard, graying at the chin. He was described by different contemporaries as "massive," "leonine," and "someone who made his presence felt before he spoke a word."[7]

While his arrow wound was still healing, Thomas suffered another injury that would plague him the rest of his life. Traveling on leave to visit his family in New York, Thomas stepped off a train in the moonlight, lost his footing and fell down a steep embankment. He was laid up for six weeks with an injury to his spine and suffered afterward from chronic pain and stiffness in his back. This made him walk with a slow, ponderous step and earned him the nickname "Old Slow Trot" for his deliberate style of riding. But the outward demeanor was deceptive; Thomas always proved himself nimble-minded in battle, and his strategic planning could be downright audacious.

In January 1861, Thomas traveled to Washington, D.C., to report in person to the general in chief, his fellow Virginian, Winfield Scott. By that time South Carolina had already voted to secede from the Union and five other Deep South states would follow by the end of the month. Thomas warned Scott that Twiggs, a Georgian, "meditated treachery," but his warning went unheeded.[8] When Texas seceded the following month, Twiggs turned over Federal installations and supplies to Ben McCulloch of the Texas Rangers. Later Twiggs accepted a commission in the Confederate army.

Because of his injury, Thomas assumed his military career was over, and he applied for the position as commandant of the Virginia Military Institute. Though that position had been filled, he received a letter in March from Virginia governor John Letcher, asking him to resign from the Federal army and accept a position as chief of ordnance for the state militia. Though Thomas had been strongly denouncing extremists in both North and South for months, he had not taken sides. In a carefully worded reply to Governor Letcher, Thomas thanked him for his offer but said he would not resign his commission so long as Virginia stayed in the Union and so long as he was not "required to perform duties alike repulsive to honor and humanity."[9]

Like many Virginians, including Robert E. Lee, Thomas took a wait-and-see attitude in the early spring of 1861. After the surrender of Sumter in April and Lincoln's call for seventy-five thousand volunteers to put down the "combinations too powerful to be suppressed by the ordinary course of judicial proceedings," Virginia made its choice and so did most Virginians. Lee resigned his commission and soon reported to Confederate authorities at Richmond. Thomas was at Carlisle Barracks near Harrisburg, Pennsylvania, when he heard the news from Sumter. He immediately wired his wife and his sisters in Virginia that he intended to stay in the Federal army. Some have wondered if Thomas's Northern-born wife prevailed on him to cast his lot with the Union, but she later said the two of them never discussed the matter, his decision was based on his own sense of honoring his oath of allegiance. As for George's sisters in Southampton County, they burned all his letters, turned his portrait to the wall, and ceased to acknowledge him as their brother.

Upon reporting for duty, Thomas was assigned to train cavalry at Carlisle Barracks. With so few Southerners remaining in the Federal army, there were continuing questions about Thomas's loyalty and his intentions. To quiet camp gossip, he voluntarily appeared before a local judge and renewed his oath of loyalty to the United States and its flag. When he was promoted to fill Robert E. Lee's vacated position, he again took an oath of loyalty. Ten days later, he was promoted to full colonel, filling Albert Sidney Johnston's vacated position, once again repeating his oath. Though this was according to army regulations, a friend asked Thomas if he was getting tired of all this. "I don't care a snap of my fingers about it," Thomas answered. "If they want me to take the oath before each meal, I am ready to comply."[10]

Besides demonstrating his loyalty, Colonel Thomas also had to deal with divided loyalties among his men. After Massachusetts Gen. Benjamin F. Butler's defeat at Big Bethel, Virginia, in June 1861, one of the junior officers in Thomas's brigade said he was glad "the damned old abolitionist was whipped."[11] Another officer considered this a treasonous remark and challenged the other to a duel. Thomas put a stop to the duel and the bickering by calling his officers to attention, telling them emphatically that anyone who wished the defeat of Federal soldiers was indeed fighting on the wrong side, adding that there was to be no more talk about this being a war to abolish slavery.

This was not just a theoretical issue for Thomas, as he had grown up in a slaveholding family and he had a black body servant and a female cook with him when he was stationed in Texas. They became an encumbrance to him once the war started, but he said he "could not sell a human being" and he was never certain how humanely they might be treated by another owner.[12] Thomas sent his slaves to his home in Virginia for the duration of the war. After the war, the cook and her family did not want to part from the Thomases. George kept her on as a paid servant until 1869, when he was ordered to the Pacific Coast, and he sent her to work for his brother Benjamin in Vicksburg.

Though Robert E. Lee said that he could never draw his sword against his native state, Thomas was called upon to do so during the first summer of the war. His cavalry brigade was attached to the force of Gen. Robert Patterson, whose assignment was to keep Confederate Gen. Joseph E. Johnston's force tied up in the western part of the state, unable to reinforce P. G. T. Beauregard at Manassas Junction. (Patterson failed miserably, partly because he ignored Thomas's warnings that a large detachment seemed to have left Johnston, headed for Manassas.)

As a former instructor at West Point, Thomas's teaching duties did not end once the war began. In his brigade's first engagement, at Falling Waters, Virginia, against the cavalry of Thomas J. Jackson (not yet called "Stonewall"), a section of Union artillery kept firing enthusiastically at Rebel troopers who were no longer in sight. When one of Thomas's officers shouted out that the brigade to his right seemed to be hotly engaged, the colonel cocked his ear for a moment and then noted dryly that all the noise was coming from their own guns, that there was no return fire.

While he was in camp near the Potomac, Thomas was visited by his old West Point roommate, "Cump" Sherman, now a colonel, and his brother, John Sherman, a senator from Ohio. Sherman was ostensibly on an inspection tour, but he also sought reassurance, yet again, about Thomas's loyalty to the Union. Thomas responded in words that suited him perfectly. He said he would "stand firm" in his service to the federal government.[13] Then the two of them unrolled a map of the United States and talked about how the war was likely to develop strategically. Senator Sherman recalled afterward that his brother and Thomas put a dot on Richmond, then looked out west and pointed to Chattanooga, Nashville, and Vicksburg. He marveled later at their prescience about where the key battles would be fought, not knowing then what role they themselves would play in those battles.

Shortly after this meeting, Gen. Robert Anderson, lately the stalwart defender of Fort Sumter, was given command of the Department of the Cum-

Robert Anderson

LIBRARY OF CONGRESS

berland, based in Louisville, Kentucky. When choosing his immediate subordinates, Anderson asked for Sherman of Ohio, Don Carlos Buell of Kentucky, and George Thomas. The first two names caused no objections, but several politicians in Washington still weren't sure about Thomas the Virginian. They suggested instead another Kentuckian, Simon Bolivar Buckner. But Sherman recounted his recent conversation with Thomas, and Anderson too vouched for the Virginian's loyalty. So Thomas was promoted to brigadier general of volunteers in August 1861 and posted to the Department of the Cumberland. (Ironically, the politicians' first choice, Simon Buckner, resigned his commission and joined the Confederates. It was Buckner who surrendered Fort Donelson to Ulysses S. Grant in February 1862.)

Thomas was assigned to train and lead six thousand new recruits from Kentucky and Tennessee, volunteers who would become the core of the sixty-thousand-man Army of the Cumberland, the largest army in the western theater. This was about the time the broad-shouldered, graying Thomas became known affectionately among his troops as "Pap."

Thomas's first independent command in battle came in January 1862. His prewar commander in the cavalry, Albert Sidney Johnston, was by then the highest-ranking Confederate general in the field, charged with defending a five-hundred-mile line that stretched from the Cumberland Gap in eastern Kentucky through southern Missouri to the Mississippi River. The linchpin of Johnston's strategic line on the right was a force of four thousand men under Brig. Gen. Felix Zollicoffer, a former Tennessee newspaperman and congressman. Zollicoffer was charged with guarding the approaches to the Cumberland Gap and blocking any Federal attempts to march on Knoxville. He was ordered to Mill Springs, Kentucky, on the south bank of the Cumberland River, but to his inexperienced eyes, the north bank looked like a better place to make camp.

On the last day of 1861, Thomas left the outskirts of Louisville with five thousand men, intent on prying loose the right anchor of Johnston's line. The hundred-mile march to meet Zollicoffer's forces turned out to be a greater trial for Thomas's untested troops than the battle itself. Cold winter rains turned the roads to mush, making weary soldiers sink to their shins in mud and baggage wagons up to their axles. It took two weeks to cover the distance, and one-fifth of Thomas's force didn't make it, some dying in route and others joining the sick list or receiving medical discharges. Finally, on January 17, 1862, Thomas's division made camp near Logan's Crossroads, on both sides of a swollen stream called Fishing Creek, about nine miles north of the Confederates near Mill Springs. (The battle that took place

Felix Zollicoffer

two days later is called by all three names: Mill Springs, Logan's Crossroads, and Fishing Creek.)

Zollicoffer's regional commander, George B. Crittenden, arrived on the scene a few days before the battle, astonished to find the Confederate troops on the north side of the Cumberland with the enemy to their front and an unfordable river at their back. By then it was too late to withdraw, with Federal forces so nearby, but he also considered it unwise to wait for Thomas to strike, because Zollicoffer's chosen position left no room for maneuver or retreat. At midnight on January 18, Crittenden and Zollicoffer set out in a pelting rain with eight regiments of infantry, a six-gun battery, and a battalion of cavalry. Crittenden hoped to surprise Thomas's troops, still drying out and resting from their arduous march and divided by the unpassable Fishing Creek. But Thomas turned out to be not so easily surprised as Crittenden hoped, nor Fishing Creek so heavily flooded.

All that night, the Confederates fought the same elements the Federals had been fighting the past two weeks—cold, wetness, mud, and fatigue. They didn't arrive at the fringes of the Federal encampment till 5:30 the next morning, and Thomas's cavalry videttes galloped back to Logan's Crossroads with the news that a gray column was approaching. The leading Confederate regiments quickly formed a battle line, discovering not only that they had lost the element of surprise but also a good deal of their firepower. Those among them carrying flintlocks could not fire their rain-soaked weapons and had to be sent to the rear. Even so, Crittenden's initial charge drove the Federal front line back to the edge of the woods. But Thomas quickly sent in reinforcements, as he had disposed his troops so that each wing could be reinforced by the other at places where Fishing Creek could be forded.

As the firing intensified, Zollicoffer's inexperience cost him his life—and cost Crittenden his reputation. Zollicoffer went to the front to take command personally, even though his vision was poor and he wore a white raincoat over his uniform. Thus he had trouble spotting the enemy, but they had no trouble at all spotting him. Riding too close to a clump of Federal officers, Zollicoffer was shot down at close range in full view of his men. Already weary from their all-night march, the Confederates gave way soon afterward, some crying out, "We are betrayed!" as they scattered to the rear.

Not content simply to repulse the dawn assault, Thomas quickly organized a pursuit. His troops pressed the retreating graybacks all the way to the

Cumberland River, where a remnant escaped on an old stern-wheel steamer and two flatboats, abandoning their camp at Mill Springs. Crittenden lost 500 men in the battle as well as 12 cannon, 1,000 horses and mules, 150 wagons, and 6 regimental flags. (Thomas reported 247 casualties, meaning that he lost four times as many men marching to the battle as he did in fighting it.)

This was the first Confederate defeat of the war, and its commander paid dearly for it. People couldn't understand how Crittenden could lose a battle in his home state of Kentucky, and they darkly recalled that his brother was a general in the Union army. He was arrested and accused of drunkenness during the battle. Though the charges were baseless, Crittenden eventually resigned his commission.

In retrospect, it seems that Crittenden lost more in the battle than Thomas gained. In similar circumstances during the war, many other commanders received battlefield promotions. But after its decisive victory, Thomas's army received a letter of commendation from Lincoln's new secretary of war, Edwin M. Stanton, but Thomas was not specifically mentioned as their leader. It was rumored that Lincoln himself had dismissed the idea of promoting Thomas with the words, "Let the Virginian wait."[14] (This rumor is certainly open to question. Lincoln had high regard for the judgment of another Virginian, Winfield Scott. And it is well known that he preferred fighting generals over those favored by Washington or West Point cliques. But unlike generals from Northern states, Thomas had no one in Congress to champion his cause.)

Apart from personal advancement, Thomas did not see the strategic gains he had hoped for from his victory at Logan's Crossroads. Crittenden's army, depleted by desertions, fell back to Chesnut Mound, sixty miles from Nashville. This left the way wide open for Federal troops to occupy east Tennessee and give support to the Unionist enclave there. But Thomas's force was too small, his rations too low, and the roads too bad for him to make an immediate advance. In February 1862, he asked for twenty thousand men in order to march into east Tennessee. Apart from returning this region to the Union, he also thought it would make an excellent staging area for a strike into the heart of the Deep South. But his proposals went unheard, and soon the opportunity was lost. It would be nearly two years and many more battles—Shiloh, Perryville, Stones River, Chickamauga, Chattanooga—before the Federals could successfully thrust southward from Tennessee deep into Georgia.

In the summer of 1862, it was the Rebels who successfully launched a major offensive out of Tennessee, headed north in hopes of reclaiming Kentucky for the Confederacy. In mid-August, Gen. Edmund Kirby Smith left Knoxville, marched north, and occupied Lexington with ten thousand troops, gaining control of the Bluegrass region in the central part of the state. For a time, Smith's army met so little opposition that panicky officials in Cincinnati, Ohio, cobbled together a makeshift home guard. It appeared the Confederate tide in the western theater might flow all the way up into the Northern states. Confederate Gen. Braxton Bragg soon followed, marching north from Chattanooga with twenty-two thousand men, taking control of western Kentucky and stopping long enough to install a provisional Confederate governor in the state. Union Gen. Don Carlos Buell eventually gave chase, reaching Louisville late in September, while Bragg turned east to join forces with Smith in the middle of the state.

Officials in Washington were dismayed that Buell could allow two Confederate armies to slip behind him and that he seemed so slow to respond to the crisis at hand. On September 30, Buell was relieved as head of the Army of the Ohio, and George Thomas, Buell's second in command, was ordered to replace him. Thomas demurred, explaining that Buell was on the verge of launching his offensive against Bragg and that it wasn't fair to either of them to change leaders on the eve of battle. Buell was restored to command the next day, and he marched out of Louisville with sixty thousand men, intent on coming to grips with the forces that had given him the slip earlier in Tennessee. The two armies came together almost by accident on October 8, fighting haphazardly and inconclusively near Perryville, south of Lexington. When Bragg withdrew to the south to shorten his supply lines, Buell's languid pursuit allowed the outnumbered Confederates to escape unmolested.

By the end of October, Buell's grace period was over. He seemed to have spent less time that summer and fall fighting Confederate forces than he had trying to find them. Instead of giving command of the Army of the Ohio to Thomas, however, the Virginian was passed over in favor of Maj. Gen. William S. Rosecrans. Apparently, once the emergency had passed, Thomas was not considered the best choice because of lingering doubts in Washington about his "loyalty, earnestness in the war, or capacity as a general."[15]

Thomas protested this decision because he outranked Rosecrans and because he was already familiar with the command structure of the Army of the Ohio. He explained that he had declined the command a month earlier because of the untimeliness of the order, not because of doubts about his own fitness. But Gen. Henry W. Halleck, the Federal army's administrative head in Washington, replied that the decision had been made by higher authorities (presumably Lincoln or Stanton). With typical stoicism, Thomas reconciled himself to being passed over. As he concluded to Halleck, "I have made my last protest while the war lasts. You may hereafter put a stick over me if you choose to do so. I will take care, however, to so manage my command, whatever it may be, as not to be involved in the mistakes of the stick."[16]

It is a tribute to Thomas's character that he served so ably as a corps commander under a general whose job he thought should be his own. In the early months of the war, Thomas had told his friend Sherman that he intended to "stand firm" in his service to the Union. Thomas did just that, for all the world to see, in the two major battles he fought under Rosecrans: Stones River and Chickamauga.

By December 1862, the Federals under Rosecrans were at Nashville and the Confederates under Bragg were at Murfreesboro, about thirty miles southeast of the Tennessee capital. Rosecrans worked feverishly to refit and resupply the depleted Army of the Ohio, but authorities in Washington urged him night and day to do something about the forty thousand Confederate so near his front. So Rosecrans moved out with forty-five thousand men on the day after Christmas, with Thomas commanding four divisions in the army center, Alexander McCook commanding the right wing, and Thomas Crittenden in charge of the left.

Rosecrans's army set out to confront Bragg at Murfreesboro almost exactly a year after Thomas's trek to defeat Thomas Crittenden's brother George at Mill Springs, about 165 miles to the northeast. It was the same kind of marching weather, and it took the Federals five days to cover thirty miles, slowed by muddy roads and dense fog, as well as slashing attacks by the Confederate cavalry. Bragg too was on the move, leaving Murfreesboro and crossing the meandering Stones River, forming a defensive line that faced north and northwest. As Rosecrans's brigades came up, they created a battle line that resembled a great bird, with its wings lifted at a slight angle, four miles from tip to tip.

As the two armies faced each other across the rugged terrain, broken by rocky hillocks and stands of cedar, their commanders formulated similar battle plans: to hold with their right and strike a crushing blow with their left. The next morning, on the last day of the year, Bragg's army moved first.

Just after 6:00 a.m., he sent two divisions forward, nearly nine thousand men, against unwary Federal brigades, some of whom were still cooking breakfast when they were overwhelmed by the advancing graybacks. McCook's corps was driven back three miles in the early morning assault. If that wing could be broken and if Confederate cavalry could swing around to block the Nashville turnpike, Rosecrans's army would be a flightless bird pinned between Bragg's forces and the rising waters of Stones River.

Near the center, a Union divisional commander, Philip H. Sheridan, slowed the Rebel advance with well-aimed artillery fire and a fierce counterattack. But he was in danger of being surrounded on three sides and so withdrew to stay in touch with elements of the collapsing Union right wing. As the morning wore on, the great Confederate turning movement began to lose its momentum, and the Federals, reinforced from their left, held their ground within shooting distance of the turnpike, their avenue of escape. George Thomas, who always had an eye for good ground, had seen early in the battle that the key to holding this position was a four-acre patch of

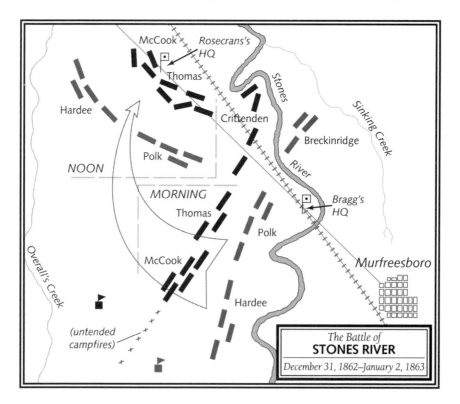

The Battle of
STONES RIVER

December 31, 1862–January 2, 1863

woods known locally as the Round Forest. The Federal line had been squeezed into the shape of a spearhead, and Thomas packed the tip of the spear, the Round Forest, with entrenched infantry and field guns standing nearly hub to hub.

The first to charge the Round Forest was a brigade of Mississippians under Brig. Gen. James R. Chalmers. They came on the run but were torn apart by a thunderous volley of rifle fire. Reforming, they tried again, but were blasted at close range by Thomas's massed artillery. The din of battle became so deafening that men stopped to stuff cotton in their ears before advancing. Terrified rabbits raced out of the thicket and tried to wriggle under prone men for safety. In the end, Chalmers was killed. The field was so thickly strewn with the bodies of his men that this part of the battle-ground became known ever after as the "Mississippi Half-Acre."[17]

The Round Forest could not be taken, and at the end of the day's fighting, Rosecrans's army still had a center, two wings (one pinioned), and a secure line of retreat to Nashville. But the Federals had lost a fourth of their number in killed, wounded, and missing and had given up twenty-eight pieces of artillery. That night Rosecrans called his ranking officers together for a council of war, clearly contemplating a withdrawal. As the discussion dragged on toward midnight, the exhausted Thomas began to doze. When Rosecrans asked him directly if his men could act as a rear guard in a retreat, Thomas stirred himself, declared "This army can't retreat," and fell back to sleep. The other corps commanders agreed, so Rosecrans decided to hold his ground for the time being.

Historian John R. Peacock has speculated that the words, "This army can't retreat," uttered by a half-dozing man, might be arguably one of the turning points of the Civil War.[18] The Yankees had just suffered one of their most one-sided defeats of the war at Fredericksburg in mid-December, and Grant's first attempt to take Vicksburg (Sherman's assault on the bluffs north of town) had been bloodily repulsed only a few days before the fight at Stones River. If the Federals were driven out of Tennessee as well, the Northern press and public might decide that the price of preserving the Union was too high, that it was time to let the Confederate states go their own way. Simply by staying put, Rosecrans turned a near-disaster into a kind of victory by default.

Bragg's forces were every bit as battered as their foe, with nearly a third of the army out of action after the day's savage fighting. Bragg would have much more trouble getting reinforcements than Rosecrans, and Stones River was rising at his back. After the fighting on December 31, in which he had driven back one wing of Rosecrans's army, Bragg wired Richmond exultantly that he had won a major victory. But the Yankees were still in front of Bragg the next day, apparently ready to receive another attack. After glaring across the picket lines on January 1, Bragg ordered a halfhearted assault on the other wing of the Federal army, which cost him another eighteen hundred casualties. The following night his army, unbeaten but unable to renew the fight, withdrew across Stones River, trudged through Murfreesboro, and headed south.

Lincoln later wrote a personal letter to Rosecrans, congratulating him for a "hard-earned victory."[19] But the victory, such as it was, may have belonged more to Thomas, commanding the center, as well as hard-hitting divisional commanders such as Philip H. Sheridan. As one of his staff officers concluded, "General Thomas gained greater distinction in other battles, but never did he meet a crisis with more promptness and skill" than at Stones River.[20]

The battle in which Thomas gained greatest distinction, earned in fact unfading renown, was fought between the same two armies under the same two commanders, Rosecrans and Bragg. After that desperate contest, Thomas also gained his most famous nickname; "Pap" or "Old Slow Trot" was thereafter best known as "the Rock of Chickamauga."

After Stones River, both armies were bled white, and both took the first six months of 1863 to recover. Like Buell the previous summer, Rosecrans was constantly harried by his superiors in Washington to do something about Bragg's Army of Tennessee. Once he had perfected his preparations, Rosecrans did move with surprising speed in late June, bewildering Bragg with a series of feints and flanking maneuvers that caused him to withdraw to Chattanooga and then through the mountain gaps into north Georgia.

In the first week of September 1863, Thomas advised Rosecrans that his army, now called the Army of the Cumberland, should pause in Chattanooga (abandoned by Bragg without a fight), secure their supply lines, and reconnoiter just what the Confederates were up to beyond the screen of mountains south of the city. But Rosecrans, influenced perhaps by ceaseless prodding from Washington, was convinced that Bragg's army was demoralized and in full retreat. Still, Thomas recommended that the army proceed cautiously through the mountain gaps, that their marching columns stay close enough together for mutual support in case of trouble. Rosecrans again did not see the need, believing by then that the Army of Tennessee would not stop to look over their shoulders till they got all the way to Atlanta. Thomas was generally a taciturn individual, not one to insist on his way once his counsel had been rejected. There was probably no general on either side during the war who so often had good advice to offer, but whose advice fell on deaf ears because of the quiet, undemonstrative manner in which he offered it.

Rosecrans temporarily left a portion of his army under Crittenden in Chattanooga, sending Thomas to one gap in the long ridge of Lookout Mountain twenty miles south of town and McCook to another gap twenty miles farther on. Thus the three segments of the Army of the Cumberland were spread out over forty miles on the assumption that the Rebels were hastily withdrawing farther south. But Bragg's army was not demoralized, nor was it in retreat. It lay in wait at McLemore's Cove, positioned to shatter Thomas's column before either Crittenden or McCook, both two days' march away, could come to his aid. The Army of Tennessee, gaining reinforcements every hour from as far away as Virginia and Mississippi, would eventually reach a strength of sixty thousand, one of the few times in the war when a Confederate army outnumbered the Federal force it opposed.

Unfortunately for the Rebels, Bragg's contempt for his corps commanders was matched only by their contempt for him. Twice his orders for a surprise attack on Thomas's leading brigades misfired because of his balky subordinates. By September 12, Rosecrans realized his danger, and he ordered Crittenden south and McCook north to join Thomas in the middle. Bragg's attempts to prevent the three segments of the Union force from reuniting were again frustrated by miscommunications with his corps commanders. So the Federal Army of the Cumberland drew up in line of battle west of Chickamauga Creek, barely able to make out the Confederate dispositions across the way because of wooded thickets that covered most of the ground.

Bragg's battle plan was a mirror image of the one he had devised at Stones River. This time he planned a crushing blow on his right, where Thomas's corps was positioned, hoping to drive it until the line of retreat, the road back to Chattanooga, was cut off and it was trapped in the cul de sac of McLemore's Cove. The battle opened on September 19, but it went according to no one's master plan. The leafy woods, narrow country roads, and dense underbrush prevented the orderly advance of troops or the effective use of artillery. It was a soldier's battle, ferocious charges and desperate stands by isolated brigades and regiments, with neither commanding general able to do much more than feed fresh troops into the melee. Thomas's position on the Federal left, the north end of the battle line, was hardest hit, as that was the wing Bragg hoped to break in order to cut off Rosecrans's line of retreat. Though the fighting was ferocious all that day, it was inconclusive, both sides suffering fearful casualties but neither side gaining a clear advantage.

As at Stones River, Rosecrans called a council of war at the end of the first day's fight. Having been heavily engaged all day, Thomas again had trouble staying awake, mumbling only, "I would strengthen the left," and then drowsing some more. Once more it was decided that they should maintain their positions and see what the next day would bring. This time, though, Bragg had the larger army, and it was he who would get reinforcements. That night, September 19, Gen. James Longstreet and six thousand hard-fighting veterans arrived by train from Virginia, joining another six thousand who had been detached from Lee's army and had arrived the day before. The second day's fighting at Chickamauga seemed for a while like a mere continuation of the first, a series of fierce but uncoordinated attacks on the Federal line, especially on the Union left under Thomas. Rosecrans kept sending more and more reinforcements to Thomas's flank, which at times was under attack from both front and rear. Amid all the confusion and shifting of troops, one of the divisions on the right side of the front, Crittenden's, pulled out of line, not realizing they had left a half-mile-wide gap in the Federal defenses. At just that moment, Longstreet sent five fresh divisions forward, sixteen thousand men driving through the gap like floodwaters rushing through a break in a dam. The Federal right collapsed, its scattered remnants scurrying north, headed for a crossroads five miles in back of the battlefield, hoping to reach the safety of Chattanooga. Rosecrans himself, along with corps commanders McCook and Crittenden, joined in the shambling retreat, assuming the entire Federal line had been broken. The last they had heard from Thomas, he was under savage attack from two sides, so they believed his half of the line must have been engulfed by now.

But Thomas's position had not been overrun. In fact, his line had not been broken. As he had done at Stones River, Thomas had pointed out before the battle what he considered the key to his position. This time it was a little knoll known as Snodgrass Hill that was joined by long rise called Horseshoe Ridge. Seeing the right half of the Federal army falling back in disarray, Thomas contracted his lines into a U-shape on the high ground,

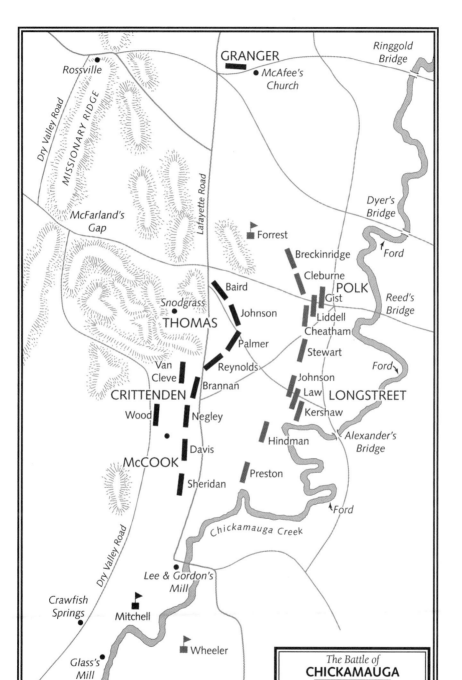

The Battle of
CHICKAMAUGA
September 19, 1863

deciding he would try to hold out till nightfall, covering the withdrawal of the shattered remnants of Rosecrans's army.

Thomas still had about one-third of the Army of the Cumberland arrayed in a semicircle on the hill, and all that afternoon Gens. James Longstreet and Leonidas Polk, each with about twenty thousand men, charged the position from both sides of the incline. Outnumbered more than two to one and running low on ammunition, Thomas's position seemed within minutes of collapsing when he saw a column of dust from a large body of marching men directly in his rear. He raised his field glasses for a moment to see if he could make out who they were. If they wore blue,

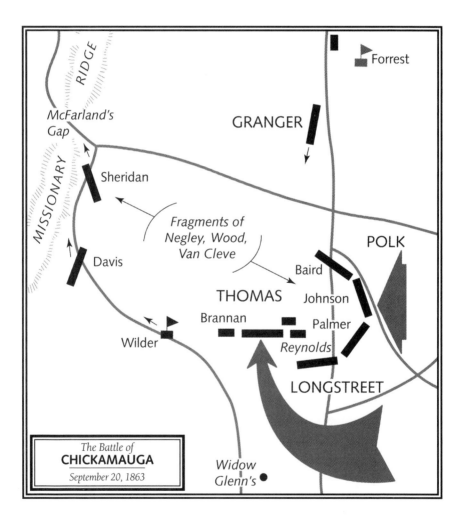

The Battle of
CHICKAMAUGA
September 20, 1863

they might just help him stave off defeat. If they wore gray, then he was surrounded, and his whole corps would be killed or captured.

Still peering at the column of dust, he handed the glasses to an aide, saying that perhaps someone with a steadier hand could make out if the approaching column was friend or foe. Still, it was impossible to tell, until their leader, Union Gen. Gordon Granger, appeared, bringing thirty-five hundred men and much-needed ammunition. Thomas immediately sent Granger to drive back a Confederate line that had already begun another charge up the north side of the hill.

Granger and his reserve brigades had been posted four miles north of the battlefield, and all morning they had stood idle while hearing the boom of cannon and the rattle of rifle fire. Finally, without orders and on his own initiative, Granger concluded that Thomas's command must be nearing the breaking point, and he marched his men toward the sound of the firing. The reserves did indeed allow Thomas to maintain the integrity of his line, sometimes in hand-to-hand fighting. By the end of the day, nearly half of the men Granger brought to Snodgrass Hill would be killed, wounded, or missing.

As the sun descended toward the horizon, Thomas began an orderly withdrawal with no letup in the intensity of the fighting. By nightfall, he had his men on the road to Chattanooga, joining the rest of Rosecrans's army, including the dejected leader himself, corps commanders Crittenden and McCook, and more than half the Army of the Cumberland. They had scattered from the field in a scene of utter chaos, but they had been given all afternoon to retreat in relative safety because of Thomas's rear-guard action. The Army of the Cumberland had suffered one of the worst Union defeats of the war, but it had not been annihilated.

Bragg's army was badly cut up too. Though they unquestionably held the field, the attackers had actually suffered about two thousand more casualties than the routed defenders. (Both armies lost about one-third of their effectives on the field, eighteen thousand and sixteen thousand, respectively, the highest casualty rates of the war after Gettysburg and the Seven Days' battles.) Bragg did not think his army was in any shape to engage in an active pursuit. Instead, he allowed Rosecrans to fall back to Chattanooga, then he invested the city from the south, commanding the heights of Lookout Mountain, Missionary Ridge, and Tunnel Hill. Though they did not have the city encircled, the Confederates controlled nearly all of its supply routes and effectively had the Union army besieged.

Rosecrans seemed stunned by his defeat and was widely reported to be confused and indecisive about what to do next. In mid-October, Lincoln met with Gen. James B. Steedman, one of the Granger's brigade commanders who had joined the desperate fight on Snodgrass Hill. When the president asked if Rosecrans should be replaced, Steedman reluctantly replied that he should. When asked who should replace him, Steedman answered without hesitation, "General George H. Thomas." Lincoln nodded in agreement, but he explained that "a powerful New York delegation" had come to him the previous day, protesting that anyone from a Rebel state should be elevated to so high a position as commander of a Federal army.[21] This was the third year of the war, after Logan's Crossroads and Stones River. Thomas was already being called "the Rock of Chickamauga" for his heroic stand on Snodgrass Hill. And yet, in the minds of some Northern politicians, he was still "the Virginian." Until the last year of the war, Thomas's allegiance to the federal government was much more apparent than the federal government's allegiance to him.

Lincoln turned the decision over to Ulysses S. Grant, who he had just named commander of the western theater. On October 19, Grant relieved Rosecrans of command and turned the Army of the Cumberland over to Thomas. Though he served capably in that position till the end of the war, Thomas is still most remembered as the Rock of Chickamauga. It was the soldiers in the Army of the Cumberland who decided, without orders, to storm the slope of Missionary Ridge, crying "Chickamauga!" as they drove the Confederates back into north Georgia. During Sherman's campaign in the summer of 1864, driving from Chattanooga to Atlanta, Thomas's Army of the Cumberland, made up three-fifths of the Union force of one hundred thousand, usually occupying the center. After the fall of Atlanta, Sherman made his famous March to the Sea with sixty thousand handpicked troops, leaving Thomas in command out west to deal with the remnants of the Confederate Army of Tennessee, now under John Bell Hood. Named head of the Military Division of the Mississippi on October 19, 1864, exactly one year after he had been named commander of the Army of the Cumberland, Thomas assembled his defenses around Nashville and decisively defeated Hood's armies in a two-day battle, December 15–16.

Though he is sometimes described as ponderous, Thomas acted with remarkable celerity in the defense of Nashville. The forces assembled there were described by one colonel as "an ill-sorted and heterogeneous mass, not yet wielded into an army [suitable] to undertake an aggressive campaign."[22]

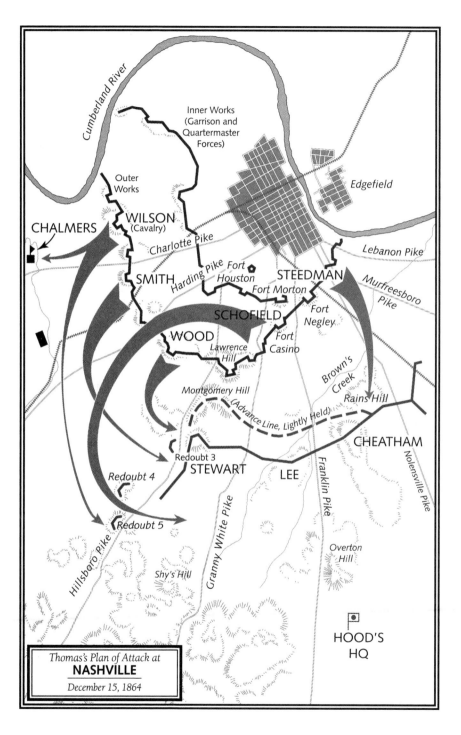

Thomas's Plan of Attack at
NASHVILLE
December 15, 1864

Yet when Hood's army arrived at the gates of Nashville on December 2, Thomas took only eight days to devise a plan for leaving the safety of the city and driving back the Confederates on the hills south of town. Delayed five days by an ice storm, Thomas was finally able to strike on December 15, following up the next day with one of the most one-sided victories of the war. Even Hood, who had a tendency to downplay his losses, said of the second day's fighting below Nashville, "I beheld for the first and only time a Confederate army abandon the field in confusion." Though no one knew it at the time, Nashville was the last full-scale battle of the Civil War. Thomas gave the Union its last major victory, as he had given the North its first western victory at Logan's Crossroads nearly two years earlier. Thomas was promoted to major general in the regular army for his victory over Hood, and he was offered the official Thanks of Congress by a joint resolution of the House and Senate.

After the war, George Thomas stayed in the army and was assigned to command of the Department of the Pacific. Though he was reconciled with his brother Benjamin in Mississippi, he never again spoke to his sisters in Southampton County, Virginia. The only time they wrote him was to ask that he change his surname so as not to bring shame to the family. While on duty in San Francisco, Thomas died of a stroke in 1870, the same year Robert E. Lee passed into history. Of course, Lee was lionized after his death throughout the South, but Thomas has been seldom mentioned. And yet in the opinion of the distinguished Civil War historian Bruce Catton, "When the Union army got Thomas, it gained very nearly as much as it had lost when it failed to get Lee."[23]

* * *

On balance, Southerners who fought for the North were a much more significant military factor than Northerners who fought in Confederate gray. The Federal hosts included more than one hundred thousand white Southerners, three-quarters of them from the rugged mountain country of western Virginia, east Tennessee, north Georgia, north Alabama, and northeastern Arkansas.[24] The Union also benefited more from the vigorous leadership provided by its commanders who had crossed over from the South: Charles Steedman, Winfield Scott, John Gibbon, and most especially, David G. Farragut and George H. Thomas.

3

WEST VIRGINIA
THE STATE THAT SECEDED FROM
THE CONFEDERACY

W E HAVE [IN THIS movement] insurrection, revolution, and secession. . . . To admit a state under such a government is entirely unauthorized, revolutionary, subversive of the Constitution and destructive of the Union of States."[1] These heated words were not spoken by Abraham Lincoln or anyone in his administration, and the subject was not any state in the Confederacy. Rather this statement comes from Jefferson Davis, writing after the war, condemning the leaders of northwestern Virginia for seceding from the Old Dominion and declaring their region to be a new Union state called West Virginia.

Actually, the idea of carving a new state out of part of an existing one created a problem for authorities in both Richmond and Washington. Jefferson Davis had declared in his inaugural speech as president of the Confederacy in February 1861 that "governments rest on the consent of the governed, and that it is the right of the people to alter or abolish them."[2] Yet here were a people who had consented, by a margin of two to one, to stay in the Union, not to join the Confederacy. But Lincoln, in his inaugural speech the following month, had declared, with all the lawyerly ingenuity he could muster, that secession was unconstitutional. So how was he to sanction a new state being created out of part of an old one without the approval of state officials who were being asked to cede this part of their territory? This was explicitly prohibited in the U.S. Constitution, article 4, section 3. (It was also forbidden in the Confederate Constitution.) Lincoln had a legal problem, and Davis had a political one. Ultimately, as so often happened in the years 1861–65, issues of law and politics were submitted to a tribunal of blood and iron.

Just as there were three Souths at the beginning of the Civil War—upper, middle, and lower—there were also three Virginias, running east to west. Eastern Virginia was dominated by the planter aristocracy, with a black population of 40–50 percent, mostly slaves. Western Virginia was separated from the east by two mountain barriers, the Blue Ridge and the Alleghenies (both part of the Appalachians, the continental range that runs from southern Canada to northern Georgia). Its population contained a large proportion of Scots-Irish and German immigrants who had come from the North, not west from Tidewater Virginia. In the northwestern counties, less than 5 percent of the population were slaves. Between the Alleghenies and the coastal plain lay a middle Virginia, with about 25 percent enslaved. This was the fertile Shenandoah Valley, a strategic natural corridor that was very much in the middle of things once the fighting began.[3]

Historically, regional conflicts in the colonies erupted more often between east and west than between North and South. The most serious of these was the Regulator movement that emerged in the Carolinas just before the American Revolution. The Regulators were farmers on the frontier in the mid-1760s who complained that the colonial government was collecting revenues from them but not providing marshals or courts to maintain the rule of law. If they had adopted a rallying cry, it might have been "No taxation without regulation." That is, they didn't see why they should be expected to pay for government services if none were being provided. Consequently, they created their own local sheriffs and law courts and chased away tax collectors sent from the coastal government.

In May 1771, more than 1,000 British troops marched upcountry and crushed a ragged militia of Regulators at the battle of Alamance Creek, killing more than 200 mountaineers. Despite this victory, the English continued to struggle to enforce their jurisdiction over the colonists in Appalachia. The Regulator spirit of the Southern mountains re-emerged as Revolutionary spirit later that in the war for American independence. In 1780, the people of the western Carolinas, joined by 300 "Over-Mountain Men" from east Tennessee, soundly defeated the British at King's Mountain, killing 150 redcoats and taking 1,000 prisoners.[4] But after uniting to defeat a common foe, eastern planters and western farmers again found themselves at odds in the decades after the American Revolution.

In the state of Virginia, tensions between east and west became evident almost as soon as the war for independence had begun. In 1776, pioneers on the Allegheny plateau sent a petition to Congress asking that their region be established as a new state, Westsylvania. As their proposed name suggests, the people there saw their settlement to be as much a southern extension of Pennsylvania as it was a western extension of Virginia. In the decades after the Revolution, tensions between east and west, the Tidewater and the trans-Allegheny, centered on voting rights and proportional representation. In 1830, the right to vote was limited to white males who owned at least fifty acres of land or its equivalent, leaving half the state's adult white males ineligible.[5] (Women and blacks were also ineligible to vote, of course, leaving about one-sixth of the adult population to make political decisions for the state.) The three-fifths clause of the Constitution granted even more power to the planter aristocrats. According to this provision, blacks were counted as three-fifths in each census, giving the Virginia "black belt" counties, those with the highest proportion of slaves, greater voting power than the western counties, some of which had virtually no slaves.

By the middle of the nineteenth century, there were more Virginians west of the Alleghenies eligible to vote than there were in the coastal counties. But the western majority still had one-third fewer representatives in the lower house of delegates.[6] It didn't help matters that Tidewater aristocrats sometimes defended this state of affairs as being perfectly just, explaining that the "hardy peasantry of the mountains" didn't have the intellectual capacity to govern as wisely as their social betters in the east.[7]

After South Carolina seceded in December 1860, followed within weeks by the other Deep South states, many Virginians in the northwestern counties made their sentiments clear. At a mass meeting in Parkersburg, just across the river from the state of Ohio, twelve hundred local citizens approved a declaration that the nation's well-being depended upon preserving the Union, and that Lincoln's victory at the polls, in and of itself, was no reason to forsake "the best Government ever yet devised by the wisdom and patriotism of men."[8] A similar gathering farther south, in Greenbrier County, declared that it was "unwise, impolitic, and unpatriotic not to give Mr. Lincoln a fair trial before we either secede from the Union or condemn his administration."[9] On April 17, 1861 (four days after the surrender of Fort Sumter and two days after Lincoln's call for volunteers), the Virginia convention passed an ordinance of secession by a vote of eighty-eight to fifty-five. Of the dissenting votes, nearly three-fifths came from counties west of the Alleghenies.

Having cast their votes, the delegates in Richmond also called for a state referendum on May 23 to ratify their ordinance of secession. Many regional leaders from the west quickly returned to their homes and tried to organize local Unionists. In mid-May, 435 informally chosen representatives from 27 western counties convened in Wheeling to decide what their next move should be. (Located in a sliver of Virginia jutting up between Pennsylvania and Ohio, Wheeling was not only the northernmost city in the South, it was also farther north than Indianapolis, Cincinnati, or Gettysburg.) At this gathering, later called the First Wheeling Convention, John S. Carlile, a fiery Unionist, argued that the western counties should immediately separate themselves from any portion of the Old Dominion that planned to secede from the Union. Other leaders, such as Francis H. Pierpont and Waitman T. Willey, however, urged restraint, proposing that the delegates wait until after the referendum later that month and then, if necessary, reconvene in June.

BATTLES FOR THE ALLEGHENIES

FROM THE very start, both sides could see the strategic importance of western Virginia. The Baltimore and Ohio Railroad, a vital link between the eastern seaboard and the middle west, ran through the Old Dominion for almost two hundred miles, from Harpers Ferry on the Potomac River to Parkersburg on the Ohio. And the long curving ridges of the Alleghenies provided a natural barrier for whoever controlled the region, protecting the left flank of Virginia for the Confederacy and shielding the Ohio River Valley for the Union. On May 3, 1861, Virginia governor John Letcher ordered a detachment of state militia under Col. George A. Porterfield to concentrate in Grafton, a key railroad junction where one branch of the railroad from Baltimore continued on to Parkersburg while another headed northwest toward Wheeling. When Porterfield's troops reached the small railroad town, he found the people there openly hostile to the secessionist regime at Richmond. There is "much bitterness of feeling among the people of this region," he reported, explaining that "they are apparently on the verge of civil war." He also warned that "traitors have seized the guns and ammunitions of the State, to be used against its authority," adding that local militia companies had disbanded, taking their rifles with them, apparently to be used against the Confederacy.[10]

After some trestles on the Baltimore and Ohio line were burned, the newly appointed head of the Union Department of the Ohio, Gen. George B. McClellan, ordered his troops to advance and drive the Rebels out of Grafton. When the Union army occupied the town on May 30, it was one of the few times in the war that Federal troops would march into a Southern district and be greeted by cheering men and smiling women. Four days later, the Federals launched an early-morning attack on Porterfield's detachment, which had withdrawn to Philippi, fifteen miles south. The Confederates were taken completely by surprise, and they scurried farther south in slashing rain, abandoning most of their equipment, some retreating in their underwear. Though it was only a skirmish, with none killed and fewer than twenty wounded on both sides, the attack at Philippi is sometimes called the first battle of the Civil War. (Others reserve this distinction for a larger engagement the following week at Big Bethel, fought on the other side of Virginia, on the York-James Peninsula.)

Though it was only a minor clash militarily, the Federal victory at Philippi had important consequences. For one thing, it provided a much-needed morale boost in the North, where newspapers exultantly referred to the Confederate rout as "the Philippi races." The triumph of Federal arms in the region also emboldened local Unionists to take the next step in breaking away from Richmond. In the referendum of May 23, Virginians statewide had ratified the ordinance of secession by a six-to-one margin (though Unionists claimed thousands of their votes had not been tallied).[11] In the western counties, the vote had been two-to-one *against* secession. The week after the Confederates were chased out of Philippi, Unionists from the western counties

Almost as soon as the sun was beginning to rise on June 3, 1861, a shell exploded in the Confederate camp at Philippi in northwestern Virginia. The raw Rebel recruits fled as five Federal regiments advanced on the site. The Union success was the beginning of Federal control of this region of the Old Dominion.

HARPER'S WEEKLY

reconvened at Wheeling, declaring all state offices vacant and creating a new "Reorganized Government of Virginia," with its capital in Wheeling. The delegates at the Second Convention selected Waitman Willey and John Carlile as Virginia's new senators in Washington and named Francis H. Pierpont, a wealthy lawyer and merchant, to be its interim governor. In that first summer of the war, the delegates at Wheeling did not see themselves creating a new state or seceding from Virginia. Rather they declared that they *were* the state of Virginia, that the assembly in Richmond represented nothing more or less than a state of rebellion.

Of course, the authorities in Richmond were having none of this, considering the dissidents in Wheeling to be traitors and rebels. And at least a third of those living in the western counties did not acknowledge Restored Virginia either. While Unionists in Wheeling were naming new state leaders, other residents of the trans-Allegheny region were reaffirming their allegiance to the Old Dominion. Thirty delegates from the western counties continued to serve in the state legislature at Richmond, while others from western Virginia towns such as Clarksburg, Shepherdstown, and even Wheeling accepted positions in the Confederate House of Representatives.

Of course, it is one thing to declare one's independence and quite another thing to defend it. From the start, the Unionists at Wheeling called for Federal protection from any forces that Richmond might send against them. Geography was on the Unionists' side, as Federal forces were ready and waiting just across the river in Ohio, while Virginians in the east would have to toil many miles over primitive mountain roads to reach the opposite end of their own state. The westerners were also fortunate that the troops sent to help them were commanded by a handsome and capable young general who seemed that summer to be the American Napoleon. George McClellan, then thirty-four, would become known later in the war as the most maddeningly deliberate of Union generals. But his campaign in the mountains of Virginia was a model of speed and efficiency.

In western Virginia, the Alleghenies form a series of long ridges running northeast-southwest, broken by widely spaced gaps, or passes. This terrain creates a mountain maze for anyone passing through, especially for two armies seeking to come to grips with each other. After Philippi, Confederate forces, about five thousand men commanded by Gen. Robert S. Garnett, tried to block the two nearest mountain passes: Rich Mountain, about ten miles south, and Laurel Mountain, an equal distance to the east. In early July,

McClellan sent five thousand men to hold the Laurel Mountain defenders where they were and led another ten thousand himself to the Rich Mountain gap. There he split his army again, keeping half his men at the base of the mountain to fix the defenders' attention. He sent the other half, under Brig. Gen. William S. Rosecrans, over a rugged, almost forgotten wagon trail and up the steep slope of Rich Mountain to fall upon the Confederate flank and rear. After a gallant but short-lived stand, the Rebels fell back in disorder, leaving be-

William S. Rosecrans

hind most of their equipment and six hundred men, who were taken prisoner. Hearing that McClellan had stormed Rich Mountain, Garnett tried to pull back from the Laurel Mountain gap, withdrawing to the east. He was killed during a rear-guard action at Corrick's Ford on July 13, the first general officer on either side to fall in battle.

McClellan's assignment had been to secure the railroad lines in the western Virginia mountains and to protect the Unionist enclave there. These tasks he accomplished in about six weeks. In mid-July 1861, he wrote to Washington, saying he could either move east into the Shenandoah Valley, threatening Richmond from the back door, or he could march south into eastern Tennessee, supplying the Unionists there with ten thousand rifles, perhaps allowing them to break away from the Confederacy as the western Virginians had done. Later that same month, however, came the Union debacle at Manassas, and McClellan was called to Washington to train and reorganize the shattered Army of the Potomac. Rosecrans was given command of all Union troops in the Alleghenies, now styled the Army of Occupation, West Virginia.

Confederate leaders were by no means willing to surrender the western third of Virginia to Union forces and Unionist insurgents. In August 1861, Jefferson Davis sent what many considered the South's best general, Robert E. Lee, to the Alleghenies to reclaim the lost territory. However brilliant his reputation, Lee could see as soon as he arrived that his prospects were not favorable. In the first place, he was not given command of the four small Confederate armies operating independently in the region; rather he was sent in an advisory capacity. The troops there were demoralized by defeat,

To support the Unionists in Virginia's western counties, Union Gen. George B. McClellan advanced on Confederates entrenched on Rich Mountain. On July 11, 1861, Federal troops overwhelmed the Confederate position.

LIBRARY OF CONGRESS

disease, and a never-ending drizzle, and the nearest supply base was seventy miles behind them in the Shenandoah Valley. Of the four commanders Lee was supposed to blend into a team, three had no experience leading armies. Henry R. Jackson was a diplomat, and John B. Floyd and Henry A. Wise were two former governors of Virginia. They battled each other more fiercely than they battled the Yankees. The one professional soldier of the four commanders was W. W. Loring, and he had only arrived the week before. Loring, however, resented Lee's presence, taking it as a sign that Jefferson Davis had doubts about Loring's military capacity.

Lee did the best he could with what he had, attempting first to drive the Federals off Cheat Mountain, a long ridge south of Corrick's Ford, where Garnett had been killed. Lee's plan looked brilliant on paper—a surprise attack involving five converging columns from the armies of Loring and Jackson. He got the men into motion on September 11, but the terrain was rugged, the men ragged, and the rain unceasing. Loring questioned his part in the plan, Jackson misunderstood his part, and the men were tired, hungry, and soaking wet. To add to the confusion, one company marched on almost no sleep, because a bear had wandered into camp the night before, scattering the men in every direction in the drizzly darkness. All chance for surprise was lost, and the advance on Cheat Mountain by Lee's weary, waterlogged men turned into more of a demonstration than an attack. It was soon called off.

Deciding that nothing more could be done in this part of the mountains, Lee left a detachment to keep an eye on the Yankees at Cheat Mountain and marched the remainder of his army sixty miles south, hoping to drive the

On July 13, one of McClellan's brigades caught up with the withdrawing Confederates at Corrick's Ford. During the ensuing skirmish, the Confederate commander, Robert S. Garnett was killed. To replace him, Richmond dispatched Robert E. Lee.

FRANK LESLIE'S THE SOLDIER IN OUR CIVIL WAR

Federals out of the Kanawha River Valley. If the Union force there, led by Rosecrans, could be defeated, then at least the southern half of western Virginia could be reclaimed for the Confederacy. But the two ex-governors there were already locked in a fierce stalemate, camped twelve miles apart, with each one demanding that the other come join him. Floyd had the higher rank, but Wise was sure he had chosen the better tactical position, a summit called Big Sewell Mountain. Lee did not have the authority to issue commands, and his attempts at mediation were fruitless. He reported to Richmond that one of the two generals had to go, and soon afterward Wise was recalled to the capital. Wise had been right about the terrain, however, and Lee persuaded Floyd to join him at Big Sewell Mountain, creating a combined force of about four thousand men. Rosecrans's army was twice that large, but when he saw the strength of Lee's position, he declined to attack. After all, his job was to protect what the Federals had already won; if the Confederates wanted it back, they would have to come and take it.

Lee's little army was in no condition to drive away an army twice its size and well fortified in a position of its own choosing. So there was no battle at Big Sewell Mountain, just as there had been virtually no battle at Cheat Mountain. By then the summer had passed, and the conditions for campaigning, bad as they had been, would soon get even worse. So Lee returned to the capital, leaving western Virginia without ever coming to grips with the enemy during his three-month stay. While Richmond newspapers decried Lee's lack of aggressive instincts (a judgment to be revised later) and detractors called him "Granny Lee" behind his back, the general wrote to his wife: "I am sorry . . . that the movements of our armies cannot keep pace with the expectations of the editors. . . . I know they can arrange things satisfactory to themselves on paper. I wish they could do so in the field."[12]

After the summer campaign of 1861, Virginia's Allegheny mountains and plateau remained securely in Federal hands. The Confederates staged spectacular cavalry raids in 1862 and 1863, but they never seriously threatened to drive the Federals back across the Ohio River. The North, it seemed, had discovered two daring and enterprising generals: George B. McClellan and William S. Rosecrans. The South's Robert E. Lee, the brightest star of them all, seemed to have fallen from the sky. But first impressions can be a part of the fog of war. Within three years, McClellan and Rosecrans would both fall from grace beyond recall, neither one ending the war in command of men at arms. Lee, of course, would eventually take his place among the most distinguished and revered commanders in military history. In the meantime, though, western Virginia had become West Virginia.

WARD HILL LAMON AND THE "FIRST VIRGINIA UNION VOLUNTEERS"

APART FROM its strategic value, both sides also saw western Virginia as an important source of manpower. There were at least fifty thousand men of military age in the trans-Allegheny, many of whom had not yet decided that first summer which side to fight for or whether to fight at all. Long before either side passed conscription acts (the Confederacy in April 1862, the Union in March 1863), state militias were pressing young men into military service, stretching the word *volunteer* about as far as it could go. Within a month of Virginia's ordinance of secession in April 1861, some western men had already joined the state militia while others had fled to Ohio, Pennsylvania, or Maryland to avoid being "volunteered."[13]

Fully aware of the strong Unionist sentiment in the mountains, the United States was also scouring the western counties of Virginia for recruits. In June 1861, the same month McClellan's troops won their first battle at Philippi and the delegates at Wheeling created a "restored Virginia," Lincoln authorized special agents to recruit western Virginians. Among the president's most successful enrollment officers was his old friend from Illinois and personal bodyguard, Ward Hill Lamon. It may seem odd that an outspoken Republican and personal friend of Lincoln should be sent to raise an army in any Southern state, least of all the one whose capital had already been selected as the Confederacy's capital. But Lamon had been born and raised in Virginia, and his family still lived twenty miles south of Harpers Ferry.

Lamon was born near Winchester, at the northern end of the Shenandoah Valley. He grew up in nearby Berkeley County, which would later become a part of West Virginia. Lamon left Virginia at the age of twenty-one to study law in Kentucky, then moved to Danville, Illinois, where he was admitted to the bar in 1847. It was in Danville that

Ward Hill Lamon

Lamon first met Lincoln, then a circuit-riding attorney in his early forties, and the two became lifelong friends. Lamon wasn't well suited for the legal profession; his most notable achievements were in the barroom, not the courtroom. Lincoln biographer Stephen Oates describes Lamon as a "legendary boozer, who spent much of his time in the saloon under his office, where he sang lewd and comic songs and got into brawls."[14] Another Lincoln biographer, David H. Donald, says Lamon was "famous for his rendition of southern songs, for his wide assortment of smutty jokes, for his vocabulary of profanity, and for his capacity for liquor."[15] However different the two men were, Ward Hill Lamon had an almost doglike devotion to Lincoln, and Lincoln returned his affection and loyalty. Lincoln used to defend his friend's notorious escapades with the observation that "folks who have no vices have generally very few virtues."[16]

Lamon was among the founders of the Republican Party in Illinois. He was not a radical by any means; he despised abolitionists and disunionists equally. Like Lincoln himself, he thought there was a clear distinction between the *existence* of slavery, which was protected in the Southern states by the Constitution, and the *extension* of slavery into the northwestern territories, a question Republicans believed had been settled by the Missouri Compromise of 1820.[17] Like many others, both North and South, Lamon hoped to preserve the status quo, allowing slavery to continue in the South so that the Union might also continue.

Lamon worked tirelessly in Lincoln's senate campaign against Stephen A. Douglas in 1858 and again in the presidential campaign of 1860. After Lincoln's election in November, Lamon accompanied the president-elect on his long train trip from Springfield to the national capital. As they neared Washington, Lincoln's traveling party heard disturbing and credible evidence that a pro-Confederate gang in Baltimore called the "plug-uglies" planned to assassinate the president-elect on his way to Washington. Railroad detective Allan Pinkerton (later to become McClellan's head of military intelligence) devised a plan whereby Lincoln would slip quietly into the nation's capital in the early morning hours. Mary Todd Lincoln insisted that Lamon go along as bodyguard. A big, burly man with a drooping walrus mustache, Lamon was known as a good man in a fight, and he seemed the right man for the job. So the president-elect entered Washington City disguised in an overcoat and droopy hat, accompanied by his friend from Virginia, Ward Lamon, who had armed himself with two revolvers, two derringers, and a pair of hunting knives.

During the crisis over Fort Sumter in the spring of 1861, Lamon was one of the emissaries Lincoln sent to Charleston, along with another transplanted Southerner, Stephen A. Hurlbut, a native South Carolinian who, like Lamon, had moved to Illinois, becoming a lawyer and a friend of Lincoln. Lamon met with South Carolina governor Francis W. Pickens, and with Maj. Robert Anderson, stationed on the island fort in Charleston Harbor. Apparently, Lamon was a better man in a fight than in preventing a fight. His visit only aggravated the situation, as he gave both Governor Pickens and Major Anderson the erroneous impression that the president had decided to surrender the fort rather than risk a war. On returning to Washington, however, Lamon correctly reported to Lincoln that Union sentiment in South Carolina was all but dead and that any attempts to provision the fort would probably bring on a battle.

That same spring Lincoln also chose Lamon to be U.S. marshal for the District of Columbia. This was not a popular choice for many in Congress, who didn't believe Southerners should be awarded political appointments and who complained that Lamon was overly enthusiastic about enforcing the Fugitive Slave Law in his jurisdiction. No one would ever accuse Lamon of being an abolitionist, but he was most certainly a Unionist. After Virginia passed an ordinance of secession in April 1861, Lamon wrote to his mother in the Shenandoah Valley, warning that his three brothers, all members of a local militia, might be required to fight for the Confederacy. He pleaded with her to remind them of what she had always taught them: that they should obey the nation's laws. He explained that he was not asking his brothers "to defend a Republican President," but rather "to defend their *Country*."[18]

After Federal armies crossed the Ohio River and occupied Grafton, Virginia, in May, Lamon wrote to Lincoln, reminding the president that Lamon had been born and bred in western Virginia, adding, "Since that time I have associated intimately with those that I knew there in my boyhood, and I know there are thousands of men who are at heart loyal to the Union and to the Government."[19] Lamon proposed to go to what he called "the valley of Virginia" and raise a regiment, one thousand men to be placed under his personal command. Lincoln gladly accepted the offer, and Lamon soon set up a recruiting post near Williamsport, Maryland, across the Potomac from the Shenandoah Valley.

Lamon recruited Virginians on both shores of the Potomac, and by the end of the summer he had enrolled twice as many men as he had originally proposed, creating not one regiment, but two, including a regiment of cavalry and one of mixed infantry, cavalry, and artillery. Though his official rank was that of a colonel of state militia in Illinois, Lamon began signing his letters (except to Lincoln) as Colonel Lamon or even General Lamon.[20] He also began talking about Lamon's Brigade, consisting of several more regiments besides those he had already enlisted. But by then the local recruiting pool seemed about tapped out. In his eagerness, Lamon began adding Pennsylvanians to his rolls, a practice to which the governor of Pennsylvania strenuously objected, since he had his own enlistment quotas to meet. Lamon also traveled to Illinois seeking more recruits, and tried to have an Illinois regiment already assigned to John C. Frémont in St. Louis detached to the Lamon Brigade training at Camp Lamon along the Potomac in Maryland. Lamon's unorthodox recruiting practices and his questionable method of financing his travels brought on a congressional investigation. Though he was never convicted of wrongdoing, Lamon lost any chance for an appointment in the Federal army. His recruits were mustered into existing units in Maryland and Pennsylvania, and he returned to Washington, D.C. Though his recruiting tactics were characterized more by zeal than discretion, Lamon's enrollment efforts gave a vigorous start to a program that would eventually add more than thirty thousand western Virginians to the Federal army.

For the rest of the war, Lamon continued his duties as U.S. marshal of the District of Columbia. Having acted as Lincoln's personal bodyguard on the day they entered the capital, Lamon became the president's self-appointed security head for the next several years. Lincoln used to joke that his friend from Virginia was a "monomaniac on the subject of my safety."[21]

Indeed, Lamon's concern for the president's welfare sprang from somewhere deeper than a stern sense of duty. He seemed personally anxious about losing his great friend: the tall, ungainly man with the sad, kindly face. Lamon's fears, of course, were not without foundation. During his first term, Lincoln received so many death threats that he had a special folder marked "Assassination."[22] According to Lamon, Lincoln once heard a pistol shot in the dark as he rode alone one evening in Washington, D.C. Feeling his tall hat go flying off, he picked it up to find it punctured by a bullet. On the night of Lincoln's re-election in November 1864, Lamon curled up in a blanket outside the president's bedroom door in the White House. Armed again with pistols and knives, Lamon slept there till sunrise, afraid someone might try to assassinate Lincoln rather than allow him another four-year term.[23] Lamon was on duty in Richmond on April 14, 1865, guarding Secretary of War Edwin M. Stanton on the evening Lincoln was shot by John Wilkes Booth at Ford's Theatre in Washington. For the rest of his life, Lamon always regretted that he had not stayed at Lincoln's side, feeling that he could have protected the president when others had failed.

Lamon returned to the practice of law after the war, again without any particular distinction. He allowed a Lincoln biography to be issued under his name in 1872, but it was ghostwritten by a Democrat unsympathetic to Lincoln and based upon highly flawed research notes purchased from another of Lincoln's old law cronies back in Illinois, Billy Herndon. The biography, which covered Lincoln's early years before his presidency, was a critical and popular failure, and Lamon abandoned his original idea of producing a sequel about Lincoln's war years. Lamon died in 1893 near Martinsburg, West Virginia, not far from where he grew up. He is now remembered mainly as Lincoln's personal body guard, one of his best friends, and one of his worst biographers. But perhaps the greatest service Lamon performed for the man he loved like a brother was to raise two regiments for the Federal army from the region in western Virginia where he had been born and raised.

FRANCIS H. PIERPONT, THE FOSTER FATHER OF WEST VIRGINIA

WHEN WARD LAMON was raising regiments from the trans-Allegheny in the summer of 1861, he was acting as a special agent commissioned by Lincoln himself. By the fall of that year, however, such special agents were no longer needed, as Restored Virginia had its own government in place, an unofficial state that nevertheless sent more soldiers to the North's army in the first year of the war than did Connecticut, New Hampshire, New Jersey, Rhode Island, or Vermont.[24] Much of the trans-Allegheny's success in becoming a new Union state must be credited to its energetic and efficient interim governor, Francis H. Pierpont. (The name was spelled *Peirpoint* during the war, but Francis considered this a corruption of his family name, and he offi-

Francis H. Pierpont

cially changed the spelling to *Pierpont* in 1881. Historians generally follow his preferred spelling.) Though Pierpont is often called the Father of West Virginia, he might be more properly termed its foster father. Pierpont was governor of a jurisdiction called Restored Virginia during the war, and he became governor of Reconstruction Virginia in the years 1865–68. But Pierpont was never actually governor of the legally recognized state of West Virginia, either during or after the war.

Pierpont had been born in Morgantown, Virginia, in 1814, a town due south of Pittsburgh and only about ten miles from the Pennsylvania border. Like many Border State men, Pierpont's early years provided a blend of Northern and Southern influences. He grew up in Fairmont, Virginia, a few miles south of his birthplace, but he traveled north to Allegheny College in Meadville, Pennsylvania, for his education. After passing the bar in Virginia, Pierpont prospered both as a lawyer for the Baltimore and Ohio Railroad and as a businessman, successful in two important regional industries: coal mining and leather goods. Joining the business-oriented Whig Party in his twenties, Pierpont was among the western Virginians who complained about how the state constitution and laws favored the Tidewater region. For example, while the excise on all other state property was levied at a rate of $4 per $1,000 of value, the tax on "animate property" (slaves) was only $1.20 per $1,000 of value. Pierpont also pointed out that three-quarters of the state expenditures before the war were devoted to the protection of slave-owners' property, as well as internal improvements and higher education in the eastern half of the state.[25] In his thirties, Pierpont was strongly influenced by *Address to the People of West Virginia* (1847), a book by fellow western Virginian

Henry Ruffner on the economic drawbacks of the slave-labor system. In 1854, a week before his fortieth birthday, Pierpont married Julia Augusta Robinson, a New Yorker whose parents were avowed abolitionists. Though he was never a radical on the issue of slavery, Pierpont was one of those Border State leaders inclined to see the institution more as a problem to be solved than a benefit to be perpetuated indefinitely.

Already a prominent lawyer and businessman in Fairmont, Pierpont quickly rose to the forefront during the secession crisis of 1861. That year he turned forty-seven years old, a solidly built man with thick curly brown hair and full beard shaved low on his cheeks. His sturdy physique and steady gaze conveyed his strong constitution and his habit of putting in twelve- to fourteen-hour workdays without breaking for meals. Even before the First Wheeling Convention in mid-May, Pierpont was already recognized as one of the leading Unionists in the west. In its May 6, 1861, issue, the *Wheeling Intelligencer* offered generous praise, declaring Pierpont to be "one of those men well fitted for the stormy and revolutionary times that are upon us." The same editorial went on in what almost sounds like a political endorsement: "He has the moral, physical, and mental power of a leader. A truer man to the cause of the Union does not live; and he has the vigor of apprehension, that incisiveness of speech and that indomitable will and courage that carries the people with him."[26] Apparently, Pierpont's enemies felt the same way. Making the same point as the *Intelligencer* from an opposite point of view, a Confederate sympathizer complained, "Probably no man supplied a larger proportion of the moral force to secession in northwestern Virginia than did Francis H. Pierpont." That same May, Pierpont narrowly escaped a plot by Southern loyalists to capture him and carry him off to Richmond to be tried for sedition or held as a prisoner of war.[27]

Pierpont proved himself a natural leader at the First Wheeling Convention, an eloquent but moderate voice throughout the sometimes tempestuous proceedings. At the Second Convention in June, he was unanimously elected interim governor of Restored Virginia. Pierpont turned out to be an excellent choice for the task at hand. Turning over his various businesses to associates and family members, he sent his wife and children to Pennsylvania to ensure their safety, then he devoted virtually every waking hour to organizing and filling state offices, overseeing the shaky budget, and raising troops for the federal government. Delegates reconvened from November

1861 until February 1862, this time to hammer out the constitution for a new state, to be called West Virginia (or perhaps New Virginia or Kanawha).

Two major issues emerged in this convention, one legal—the question of constitutionality—and one practical—the question of slavery. The solution to the legal question was at once ingenious and disingenuous. It was decided that Restored Virginia, already recognized by the president and the U.S. Congress, did not consist merely of the western counties controlled by Unionists, but also included regions in eastern Virginia controlled by Federal armies. Admittedly, this latter region consisted of only a few Virginia neighborhoods near Washington, D.C., as well Norfolk and Fort Monroe on the Atlantic coast. But it was agreed that, constitutionally, the new state of West Virginia need not be approved by anyone in Richmond, as they had nullified the Union and the Constitution. Rather it could be legally recognized by the leaders of Restored Virginia, including Governor Pierpont (though his own jurisdiction would thereby shrink to something rivaling Rhode Island in size).

The question of slavery proved a thornier one. Some, like the influential Methodist minister Gordon Batelle, insisted that West Virginia join the Union as a free-labor state, like the states closest to Wheeling: Pennsylvania and Ohio. Others, like Restored Virginia's incumbent senator, John Carlile, argued that the state should enter on a par with the other Border States that had stayed in the Union: Delaware, Kentucky, Maryland, and Missouri. Carlile, one of the first to champion the idea of a separate state of West Virginia, was so committed to preserving slavery that he nearly scuttled the bill for creating the new state in the U.S. Senate. Finally, after much maneuvering and compromise, the new state constitution was approved overwhelmingly by popular referendum (18,862 to 514) and passed both houses of Congress, with a compromise clause on slavery that called for gradual emancipation.

When the bill to create the new state of West Virginia reached Lincoln's desk, he was uneasy about its legality. He polled his cabinet, asking, "Is the act constitutional, and is the act expedient?"[28] His advisers were deeply divided about this issue. Attorney General Edward Bates considered that creating a new state was "an original, independent act of Revolution."[29] He feared that such a precedent would "tear into pieces the regions further south, making out of the fragments a multitude of feeble communities."[30] Postmaster General Montgomery Blair concurred, saying that the Commonwealth of Virginia had not consented to this division, as the Constitution explicitly required. Secretary of the Navy Gideon Welles added that the new government was only a legal fiction, that the "records, archives, symbols, [and] traditions" of the commonwealth still lay in its capital, Richmond.

Others on Lincoln's cabinet argued just as forcefully that the president *should* sign the bill. Secretary of State William H. Seward declared that, because "treasonable authorities" had taken control in Richmond, the old government of the commonwealth had "lost its right to be recognized as the constitutional one," thereby forfeiting its right to approve the bill for dividing the state that had been passed by Congress. Secretary of War Edwin M. Stanton and Secretary of the Treasury Salmon P. Chase agreed, saying that the unique exigencies of war had created this new state, a situation without precedent, and one that would set no precedents for future generations.[31]

When it came time for him to decide, Lincoln seemed to rely as much on his heart as his head. He finally approved the bill, explaining, "It is said, the devil takes care of his own. Much more should a good spirit, the spirit of the Constitution and the Union, take care of its own. I think it cannot do less, and live."[32] Responding to the charge that this new state constitution was approved by a very small percentage of actual voters from the Old Dominion, Lincoln replied, "It is not qualified voters, but the qualified devotees who choose to vote, that constitute the real power of the State." To the argument that this represented nothing more than a new wave of secession, Lincoln answered, "There is a still a difference between Secession against the Constitution, and Secession in favor of the Constitution." Lincoln observed privately to Pierpont that the question in his mind finally turned on political expedience, not constitutional exegesis. He knew well that the government of West Virginia had been "fighting nearly two years for its existence," and he did see how it would strengthen the Union to turn aside these earnest entreaties to create a separate state.[33] Finally, on June 20, 1863, West Virginia entered the Union, more than two years after calls for statehood at the Second Wheeling Convention and more than halfway through the War Between the States.

Pierpont was invited to become governor of the new state, but he thought it would add to the appearance of impropriety to resign as governor of one state, Restored Virginia, in order to become governor of what was now an adjoining state. In so choosing, Pierpont greatly reduced his own power and influence for the duration of the war. The capital of Restored Virginia moved from Wheeling to Alexandria, just across the Potomac from Washington, D.C. Referring to Pierpont's tiny new jurisdiction, what might now be called Reduced Virginia, Lincoln himself conceded that there was a "somewhat farcical air to his dominion." But the president hastened to add that Pierpont had already served the Union well, "as earnest, honest, and efficient, to the extent of his means, as any other loyal governor."[34]

Pierpont continued on dutifully, even with the extent of his means reduced to nearly nothing. In his scattered patches of jurisdiction, Pierpont raised two new military units for the Federal army: Loudon Rangers from a Virginia county near Washington, D.C., and the First Loyal East Virginia Infantry, consisting largely of German or Scots-Irish immigrants from coastal regions under Federal control. Despite their impressive-sounding names, these two outfits together consisted of about two hundred men, a tiny fraction of the more than thirty thousand soldiers Pierpont had helped recruit from over the mountains in the first two years of the war.

After Lee's surrender and Lincoln's assassination in April 1865, Pierpont's domain suddenly expanded again. In May 1865, the new president, Andrew Johnson, greatly enlarged Restored Virginia to include what had been Confederate Virginia. Pierpont moved his capital yet again, this time to Richmond. Like most would-be moderates in the first years of Reconstruction, Pierpont was ground between two millstones: the Radicals in Congress who planned to reinvent the South—and take a good measure of revenge in the bargain—and unreconstructed Southerners who would not stand by idly and watch their traditional social order overturned.

Pierpont was simply too straightforward and guileless for the job of Reconstruction governor of Virginia. He honestly believed that, having been defeated on the battlefield, former Confederates would submit to a Northern blueprint for having their state reconstituted according to congressional guidelines. In 1865, he appointed many former Confederates to high government posts in the state, assuming they would follow directives from his office or from the legislature in Washington. Of course, Richmond hardliners would never accept Pierpont as governor, knowing well that he had led the mountain third of the Old Dominion out of the Confederacy and helped supply the Union with enough men for several well-appointed army corps. Radical Republicans, on the other hand, were outraged by how readily Pierpont seemed willing to share power with recent and unrepentant Rebels.

After three ineffective years as Reconstruction governor of Virginia, Pierpont returned to his hometown of Fairmont in the west and renewed his successful business enterprises. One biographer summed up Pierpont's political career by saying he was "an admirable and successful wartime Unionist, but a naïve and inept Reconstruction political leader."[35] Whatever his shortcomings in trying to steer a middle course for Reconstruction Virginia after the war, there is no denying his pivotal role in leading Restored Virginia during the war. Pierpont's legacy can still be seen today west of the Alleghenies and east of the Ohio River. From Wheeling in the northern panhandle to Huntington in the southwest, one still sees signs and bumper stickers throughout the state proudly proclaiming "*West*—By Choice, By God—*Virginia*."

4

TENNESSEE TORIES

THE CIVIL WAR did not bring forth a new nation, as Confederate leaders had hoped. But it did bring forth a new state, West Virginia. It did not, however, bring about a second new state called East Tennessee. Conditions in eastern Tennessee at the start of the war were very similar to those in western Virginia. In the first year of the war, both the interim governor of Restored Virginia, Francis H. Pierpont, and the Federal commander in charge of the region, George B. McClellan, assumed that eastern Tennessee might well secede from the Confederacy as did the Unionist enclave in the Old Dominion.[1] But there was one crucial difference: western Virginia was within easy reach of Federal troops just across the Ohio River. Eastern Tennessee, by contrast, was one of the most inaccessible regions anywhere in the eastern United States. By the time Federal troops began arriving in large numbers in the mountainous regions of Tennessee, there was no need for the people there to separate from the rest of the state. By August 1863, even the pro-Confederate regions of the state were in the process of rejoining the Union—by force, not by choice.

The state of Tennessee had a unique place in the Civil War. It had the shortest term as a Confederate state: the last to secede (June 8, 1861) and the first to be fully returned to Federal control. It was the only Confederate state entirely exempted from the Emancipation Proclamation in January 1863 (because Union forces already occupied most of the state), later becoming the only state to free its own slaves rather than having them freed by a Federal mandate. Tennessee spent the first half of the war with its eastern third occupied as enemy territory by Confederate troops, the last half of the war with the rest of the state occupied as hostile territory by Union troops.

In some respects, prewar Tennessee was a mirror image of Virginia, with three distinct sections—eastern, middle, and western—which even then were referred to as the state's Grand Divisions. Eastern Tennessee was a land of steep ridges and long, narrow valleys settled mainly by yeoman farmers, many of German or Scots-Irish descent, who raised corn and hogs. Middle Tennessee was mainly a flat, grain-growing region. Western Tennessee, fronting the Mississippi, derived much of its wealth from tobacco plantations.

Like western Virginia, eastern Tennessee had a long tradition of seeking independence. In 1785, delegates from three adjoining mountain counties in western North Carolina declared themselves to be a separate state known as Franklin, electing one of the heroes of the King's Mountain victory, John Sevier, to be their governor. For a time, the region had two competing administrations, one as a frontier district of North Carolina (counties now a part of Tennessee), the other as the state of Franklin, and neither set of judges or local marshals recognized the authority of the others. In 1788, Sevier was called to a hearing in the mountain village of Morganton, North Carolina, on charges of treason. As soon as he heard a guilty verdict pronounced against him, Sevier bolted from the courtroom and galloped out of town. The idea of the state of Franklin never caught on, though Sevier was later pardoned and continued to be a leading figure in regional politics. When the state of Tennessee was officially admitted to the Union in 1796, Sevier became its first governor.[2] Nearly a half century later, east Tennesseans again sought their independence. This time they looked in the other direction, petitioning the state legislature at Nashville in 1843 to allow the thirty easternmost counties to establish themselves as a separate state. This request did not receive serious discussion.[3]

When the secession crisis came to a head nearly twenty years later, Tennessee, like the other Middle South states, did not immediately follow South Carolina out of the Union. In February 1861, the call for a convention to discuss secession was soundly defeated by a margin of 55 to 45 percent in a statewide referendum. After the surrender of Sumter, though, followed quickly by Lincoln's request to the states for volunteers to suppress the rebellion, Tennessee's pro-Confederate governor, Isham Harris, replied indignantly, "Tennessee will not furnish a single man for purposes of coercion but 50,000 if necessary, for the defense of our rights, and those of our Southern brothers."[4] The legislators in Nashville felt the same way. On April 25, they approved a state declaration of independence, to be approved by a referendum on June 8. Of the twenty-five dissenting votes, eighteen were from the eastern third of the state.

Just as the western Virginia Unionists had gathered at Wheeling on May 13, five hundred like-minded brethren in eastern Tennessee met in Knoxville on May 30–31.[5] At this convention, longtime political foes such as Knoxville editor William Brownlow, an old-line Whig, united with Democrats such as Andrew Johnson to denounce secession. (The Whigs favored a stronger federal government, a national economic plan, and laws to promote business; the Democrats envisioned a more decentralized, agrarian America.) When the vote came on June 8, eastern Tennessee's distinctness from the rest of the state became jarringly clear. Western and middle Ten-

Isham Harris

nessee voted to leave the Union by a count of nearly six to one, but in eastern Tennessee, 69 percent voted to stay in the Union.[6] On June 17–20, many of same Unionist delegates who had met in Knoxville in May reassembled farther east in Greeneville, making it clear they did not intend to go along with the state majority. After much discussion, the delegates at Greeneville passed a unanimous declaration stating their position in no uncertain terms:

> We prefer to remain attached to the government of our fathers. The constitution of the United States has done us no wrong. The Congress of the United States has passed no law to oppress us. The President of the United States has made no threat against the law-abiding people of Tennessee. Under the government of the United States, we have enjoyed as a nation more of civil and religious freedom than any other people under the whole heaven. . . . The cause of secession or rebellion has no charm for us, and its progress has been marked by the most alarming and dangerous attacks upon public liberty. . . . Its whole course threatens to annihilate the last vestige of freedom.[7]

Acting on this declaration, the delegates at Greeneville also petitioned the legislature in Nashville to allow eastern Tennessee to become a separate state. Once again, the request was set aside. On July 22, the state of Tennessee—all of it—officially joined the Confederate States of America. But the majority of those in east Tennessee were just as resolute about staying out of the Confederacy as the majority of other Tennesseans were about joining it. Observing the attempts of their Northern neighbor Kentucky to declare its neutrality, some east Tennesseans talked about forming a new

Confederacy, not the Southern one, but a Border State Confederacy, a buffer zone between North and South.[8]

But both Kentucky and Tennessee were far too important strategically to be simply bypassed in a sprawling conflict that stretched from the Atlantic seaboard to the Mississippi Valley. Tennessee would see more battles and skirmishes in the Civil War than any other state except Virginia. In part, this was because eastern Tennessee contained a vital railroad line connecting Virginia directly to the Gulf States, with branch lines leading westward to Nashville and Memphis. The area also contained vital deposits of lead, copper, and saltpeter (needed for making gun powder). As for daily bread, the Appalachian Valley of east Tennessee was second only to Virginia's Shenandoah Valley in its wheat production.[9]As for manpower, east Tennessee's white population of 380,000 was larger than that of five Southern states already out of the Union—Arkansas, Florida, Louisiana, Mississippi, and South Carolina.

After the popular referendum in June ratified the legislature's work, it was clear even to Tennessee Unionists that the state would neither remain in the Union nor would it remain neutral. What had been political opposition to secession before June 8 became military opposition after that date. Those who had been called Unionists or "cooperationists" before Tennessee's popular vote were now accused of being tories or even traitors. They were also suspected, with good cause, of being potential saboteurs or recruits for the Federal army that was being organized and trained at Camp Dick Robinson near Lexington, Kentucky.

In late July, Felix Zollicoffer was appointed as the Confederacy's district commander in eastern Tennessee. Zollicoffer was a Nashville newspaperman who had begun his journalistic career in Knoxville, and that first summer of the war, he adopted a conciliatory stance toward the local population. Zollicoffer believed that Unionism of the region was not deeply rooted, that demagogues like Knoxville editor William Brownlow had been stirring up needless antagonism. Zollicoffer's first unpleasant surprise came in the state elections of August 1861. Though Governor Isham Harris was reelected by a two-to-one margin in western and middle Tennessee, he was defeated by the same margin in the mountain counties. Furthermore, eastern Tennesseans insisted on nominating and electing congressmen to represent them in Washington, ignoring the fact that the state now belonged to the Confederacy.[10] Senator Andrew Johnson, from

Greeneville, never vacated his position in the national capital, continuing to represent his state, even though it had left the Union.

At the same time Zollicoffer was trying to win east Tennesseans over to the Confederacy, Lincoln was trying to recruit them for the Union. The president sent enlistment officers to the Cumberland Valley in June 1861 (the same month he sent Ward Hill Lamon to western Virginia), calling for the enrollment of ten thousand men from the state of Tennessee.[11] But it soon became clear that most of these potential recruits could not make the trip north through the Cumberland Mountains, on the Tennessee-Kentucky border, because the passes were guarded by Confederate patrols. Prominent in these early recruiting efforts were three brothers from Carter County, on the eastern edge of Tennessee. These were James, Samuel, and William Carter—each a staunch Unionist, but each with his own idea about how their part of the state could be returned to the Union. James Carter wanted to carry rifles and ammunition into east Tennessee so that the Unionists could stage an uprising. He traveled to Washington and met with Secretary of War Simon Cameron and with Senator Andrew Johnson, obtaining their approval for his arms-smuggling operation. But Carter was careless about discussing his plans after he returned to Tennessee, and a Federal officer in Kentucky complained that James's "blabbing" had done more harm than any five thousand secessionists could have done.[12]

James's more discreet brother, Samuel P. Carter, was a naval lieutenant transferred to the army to help recruit east Tennesseans. (The P. stood for Powhatan, based on the Carter family tradition that their family included Powhatan and his famous daughter, Pocahontas, in their lineage.)[13] By the end of the summer, Samuel Carter had helped arm and train two thousand fugitives from his home state, men eager to march south and liberate their families in the mountains of Tennessee.[14] (Samuel Carter rose to the rank of major general during the war, returning to his original branch of the service in 1865. He is the only person in American history to serve both as a major general in the army and a rear admiral in the navy.)

While James Carter conspired to smuggle arms and Samuel Carter worked on regular army recruiting and training, the third brother, William Carter, had yet another idea: sabotage. On September 30, 1861, William met with Gen. George H. Thomas, commanding at Camp Dick Robinson, and proposed a scheme for burning nine key railroad bridges in eastern Tennessee. Carter believed the bridge burnings would ignite a general uprising among mountain Unionists, who would be supported by Federal troops from Kentucky, including the newly trained regiments from Tennessee. Thomas liked the idea and sent William Carter to Washington to meet with Lincoln, Secretary of War Cameron, and general in chief George B. McClellan. All three were impressed, and Carter returned with twenty-five hundred dollars to implement the plan.

Back in Kentucky, however, Carter discovered that the commanding general of the Department of the Cumberland, William T. Sherman, didn't support the scheme. Sherman believed everyone was underrating the difficulties of getting a Federal force through the Cumberland Mountains to eastern Tennessee. The idea was revived in November when Sherman, on the verge of nervous collapse, was replaced by Gen. Don Carlos Buell. But Buell didn't believe in the plan any more than Sherman had, and he resisted intense prodding from both Lincoln and McClellan to do something about east Tennessee. In the meantime, William Carter decided to proceed with or without the army's help, and he slipped over the Kentucky-Tennessee border and began organizing Unionist partisans.

Even though they had no assurance that Federal forces were anywhere nearby, Carter's saboteurs struck on the night of November 8. They had planned to burn nine key railroad bridges on the east Tennessee and Virginia line, all the way from the northernmost bridge near the Virginia border to one near the Georgia border. It was an ambitious plan and proved to be surprisingly successful, considering that it was conceived, funded, and executed in less than two months. Of the nine bridges the Unionists hoped to destroy, they succeeded in burning five. Three others were found to be too well guarded. At the ninth bridge, a rather timid band of thirteen would-be saboteurs was turned away by the sight of a lone Confederate sentinel.[15]

The five railroad bridges that burned during the night of November 8 were intended as a signal flare, both for local Unionists and for Federal forces in Kentucky. The next few days there were reports and rumors of armed bands all over eastern Tennessee—a thousand armed Unionists north of Knoxville and five hundred more in Hamilton County, a southern county bordering Georgia. A resident of Jonesboro reported to Jefferson Davis, "The whole country is now in a state of rebellion. Civil War has broken out at length in East Tennessee."[16]

Confederate authorities responded swiftly and harshly to the potential uprising. From Richmond, Secretary of War Judah P. Benjamin sent instruc-

Unionist guerrillas in east Tennessee were depicted in *Harper's Weekly* as taking an oath of allegiance prior to the 1861 campaign of bridge burning. Nine bridges were targeted; five were burned.

tions that captured bridge burners should be "summarily tried by drum-head court-martial, and if found guilty, executed on the spot by hanging." Benjamin also advised that the bodies be left in the vicinity of the burned bridges.[17] Though William Carter himself escaped and made his way back to Kentucky, a thousand others were arrested and four hundred were sent to a military prison in Tuscaloosa, Alabama.[18] Four were hanged close to the railroad bridges, as instructed, and train engineers slowed down as they passed, so that passengers could get a good look at the fate of bridge burners. As the cars went by, some angry passengers reached out and struck the dead bodies with their canes, or leaned out from the rear platforms to kick at the dangling corpses.[19]

Despite scouring the region and making mass arrests, Confederate authorities still could not find the man they wanted most, a Unionist that gray-clad soldiers had orders to shoot on sight. This fugitive was not a bold partisan ranger or a wily saboteur, but rather a slender, stoop-shouldered newspaper editor named William Gannaway Brownlow.

THE FIGHTING PARSON:
WILLIAM GANNAWAY BROWNLOW

It was the Knoxville editor William G. Brownlow who famously declared of secessionists that he would "fight them till hell freezes over, then fight them on the ice." But in November 1861, the Confederate commander in eastern Tennessee wanted to talk to Brownlow not about ice but about fire. It was generally believed that Brownlow might have instigated the bridge burnings, and if not, his fiery editorials in the *Knoxville Whig* had certainly helped inspire the plan. It is one of those peculiar twists of history that Brownlow found himself on the Confederacy's most-wanted list in late 1861. Only three years earlier, he had been known throughout the nation as one of the most flamboyant defenders of all things Southern, most especially the institution of slavery.

William G. Brownlow

William Gannaway Brownlow was born in 1805 in Wythe County, Virginia, in the southwestern corner of the state. His family moved to eastern Tennessee in 1816, but both parents died while William was still a boy. He was raised on a farm by an uncle and then apprenticed in carpentry by another uncle. At the age of twenty, he had a conversion experience at a Methodist camp meeting and decided upon the life of an itinerant preacher.

Even as a young man, Brownlow was pugnacious and quickly drawn into local controversies. At first glance, he seems not at all suited to the life of a country parson. His speeches and writings seldom evoked faith, hope, or love; his specialties were argument, accusation, and invective. Yet, as his biographer, James C. Kelly, explains, religious and political controversies in nineteenth-century Appalachia, while taken with deadly seriousness, also contained an element of entertainment or sport, almost the verbal equivalent of "wrestling matches or cockfighting."[20] Kelly notes, "On the frontier, at least, religious controversy was often merely a form of eye gouging and ear biting. Every uncharitable word was spoken. Every unchristian thought was thought."[21] Though the doctrinal or policy issues under discussion might not actually be that far apart, listeners or readers seemed to expect, and enjoy, a certain extravagance of expression, what Brownlow himself called "piling on epithets."[22]

As a circuit rider, Brownlow traveled over many counties, preaching to scattered settlements too small or remote to have their own church. As a Methodist, he seemed to have less to say about unbelievers than he did about Baptists, Catholics, Mormons, and Presbyterians,. He was unstinting in his criticisms of all these denominations, often moving from disputation to vilification, from arguments to ad hominem attacks. Of Roman Catholics,

Brownlow calculated that, through the centuries, they had spilled precisely 272 million gallons of Protestant blood.[23] Against the Baptists, he argued that full-immersion baptism could be harmful or even fatal in polar regions, where new converts might freeze to death in the icy waters. Brownlow accused one Baptist preacher of distributing Bibles for personal gain. He was sued for libel, lost the case, and had to give up his horse, saddle, bridle, plus five dollars as a settlement.[24] Brownlow's greatest scorn, however, was reserved for Mormons, of whom he said darkly he wouldn't mind seeing the whole lot of them exterminated.[25] Even by the rough-and-ready standards of that time and place, Brownlow seems to have pushed things to an extreme. Despite his undeniable effectiveness as a preacher and propagandist, his superiors in the Methodist hierarchy told him to tone it down, to focus more on building up the faith of his listeners rather than tearing down the beliefs of others.[26]

If Brownlow's religious views were steeped in politics, his political views were defended with religious fervor. Throughout his lifetime, he displayed an intense devotion to the Union as something almost sacred. Brownlow rode the circuits of the southern highlands for ten years, spending most of his time in eastern Tennessee and western North Carolina, but he also visited Georgia, South Carolina, and Virginia. In his frequent travels, Brownlow developed an almost mystical conviction that the country was all one, that states were made only by drawing surveyor's lines on a map. He was visiting South Carolina during the nullification crisis of 1831, and he was thoroughly disgusted that anyone would threaten to dismantle the United States. Since the badge of those who supported nullification was a purple ribbon worn on the hat, Brownlow's initial response was to catch a stray dog in one South Carolina town and tie a purple ribbon to its tail. The combative parson also published a pamphlet attacking the theory of nullification, and he nearly got himself hanged for the unbridled vehemence with which he expressed his opinions.[27]

Like other itinerant preachers in the southern Appalachians, Brownlow often fulminated against whiskey, card playing, and tobacco. But unlike many of his fellow preachers, he had nothing to say against slavery. Early in the nineteenth century, eastern Tennessee stood out as a center for antislavery activism in the South. In 1816, the *Manumission Intelligencer* was published in Jonesboro, followed soon by the *Emancipator*, edited by Elihu Embree. Benjamin Lundy published *Genius of Emancipation* in the early

1820s out of Greeneville, though he later moved it to Baltimore.[28] Brownlow imbibed none of this antislavery spirit. His mother's family had been slaveholders, and he himself owned a slave or two at various times in his life. Unlike the Quakers, most Baptists in his district, and even many of his fellow Methodists, Brownlow was a staunch defender of slavery. He viewed it as a divinely ordained institution, arguing that "the Redeemer of the world smiles alike upon the devout master and the pious slave!"[29]

When Brownlow married in 1836, at age thirty, he realized he could not support a wife and family as a circuit preacher, so he began a new career as a journalist. Taking over a small newspaper in Elizabethton, the *Tennessee Whig*, he changed its motto to suit his style, from the sedate "Life, Liberty, and the Pursuit of Happiness" to an Old Testament text, "Cry Aloud and Spare Not."[30] Brownlow cried aloud and spared not, acquiring new readers and new enemies with almost equal rapidity. He boasted in his paper that "in point of severity, and wholesale abuse of individuals, our paper is without parallel in the history of the American Press."[31] But he went on to explain that such a scathing tone was in order since he felt his duty was to expose "a disciplined corps of the most obdurate sinners, and unprincipled scoundrels, that ever annoyed any community."[32] In his first year as editor (1839–40), the paper's circulation rose from three hundred to a thousand. That same year, as he was sitting at home, two shots rang out one night, and a pair of bullets just missed his head.[33]

In 1841, Brownlow moved his newspaper to nearby Jonesboro, perhaps sensing that there would be more sinners and scoundrels to expose, as well as more subscribers, in a larger town. Before the year was out, he had engaged in a street scuffle with rival newspaper editor Landon Carter Haynes, striking Haynes with a cane and taking a bullet in the thigh from Haynes's pocket pistol. The following year, Brownlow was beaten senseless by a pair of thugs while attending a religious revival meeting. Incidents like these did not hurt Brownlow's journalistic reputation; in fact, they enhanced it. Brownlow's quarrels often did not end with words thundered from a stump or printed on a page. He reveled in his reputation as the "Fighting Parson," but it was the fight in him that stood out, not the parson.

In 1849, Brownlow took his newspaper to the largest city in east Tennessee, where it became the *Knoxville Whig*. Attracting two thousand subscribers in his first year, Brownlow had fourteen thousand subscribers by 1861, more than all other newspapers in eastern Tennessee combined.[34] In the 1850s, he continued to strike out at his old opponents in religious controversies, but he added more and more new adversaries in the arena of politics. His main target was the Democratic Party. He lashed out at his fellow east Tennessean, Democratic governor Andrew Johnson, as "an UNMITI-GATED LIAR AND CALUMINATOR and a VILLAINOUS COWARD."[35] As the parson-editor's own Whig Party began to fall apart in the 1850s, a reader (perhaps in jest) asked Brownlow if he ever considered switching to the more viable Democratic Party. Brownlow replied with a scornful eloquence that verges on poetry:

> When the sun shines at midnight and the moon at mid-day; when man forgets to be selfish, or Democrats lose their inclination to steal; when nature stops her onward march to rest, or all the water-courses in America flow upstream; when flowers lose their odor, and trees shed no leaves; when birds talk, and beasts of burden laugh; when damned spirits swap hell for heaven with the angels of light; when impossibilities are in fashion, and no proposition is too absurd to be believed,—you may credit the report that I have joined the Democrats![36]

In addition to Democrats, Brownlow also used the *Knoxville Whig* to heap scorn on abolitionists, whom he called "fiery bigots," "vagabond philanthropists," and "hypocritical freedom-shriekers."[37] He called Harriet Beecher Stowe, the author of *Uncle Tom's Cabin* (1859), a "deliberate liar," offering as well his impression of her personal appearance: "She is ugly as Original sin—an abomination in the eyes of civilized people. A tall, course [*sic*], vulgar-looking woman—stoop-shouldered with a long yellow neck, and a long peaked nose, through which she speaks."[38] (This was an odd topic for Brownlow to bring up, as he himself was notorious for his ill-favored looks. Besides his shaggy hair and eyebrows, he had a crooked mouth, turned down at one corner, giving him a permanent sneering expression.)

Apart from his slashing editorials in the *Whig*, Brownlow was eager to debate the abolitionists on their own ground in the North. An invitation came for him to do so against the brilliant African American orator Frederick Douglass, but Brownlow was insulted at the idea of sharing a public forum with a black man. When a challenge came for Brownlow to debate a much less formidable foe, Philadelphia minister Abraham Pryne, the parson politely asked before accepting the invitation whether Pryne was a "gentleman of color."³⁹ Upon confirming that he was not, Brownlow engaged Pryne in a series of five debates in September 1858, which gave him exposure throughout both North and South.

In the Philadelphia debates, Brownlow argued that the institution of slavery was scientifically justified, biblically sanctioned, and morally enlightened. He claimed that scientists had shown that a black adult had the same mental capacity as a white child, so that blacks needed to be supervised and looked after like children.⁴⁰ For biblical justification, he cited Genesis 16, a passage in which Hagar, the Egyptian handmaid of Abram's wife Sarai, runs away because she is being treated harshly. An angel appears to Hagar in the desert, telling her that she and her young son Ishmael should return to Abram and Sarai. Brownlow argued that, in this episode, the angel is acting like a U.S. marshal, enforcing the fugitive slave laws of the Old Testament.⁴¹ Brownlow also argued that blacks in Africa had a primitive religion of nature worship, that it was much better for them to become civilized by serving the Christian nations as laborers.⁴²

Brownlow charged that it was not Southern slaveholders, but Northern "freedom-shriekers" who were splitting the Union apart. He explained, "We of the South intend to fight you *in* the Union, not *out* of it!" He also added a much broader indictment of Northerners, citing statistics to show they were more likely to be debtors or army deserters, that they included "Free Lovers, Free Soilers, Abolitionists, Spiritualists, Trance Mediums, Bible Repudiators, and representatives of every crazy other *ism* known to the annals of bedlam."⁴³

Anyone hearing Brownlow's withering attacks on the North in 1858 would never have guessed that he would become one of the most despised men in the South within three years. But before all else, what he believed in most was the Union. As there was more and more talk of splitting the country in the 1850s, Brownlow was appalled by what was being said and done in both North and South. Brownlow wondered at one point if the crisis could have been averted fifty years earlier by hanging one hundred leading abolitionists in the North along with one hundred fire-eaters in the South and burying them all in a common ditch.⁴⁴ (Fire-eaters were Southern radicals hotly demanding separation from the Union.) Brownlow wrote blistering editorials against Lincoln and the Republicans, but he argued that Lincoln's election alone did not justify secession. After all, slavery was protected by the Constitution, and any radical actions by the executive could easily be checked by the legislative or judicial branches of the government. He claimed as well that secession was not the will of the Southern majority, but rather a scheme "hatched in the dead of night by fourteen Senators" from seven cotton states.[45] If he would not fight in the Confederate army, someone asked, would he at least consider serving as a chaplain? "When I shall have made up my mind to go to Hell," he replied, "I will cut my throat and go direct, and not travel by way of the Southern Confederacy."[46]

In the summer and fall of 1861, Brownlow's antisecession editorials in the *Whig* remained as vitriolic as ever, despite the fact that Tennessee's star had already been sewn onto the Confederate flag. And the fighting parson-turned-pressman continued to attack various local Confederate officials by name. Gen. W. H. Carroll was a "walking groggery." Confederate district attorney J. C. Ramsey was a "corrupt scoundrel and unprincipled knave." Another leader in Knoxville was "a goggle-eyed little scoundrel," and yet another belonged to a "villainous clique."[47] Though the government in Richmond defended freedom of the press, local authorities (some of whom were being mentioned by name in the *Whig*) were not so scrupulous. They blocked delivery of Brownlow's newspapers and began confiscating his incoming mail, including much-needed subscription payments.

Finally, with his newspaper failing financially and his safety in doubt, Brownlow shut down the *Whig* at the end of October 1861. He tried to travel north to Kentucky but found his way blocked by military patrols. So he circled back south, preaching and collecting overdue subscriptions, when the bridge burners struck on November 8. Being warned that Confederate soldiers had orders to shoot him on sight, Brownlow and several other prominent Unionists retreated to a remote camp in the Great Smokies, where they lived for several weeks on bear meat and provisions supplied by friends.[48] Though he took secret satisfaction in the bridge burnings after the fact, he had nothing to do with the scheme, and he could prove he was nowhere near a railroad bridge on the night the saboteurs struck. Brownlow wrote first to the military commander, W. H. Carroll, and then to his replacement, George B. Crittenden, asking for safe passage out of east Tennessee.

Acting on instructions from Richmond, Crittenden replied that, if Brownlow could prove his noncomplicity, he would be safely escorted to Union lines on December 7. Brownlow returned to Knoxville, but the day before he was scheduled to leave, he was arrested, not by military police, but by civil authorities, and not on the specific charge of bridge burning, but on a general charge of sedition. Behind the arrest was state attorney J. C. Ramsey. He offered as evidence an editorial Brownlow had written in May 1861, before Tennessee's secession had been ratified by popular vote, saying that if local Unionists were arrested and sent to Richmond to be tried for treason, the people ought to rise up and destroy the railroads by which the prisoners were carried out of the state. At the time, that seemed like just one more sample of Brownlow's inflammatory rhetoric. But once there was a war on and vital bridges had been burned, Brownlow's words seemed to be sufficient grounds for arrest.[49]

Brownlow was thrown into an overcrowded Knoxville jail, where conditions were appalling. The cells were jammed with 150 men, so crowded that they had to take turns standing and sleeping. The latrine consisted of two barrel halves, both of which overflowed with human waste. The drinking water came from a spring downstream from a slaughterhouse. Apart from the squalid conditions and his failing health (from bronchitis), Brownlow also faced the very real threat of execution. Four of the bridge burners had already been hanged, and one of his prison mates, Harrison Self, had already been convicted and sentenced to death. On December 27, Self was notified that he would be hanged at four o'clock that afternoon. When Self's daughter Elizabeth came to visit him one last time, she was heartbroken and distraught, and Brownlow confessed he wept openly at the poignant scene. He took a piece of paper and wrote an urgent telegram in Elizabeth's name, eloquently pleading with Jefferson Davis to spare her father's life. She hurried to send the message, and a reply came from Richmond two hours before Harrison was scheduled to be hanged, granting him a pardon. Though others had been pleading for Harrison Self's life as well, the timing suggests that Elizabeth's telegram, composed by Brownlow, was the crucial factor in Davis's last-minute stay of execution. What Brownlow didn't know was that, only a few hours earlier, the hated editor's enemies in Knoxville had offered to commute Self's sentence if he would implicate Brownlow in the bridge burnings. Self had refused to do so, even at the peril of his own life. In composing the message for Harrison Self, Brownlow unknowingly returned the favor for a man who had saved his own neck from the noose.[50]

Brownlow complained loudly about his arrest, writing directly to Confederate secretary of state Judah P. Benjamin, explaining that he had surrendered himself to Crittenden voluntarily, with the understanding that he would be escorted to Union lines. As Brownlow explained it, "A third rate County Court lawyer, acting as your Confederate attorney, took me out of his hands and cast me into this prison. I am anxious to learn which is your highest authority, the Secretary of War, a Major General [Crittenden], or a dirty little drunken attorney, such as J. C. Ramsey is!"[51] Brownlow added that he knew he was considered dangerous to the Confederacy and that Richmond authorities would like to see him expelled from the country. Even in his desperate situation, Brownlow couldn't resist ending his plea with a sardonic twist: "Just give me the passports, and I will do for your Confederacy more than the devil has ever done. I will quit the country!"[52]

Benjamin could see Brownlow's point, and he considered the case an embarrassment: even if Brownlow's arrest had been technically legal, it gave the appearance of duplicity. Benjamin instructed Ramsey to release Brownlow, explaining that it was "better that even the most dangerous enemy, however criminal, should escape than that the honor and good faith of the Government should be impugned or even suspected."[53] After spending several weeks under house arrest (released from jail because of severe bronchitis), Brownlow eventually received his passport and a guarantee of safe conduct out of Confederate Tennessee. Under heavy guard, he was escorted to Federal lines near Nashville and turned over on March 15, 1862. Perhaps not knowing it was Judah P. Benjamin who had personally intervened on his behalf, Brownlow summarized the affair in one of the most utterly graceless remarks ever spoken by a man notorious for graceless remarks. He explained he'd had some dealings with "a little Jew, late of New Orleans," but that he had counted on "no more mercy from him than was shown by his illustrious predecessors toward Jesus Christ."[54]

After passing into Union lines, Brownlow went from cellmate to celebrity almost overnight. Northern audiences were eager to have their moral fervor rekindled by tales of brutality and injustice against Unionists in the South, and Brownlow was willing to give them what they wanted in vivid detail. The newly freed editor spoke to a packed house in Cincinnati the first week of April 1862, earning $1,125 in one evening, more than he had sometimes made in a whole year.[55] That spring Brownlow spoke for handsome fees in Chicago, Columbus, Pittsburgh, and Harrisburg, concluding his triumphant tour by speaking at Independence Hall in Philadelphia. Brownlow also secured a lucrative book deal, collecting his editorials and prison diaries into *Sketches of the Rise, Progress, and Decline of Secession,* published in the summer of 1862 and usually called simply *Parson Brown-low's Book*. The work was actually a hastily edited collection of Brownlow's previous writings rather than a coherent narrative. But whatever its short-comings as a memoir, it made for excellent propaganda and sold more than one hundred thousand copies in the first three months of publica-tion.[56] Brownlow's family was allowed to join him in New Jersey, and he spent a busy two years speaking and writing in the Northern states. Though he rightfully considered himself an exile from his home country, he was among the most safe, comfortable, and celebrated of those who have ever had to endure that fate.

THE ADVENTURES OF DANIEL ELLIS, THE MOUNTAIN PILOT

WILLIAM BROWNLOW'S case was unique, in that Confederates assisted him in leaving the state, considering him much less a threat outside of eastern Ten-nessee than inside it. For thousands of others who wanted to escape that part of the country, the route was long, hazardous, and sometimes fatal. In addition to Unionists and Confederates in eastern Tennessee (eight thou-sand men from the region served in Southern armies[57]), there were a good many men in the mountains who would have preferred to simply let the war pass them by. These small farmers were mainly concerned for them-selves and their families. They didn't see the question of national sover-eignty vs. state sovereignty as an issue they wanted to fight about, on either side. They were accustomed to slavery, but it was not a major part of their lives, as only one in twelve in the eastern counties was black.[58] Local whites didn't want to risk their lives and fortunes either to abolish the institution or to defend it. That was somebody else's business.

Yet there were no sidelines in the Civil War, only battle lines—the kind one could see on a map and the kind one couldn't. Both North and South understood the strategic importance of east Tennessee, and both saw its major reserves of manpower. In this war, there were no neutrals; the old rule prevailed for both sides: If you are not with us, you are against us. In August 1861, the Confederate Congress passed an Alien Enemies Act, declaring that any citizen living within the boundaries of the new nation who refused to swear an oath of loyalty could be arrested as an "alien enemy." That same month Richmond passed a Sequestration Law, stating that the homes and

ALBERT D. RICHARDSON, *THE SECRET SERVICE, THE FIELD, THE DUNGEON, AND THE ESCAPE* (1865)

Daniel Ellis

properties of alien enemies were subject to confiscation. Both laws were aimed at Unionist enclaves such as east Tennessee, and both were energetically enforced there.[59]

For those in eastern Tennessee who wanted to escape arrest or conscription, the nearest Union lines were along the Cumberland River in southern Kentucky, 120 miles to the northwest. The route was marked by a series of steep ridges and rushing rivers, a gauntlet of natural walls and moats with its passes and bridges guarded by Confederate cavalry. Those who tried to make the trek, called "stampeders," were often captured and sent to prison, sometimes shot or hanged on the spot. Others got lost in the mountains and died of starvation or exposure. Those hiding out in the hills of eastern Tennessee began to gather in groups to wait for a mountain guide, or pilot, to lead them across the rugged terrain: someone who knew the safest places to camp and the best way to evade Confederate home guards. The pilots, also called conductors, were in great demand; at times there were up to nine hundred men camping in the Tennessee woods waiting for a guide to lead them to Kentucky.[60]

The most famous mountain pilot was Daniel Ellis of Carter County, who made dozens of expeditions, guiding a total of four thousand men to Union lines, most of whom joined the Federal army.[61] In 1862 and 1863, Ellis led parties of stampeders north and west through the corner of Virginia and up to Kentucky. He tried to hike in a straight line as much as possible, preferring to travel at night, avoiding towns and settled areas, and crossing streams at remote points where there were no bridges or well-known fords. To avoid Confederate patrols, Ellis deliberately sought out the most obscure routes, usually the most difficult, making the one-way trip in a week to ten days of arduous hiking and climbing.

According to the book he published after the war, *Thrilling Adventures of Daniel Ellis* (1867), the east Tennessee native didn't set out to become a mountain guide. In fact, he didn't know the route to Kentucky himself until after he'd made his first trip. Ellis was born in 1827, receiving a basic education in a one-room schoolhouse. In 1846, at the age of nineteen, he volunteered to serve in the Mexican War. After two years of battling disease and harsh living conditions as much as opposing armies, Ellis returned from Mexico exhausted and in poor health, hoping he would never again witness the "terrible scenes of desolation and distress" brought on by war.[62] Eventually, he recovered his strength and began making his living as a farmer and wagon maker. In 1852, Ellis married a Virginian, Martha May of Sussex County, and the two raised seven children. When the Civil War began in the spring of 1861, Ellis was thirty-four years old, a tall, slender man with dark hair and a full rounded beard.

When Tennessee formally joined the Confederacy in July 1861, Ellis was one of the Unionists in the eastern part of the state who immediately began organizing for armed resistance. On the night of November 8, he was a member of the party that successfully burned the railroad bridge over the Holston River at a town called Union in Sullivan County. In the state of Tennessee, this was high treason, punishable by death. But, as Ellis later explained, "Orders had been received from the government of the United States to burn all bridges" on the east Tennessee and Virginia line, and every "true-hearted Union man" was obliged to engage in that work.[63] The bridge burners expected Federal armies to occupy east Tennessee at any time, and they hadn't planned on what to do if left on their own. As Confederate troops began scouring the county, making mass arrests, more and more Unionists took to "scouting" (camping in remote coves and inaccessible mountain plateaus). Ellis was captured briefly by a Rebel patrol, but he escaped by bolting from the road, running up a steep slope, and hiding out in a cedar thicket. While hiding in the mountains with dozens of others waiting for relief from the North, Ellis tried to convince them that if the Federal armies would not come to east Tennessee, then east Tennesseans would have to find the Federal armies.

Finally, on August 1, 1862, he and a companion named Dolan set out on their own for Kentucky. When stopped and questioned by a squad of Confederate home guards, they said they were searching for saltpeter caves. Though he was actually one of the most-wanted men in eastern Tennessee, a known bridge burner, Ellis's story sounded plausible, and the two men were allowed to continue. Later that day, Ellis and Dolan learned from local Unionists that a party of scouters, led by an experienced guide, was leaving for Kentucky that night. They joined the group, meeting many old friends from Carter County whom they hadn't seen for nearly a year. That first trek went surprisingly well, and most of the others continued on to Lexington to enlist in one of the regiments of Tennessee volunteers in the Union Army of the Cumberland. Explaining later that he wasn't one who liked to take orders, Ellis decided that he could better serve the Union by returning to Carter County and showing others the way than by joining the Federal army himself.[64]

Ellis led the first of many excursions in November 1862, only two months after he had learned the route. For the next two years, Ellis would typically meet a group of men, numbering from twenty to over a hundred, in the early hours of the morning on a secluded ridge outside of Elizabethton. Carrying several days' provisions in haversacks but usually unarmed, they would first hike about thirty miles across the mountain plateau to White Oak Flats on the border. There they would stop at a safe house, the home of a staunch Unionist widow named Grills, who gave them a place to bed down and whatever meager rations she had on hand. From there the journey was all up and down—across the Holston River, over the steep ridge of Clinch Mountain, through the Little Poor Valley and two forks of the Clinch River. Sometimes stopping a day for rest, the party would continue over Powell's Mountain and across Wild Cat Valley. When they came to Walling's Ridge (now called Wallen Ridge), the trail was sometimes so steep they had to grab onto laurel bushes to pull themselves up the slope with their arms. In some level stretches, the briar patches were so thick that they had to crawl on their hands and knees to get through. After crossing Powell's Valley, usually by night, they reached the greatest barrier of all: the long wall of the Cumberland Mountains. Once they had conquered that last obstacle, the fugitives usually stopped for much-needed food and a good night's sleep at another safe house before making the last push to the Cumberland River and the Union camps on the other side. After resting a day or two, Ellis would retrace his steps to Carter County alone or with a single companion, then rest a short while before setting out with a new party of stampeders.

And all that describes a good trip. On most of his excursions, there were emergencies, alarms, delays, or rain and snow to impede the group's progress. On his very first trek, Ellis was looking for a freshwater spring, and he slipped on loose rock, cutting his hand on the glass jar he had been carrying. There were no doctors or surgical tools available, so one of his companions picked out the glass shards as best he could, then sewed up the palm of Ellis's hand with a needle and thread. On another trip, in November 1862, Ellis's party was caught in a violent snowstorm and nearly froze to death. At two o'clock in the morning, they were saved when they came across an abandoned cabin in the trackless woods. They found it full of hogs sleeping on a mattress of fallen leaves. They drove the hogs out to fend for themselves and took over the nest, still warm from the bodies of its recent occupants. Returning from that trip by himself, Ellis's problem was not the cold but heat. Seeking escape from a driving rain, he found a hollowed-out chestnut log and decided to crawl inside for a nap. He built a small fire at the open end of the log, hoping the warm air would dry him out as he got some rest. But he slept like a dead man, and the fire dried out the log and set it ablaze. When he awoke, the whole log was beginning to catch fire, and he was in danger of going up in smoke himself. He had to crawl through the burning hole at the base of the log, singeing his face and hair badly, to avoid being roasted alive by the fire. It was still raining, and he was still dead tired, so once he put out the blaze, Ellis crawled back inside the smoldering log and slept till morning.[65]

On his next trip the following month (December 1862), Ellis and his party, tramping through the snow at night, discovered their last water crossing, Powell's River, swollen by the winter rains. They took off their clothes and held them over their heads, wading naked through the freezing water. As they were starting to dress on the far side of the stream, they heard a dog bark nearby and then a squad of Rebel soldiers came running up to the river and began firing. Everyone in Ellis's party escaped the hail of bullets, but most did not have time to finish dressing or to pick up their shoes, caps, or blankets. After they regrouped well away from the river, the fugitives realized it would be too dangerous to try to retrieve their things. But it was a bitter cold night, and several in the group were hatless or shoeless. Since their leather haversacks were empty by then, the shivering men decided to fashion caps and moccasins out of them. The moccasins didn't work very well, and the men that wore them spent their nights in camp picking briars out of their badly cut feet. But Ellis's own haversack cap fit so well, he forgot all about it until the party reached their destination and he started getting some strange looks at his headgear.[66]

On some trips, the fugitive Unionists were their own worst enemy. On several occasions, the stampeders would do just what their name suggested—stampede. The party would be treading along quietly when suddenly the creaking of a tree branch or a glimmer of light ahead would send the men running, certain that a Confederate marksman had them in his sights or that Rebel horsemen were just about to come galloping into their midst. Even when Ellis shouted at them to stop, the spooked men would scatter in every direction and scramble out of sight. One panicked man ran so far into a briar patch, he couldn't get back out. Another ran straight into a tree, nearly knocking himself unconscious. All this wasted a great deal of valuable time and was especially irksome to Ellis, who was sure there wasn't a Rebel within miles of their remote location.

Yet Ellis did not entirely discount the danger of being surprised by Confederate patrols. On one of his expeditions, his party picked up scattered fugitives, freezing and half-starved, who said they had been ambushed by horsemen in gray who shot down some of the stampeders in the act of trying to surrender. Ellis's highly partisan account stresses the heartlessness of the pursuers, but he also notes that such misfortunes were also due to careless guides who stayed too close to the road or who traveled too often by day.[67] Even more unsettling than the stories of other fugitives was Ellis's experience while traveling alone one night on a return trip to east Tennessee. Filling his canteen at a stream, he smelled a putrid odor in the air. Thinking a dead horse or hog must be nearby, he turned around and saw by moonlight three decayed bodies hanging from a tree. Their clothes and flesh had mostly rotted away, but two of the skeletons were still intact. The third man had apparently been shot in the spine. Only his head, arms, and ribcage still dangled from the tree; the hip bones and legs lay crumpled on the ground. A local woman confirmed what Ellis had already guessed: these were fugitives who had been taken unawares while refilling their water bottles. Not realizing she was talking to the Unionist guide already known on both sides as the "Old Red Fox," she added that she hoped all "Lincolnites" would meet a similar end.[68] As a matter of fact, the Rebels had an even grimmer fate in mind for Ellis. Later in the war, he learned that a large reward was being offered for his death or capture, with the added rumor that Confederate authorities were hoping to display his severed head on a pike as a warning to other would-be mountain pilots.[69]

TENNESSEE'S RETURN TO THE UNION

WHATEVER PLANS the Confederate authorities had in mind for the Old Red Fox, it was becoming increasingly clear that their general plans for east Tennessee were not working out as hoped. After Felix Zollicoffer was killed in the battle of Mill Springs (see page 50) in January 1862, east Tennessee saw a rapid succession of military commanders, none of whom was able to pacify the local population. Zollicoffer was followed by W. H. Carroll, George B. Crittenden, Edmund Kirby Smith, J. P. McCown, Samuel Jones, Daniel Donelson, and Simon B. Buckner. In this group, the department commander who brought the most stability to the area was probably Smith. By early 1862, the Confederacy had eleven thousand troops garrisoned in east Tennessee, which Smith bluntly described as "an enemy's country."[70] Even when Gen. Albert Sidney Johnston was seeking every man he could find for a surprise attack on Ulysses S. Grant around Shiloh (April 1862), Smith said he could not release any of his troops who were guarding the railroad lines, the Cumberland Gap, and the passes leading into Kentucky. At a time when they desperately needed troops for offensive operations, the Confederates had what amounted to a full army corps tied up in east Tennessee, a region Smith considered a land of "unionism and traitordom."[71]

Besides never really gaining control of eastern Tennessee, Southern armies were continuing to lose their grip on the state as a whole. Grant had taken Forts Henry and Donelson, on the Tennessee and Cumberland Rivers, in February 1862, allowing Don Carlos Buell to occupy Nashville, the state capital, without a fight. The tide of battle ebbed and flowed in the West, but the current was generally in favor of the Federals. In April, Grant and Buell turned back a determined Confederate assault at Shiloh, in southwestern Tennessee, and advanced into Mississippi. Memphis fell to Union naval forces in June. Southern Gens. Braxton Bragg and Edmund Kirby Smith took the war into Kentucky in the fall of 1862, but by January 1863 they had fallen back to middle Tennessee. That summer, when William S. Rosecrans maneuvered Bragg out of the state without bringing on a battle, Union Gen. Ambrose E. Burnside marched into eastern Tennessee in August and occupied Knoxville in September. Though Rosecrans was driven back to Chattanooga after his defeat at Chickamauga in September, the Federals resumed their advance into Georgia after Rosecrans's replacement, U. S. Grant, drove Bragg's army off Missionary Ridge (November 26) and back into Georgia. By early 1864, all of western Tennessee and most of central Tennessee were controlled by the Federals. Though Confederate cavalry under Nathan Bedford Forrest and John Hunt Morgan mounted brilliant expeditions behind Union lines, capturing garrisons and supply depots and disrupting communications, most of the state west of Knoxville remained under Federal control for the rest of the war.

When Burnside's troops entered eastern Tennessee in August 1863, they were greeted by crowds of local Unionists as an army of liberation. Like George B. McClellan's army entering western Virginia in June 1861, Burnside's men were welcomed with wild cheering and cookies and cakes. One soldier described the throngs of women, children, and old men as "almost crazed with joy."[72] Well-wishers waved handkerchiefs and American flags, and one old woman with tears running down her cheeks cried out, "At last we are saved. . . . God bless the Yankees!"[73]

With Northern forces in control of Knoxville, it didn't take long for William G. Brownlow to resume publication of his newspaper. It reappeared in November 1863 under the expanded title *Brownlow's Knoxville Whig and Rebel Ventilator*. (In nineteenth-century parlance, "to ventilate" a topic was to subject it to intense scrutiny, to "air out" its dark corners or hidden recesses. The way Brownlow used the term, it also carried the vernacular connotations of shooting something full of holes.) Brownlow's revived *Whig* declared that anyone who had persecuted Unionists in eastern Tennessee "would do well to leave" the area entirely, naming specific people he thought should clear out. He later stated that he could think of at least twenty-five prominent secessionists in the Knoxville area who deserved hanging.[74]

After his triumphal return to Knoxville, Brownlow's star continued to rise. When Governor Andrew Johnson left for Washington to assume his duties as vice president during Lincoln's second term, Brownlow was overwhelmingly elected by the Unionist-controlled legislature to replace him.[75] Brownlow served as governor until 1869, though he was clearly the wrong man for the job. Reversing Lincoln's formula for Reconstruction, Brownlow had charity for none, even for fellow Unionists like President Andrew Johnson, and malice toward all who had opposed him during or after the war. While other governors were issuing amnesty oaths after the war, pardoning those who swore allegiance to the Union, Brownlow favored what he called "damnesty oaths," basically telling former Confederates to go to hell. After three tempestuous terms as governor, Brownlow was elected U.S. senator from Tennessee in 1869. But by then his health was so poor he had to have someone hold up his hand for him to take the oath. Brownlow completed his senate term in 1875 without much distinction and died in 1877. Though he spent much of his career being hated, and seeming to revel in it, Brownlow lived his life to the end without regrets. Looking back in his later years, he remarked, characteristically, "Had I my life to live over, I would pursue the same course I have pursued, ONLY MORE SO."[76]

The coming of Union troops to Knoxville in 1863 had a much less dramatic effect on Daniel Ellis's career. Union lines did not extend too far east of Knoxville, which is almost as far away from Carter County as the Cumberland River in Kentucky. Ellis continued serving as a mountain guide, but his route from Carter County had to change, taking him not toward Kentucky but 120 miles east to Knoxville. In order to evade Confederate patrols, Ellis had to loop around, first traveling into North Carolina, then north to little-used mountain trails near the Tennessee-Kentucky border, then west and south to reach the new Union lines.

On his new route, one of Ellis's usual stopping places in North Carolina was Shelton Laurel, a community dominated by Unionists and the scene of one of the most appalling episodes of the Civil War. In January 1863, Confederate Gen. Henry Heth, commanding in east Tennessee, sent three companies of infantry and one cavalry company to round up local tories in Shelton Laurel who had been raiding warehouses of salt (needed to preserve meat) and plundering the homes of Confederate sympathizers. The two men leading the expedition, Col. Lawrence Allen and Lt. Col. James Keith, were both North Carolinians with scores to settle, and their handling of the Shelton Laurel assignment was brutal. They whipped and strangled neighborhood women for the information they wanted, then tracked down and arrested fifteen local Unionists. Two escaped in the night, but the remaining thirteen, ranging in age from thirteen to sixty, were marched into the mountains, told to kneel in the snow, and summarily executed. Gray-clad soldiers who balked at this command were told they too would be shot if they didn't obey orders. The incident was investigated by military authorities during the war and civilian authorities afterward, but both Keith and Allen escaped to Arkansas, evading the penalty for what was essentially a mass murder. The episode near Shelton Laurel was only one of the more notorious instances of what historian James O. Hall has called "a little war wrapped up in a big war" in the mountains of eastern Tennessee and the western Carolinas.[77]

As for Daniel Ellis, he piloted Unionists from Carter County through North Carolina and back to Knoxville for more than a year, then he decided it was time to join the regulars. In January 1865, Ellis accepted a commission as a captain in the Tennessee cavalry, leading many of the same men whom he had guided to safety in the past three years. His first assignment as an army officer was to travel to Carter County and return with members of the regiment who had gone home to visit their families but had not returned on time and were officially AWOL. The following month he piloted a company of 125 men, what he called a "motley assemblage" of local Union soldiers who were "undeserting," two officers who had escaped from the Salisbury prison in North Carolina, Unionist stampeders, Rebel deserters, and east Tennessee blacks seeking to enlist in the army at Knoxville. The diversity of the group hints that the war was in its closing stages and illustrates the widespread social disruption in the Appalachians caused by the war.

Ellis spent the last months of the war skirmishing with scattered Rebel units in the mountain counties of Tennessee and North Carolina. In March 1865, he and a squad of thirty-two men, on foot but well armed, surrounded and ambushed a company of Confederate cavalry camped in a barn, capturing most of the gray troopers and commandeering their horses. The oddity of this engagement is that Ellis's blue-clad soldiers were nearly all from Tennessee, and their Rebel prisoners turned out to be from Kentucky.[78]

Ellis was honorably discharged in September 1865. He had not accepted pay for his services as mountain guide, living on small contributions from stampeders or from Tennessee soldiers for carrying letters and money from them to their families at home. In 1866, Ellis asked for, and received, $3,060 for what was essentially back pay for services rendered to the army during the war years. Of course, Ellis's services to the U.S. government during the war were incomparably greater than that amount. Though he was an unassuming man, Ellis could have justly boasted that four full regiments in the Army of the Cumberland (4,000 men) were turned from Unionist fugitives into Union soldiers because of his boldness and skill in leading them out of eastern Tennessee. By war's end, about 35,000 Tennessee whites served in the Union army, as well as 15,000 blacks. (About 140,000 Tennesseans served in Confederate armies.)[79] Despite chronic ill health and several death threats after the war, Ellis lived to be eighty years old, dying almost forgotten in 1908.

Ellis's account of his experiences was published in 1867 under the title *Thrilling Adventures of Daniel Ellis, The Great Union Guide of East Tennessee for a Period of Nearly Four Years during the Great Southern Rebellion.* Apart from his many adventures, which live up to the book's title, the most notable feature of the book is its extremely bitter tone. Like *Parson Brownlow's Book*, published in 1862, *Ellis's Thrilling Adventures* shows no disposition to follow Lincoln's advice to "bind up the nation's wounds." Rather he seems to hope a few more wounds will be inflicted, identifying particular Confederates by name as "infamous scoundrels," "bloodthirsty murderers," and "heartless desperadoes," adding that Jefferson Davis should have been shot or hanged as soon as he had been caught.[80]

A good third of *Thrilling Adventures* is taken up with lurid tales of women being beaten, young boys strangled to get information out of them, and old men pleading in vain for time to say their prayers before being executed. Some historians have dismissed many of the incidents Ellis describes as propaganda; others say that many of the episodes he describes have been confirmed by other sources.[81] Of course, the many incidents of brutality Ellis relates can be matched, story for story, by those of Confederate sympathizers describing how they were treated, both during and after the war. As shown in the work of modern histories such as Noel Fisher's *War at Every Door* (1997) and Todd W. Groce's *Mountain Rebels* (1999), the people on both sides of the war in eastern Tennessee had ample stories to tell—about being harried by armed men in uniform, by partisans on one side or the other, and by vicious criminals who took advantage of the widespread lawlessness. In a long, seething "neighborhood war"[82] such as the one that ravaged east Tennessee throughout the 1860s, there seemed to emerge, by the end, a grim equality of victimization and suffering.

5

MOSSBACKS, DESERTERS, AND GUERRILLAS

Both sides in the Civil War saw themselves as defenders of freedom. Abraham Lincoln insisted that the Union was "conceived in liberty" and that the war was being fought to settle the question of whether, in a free society, "the minority have the right to break up the government whenever they choose." But Jefferson Davis declared that the people of the South were forced to take up arms "to vindicate the political rights, the freedom, equality, and State sovereignty" that they had inherited from their Revolutionary ancestors.[1]

Officials in both the Union and the Confederacy soon discovered the paradox of "fighting for freedom." Freedom, by definition, is an individual's liberty of thought and action. But organized warfare calls for subordination of individual wills, submission to the collective will of the people as expressed in their leaders. In both the North and the South, there were tens of thousands of people whose definition of freedom was far more radical than that of their political and military leaders. In the Union, there were as many as 320,000 men unwilling to serve in the armed forces or unwilling to stay if they were forced to serve. In the Confederacy, there were about 200,000 such draft evaders or deserters.[2] But the North, with its population of 22 million and its increasing influx of black soldiers, was able to tolerate its desertion rates much better than the Confederacy, with a white population of 5.5 million.

In all armies and navies, there are those whose character or attitudes make them unsuited for military life. But the Confederacy, as the invaded region and the side with fewer resources, faced a whole series of unique challenges to its fighting forces. With its smaller reserves of manpower, the South introduced a national conscription law in April 1862, a year earlier than the North, and it enforced the law more rigorously and with fewer exemptions. The law originally applied to all white males aged eighteen to thirty-five, but the age limit was raised to forty in September 1862. In February 1864, the age range was expanded in both directions, from seventeen to fifty, and in March 1865, the last month of the war, the Confederate government took the drastic measure of authorizing slaves for combat service. During the war, the South mobilized up to 80 percent of its able-bodied white males for military service, volunteers and conscripts, and yet it still suffered from chronic shortages of men ready and equipped for duty. (The Union, by contrast, never mobilized more than half its able-bodied men.) [3]

The rule for both sides in the Civil War was that today's conscript is tomorrow's deserter. As historian Ella Lonn put it, "Men dragged into the army had no spirit to bring with them."[4] In the first two years of the war, Confederate deserters generally left the army singly or in small groups, except in the case of conscripts. In 1861, Gen. Henry A. Wise enrolled a regiment in western Virginia that he called Wise's Legion. But in falling back to the Kanawha Valley after the Confederate reversal at Cheat Mountain, Wise reported that he lost five hundred men on the march south.[5] Many of these early deserters cost the South twice: they left the Confederate army in order to join the Federal hosts. In eastern Tennessee, Confederate officers complained that it took one man to guard every conscript. In northern Alabama, an entire regiment of conscripts ran away as a body, taking their weapons with them.[6]

Soldiers in blue and gray probably suffered about equally from the horrors of battle, the rigors of forced marches, the tedium of life in camp, and the miseries of rain, snow, and mud. But in Confederate armies the trials of army life were considerably worsened by shortages of food, clothing, shoes, blankets, and medicine. Sometimes men on the march went a full day without rations, sometimes two days. On a few occasions, there were no rations distributed for a full week. Men were forced to pick persimmons or berries from the roadside, to eat corn mash originally intended for the horses, or to forage from local farmers. Soldiers baked in the summer and froze in the winter.

Rebel troops also suffered from a chronic shortage of shoes. In November 1862, Gen. James Longstreet reported that six thousand of his men were marching barefoot. In February 1864, Gen. Joseph E. Johnston reported thirteen thousand men without shoes, marching with their feet wrapped in rags or makeshift strips of cowhide. Many soldiers' feet were so blistered and lacerated from rough roads that marching columns left behind a visible trail of blood.[7]

Often, it was the plight of loved ones that drove Confederate soldiers to desert. Single-family farms needed every available hand, and it was too much for a wife to try to plow and plant and harvest on top of her already arduous household chores. And some soldiers' homes were behind enemy lines, in constant danger from prowling foragers and marauding rangers. When one desperate soldier, Edward Cooper, was tried for desertion, the only defense he presented to the court was a letter he had received from his wife:

My dear Edward: I have always been proud of you, and since your connection to the Confederate army, I have been prouder of you than ever before. I would not have you do anything wrong for the world, but before God, Edward, unless you come home, we must die. Last night, I was aroused by little Eddie's crying. I called and said, "What's the matter, Eddie?" and he said, "O mamma! I am so hungry." And Lucy, Edward, your darling Lucy; she never complains, but she is growing thinner every day. And before God, Edward, unless you come home, we must die.—Your Mary[8]

Though the court officers were moved to tears by the letter, they still handed down a guilty verdict for desertion, punishable by death. Cooper was later pardoned by Gen. Robert E. Lee. This sort of leniency on the part of high officials was common; in the course of the war, there were perhaps one thousand Confederates executed for desertion, though the actual number of deserters was more than one hundred times that many.[9]

In his classic study, *The Plain People of the Confederacy* (1943), Bell Irvin Wiley states bluntly that "the defection [of common soldiers] was probably due more to the conviction that they were being discriminated against by the privileged classes than to defeats or deprivations."[10] Even in the first six months of the war, when things were going comparatively well for the South, some soldiers felt that the wrong people were being asked to carry the burden. A letter published in the *Weekly Courier* of Rome, Georgia, in October 1861 expressed the situation as one man saw it: "Is it right that the poor man should be taxed for the support of this war, when the war was brought about on the slave question, and the slave at home accumulating for the benefit of his master, and the poor man's farm left uncultivated, and a chance for his wife to be a widow, and his children orphans? Now, in justice, would it not be right to levy a direct tax on that species of property that brought about the war to support it?"[11] Later edicts—such as the Conscription Act (April 1862), the Twenty Negro Act (October 1862) and the tax-in-kind laws (April 1863)—only deepened feelings among enlisted men that they were being asked to sacrifice far more than their share.

Commoners also resented the policy by which wealthy young men could hire substitutes, sometimes paying as much as five thousand dollars to someone willing to serve in their stead. In the course of the war, there were at least fifty thousand paid substitutes in the Confederate army before this program was discontinued early in 1864. Given their mercenary motives for serving, it should not be surprising that paid substitutes also had consistently high desertion rates. Young men from well-placed families could also avoid the rigors and dangers of army life by arranging for a comfortable post on the home front. As one prominent Mississippian complained to President Davis, "It seems as if nine-tenths of the youngsters of the land whose relatives are conspicuous in society, wealthy, or influential, obtain some safe perch where they can doze with their heads under their wings."[12] If even Davis's personal friends were concerned about exemptions and substitutions, it is not hard to see why so many common soldiers were calling this "a rich man's war and a poor man's fight."

Some Southerners didn't care whose fight it was, as they objected to war on principle. There were at least two thousand members of the Society of Friends (Quakers) in the Confederacy as well as four hundred families of Mennonites and Dunkers (Brethren) in Virginia's Shenandoah Valley. These denominations were usually antislavery as well, so they tended to be tacit Unionists—though this was expressed through passive resistance, not active rebellion. Members of the peace churches generally avoided conscription, fleeing to the North or sitting in local jails rather than serving in the military. Some pacifists chose to join the Confederate army, but not to fight. Gen. Thomas J. "Stonewall" Jackson reported that Dunkers and Mennonites in his brigade often allowed themselves to be conscripted and obeyed orders in training, but in battle, they deliberately refused to take aim and fire at the enemy. Jackson concluded the members of peace churches could better serve the Confederacy by staying home and growing food for the army rather than serving in it.[13]

Civilian and military officials tried a variety of strategies to stem the rising tide of desertions, but with little success. Besides those rare cases of execution, deserters were arrested and thrown into prison, limited to a diet of bread and water, or forced to wear a ball and chain. Some were whipped with thirty lashes, some branded with a D, and others had their names published in their hometown newspapers. But such measures often kindled resentment among the rank and file more than they deterred runaways. As early as August 1863, a conscript officer in South Carolina reported "it is no longer a reproach to be known as a deserter."[14] In March 1865, Assistant Secretary of War John A. Campbell amplified on how the problem of disaffection had spread to whole sectors of Southern society: "So common is the crime, it has in popular estimation lost the stigma which justly pertains to it, and therefore the criminals are everywhere shielded by their families and by the sympathies of many communities."[15]

The rate of Southern desertion did not climb steadily from the first year of the war to the last; there were sudden rises and then leveling-off points. There was a spurt of desertions after the Conscription Act of April 1862, as men who had been evading service were brought into the ranks. There were also more desertions at that time among soldiers who had enlisted for one year but were told their tour of duty had been automatically extended to three years. Desertions climbed again in the summer of 1863 after Lee's failed assault at Gettysburg (July 3) and Pemberton's surrender of Vicksburg (July 4) created a widespread despondency, a sense that the war was being lost. In late July of that year, the Confederate assistant secretary of war John A. Campbell estimated that there were up to 100,000 men either evading conscription or absent without leave from the army.[16] In November 1863, Secretary of War James A. Seddon reported to President Davis that one-third of the army was AWOL.[17] Vigorous efforts to round up the absentees in the first half of 1864 brought down absentee rates for a season, but in the last year of the war, desertions reached critical proportions. At the end of the war, Confederate records showed 160,000 men in the ranks out of a total of 359,000 on the muster rolls, less than half the army available for duty. Those numbers mean that, in the closing months of the war, there were more Southern soldiers away from the army, without leave, than there were in the ranks answering roll call.[18] Beginning in the summer of 1863, and accelerating after the fall of Atlanta in September 1864, a disastrous cycle was set into motion: defeats contributed to desertions, and desertions contributed to more defeats. In her classic study, *Desertion During the Civil War* (1928), Ella Lonn concludes, "The miracle is not that the South fell, but that it did not collapse in 1863."[19]

THE CAVE DWELLERS OF NORTH CAROLINA

THE PERVASIVE problem of absenteeism, both North and South, can be seen in the sheer number of labels there were for men who did not do their duty.

They were deserters, of course. But they were also called stragglers, slackers, shirkers, and skulkers. Originally, a straggler was a soldier who couldn't keep up with his fellow marchers and had to catch up with his unit later. But eventually *straggler* became a euphemism for *deserter.* Conscript officers set up straggler-collection stations in many Southern counties, especially in remote areas, offering amnesty to anyone who would come in and rejoin his regiment. But a man who falls behind his company and ends up at home, perhaps five hundred miles away from the battle front, has indeed "straggled" behind his comrades.

Though the various terms to describe deserters were often used interchangeably, the word *mossback* usually referred to someone who evaded conscription by hiding out in the woods or swamps. The colloquial term suggests that these men spent so long in the wild that moss grew on their backs. These were technically not deserters, as most of them had never reported for duty in the first place. Mossbacks could be found in every state of the Confederacy, especially in remote mountain coves, trackless swamps, or inaccessible canebrakes. While some deserters or conscript evaders put up armed resistance to military authorities, mossbacks usually avoided confrontation altogether. Their specialty was hiding, not fighting.

Perhaps the most industrious and ingenious mossbacks were those called the cave dwellers of North Carolina. In the western part of the state, men hid out in the mountains, and in the east, they took to the swamps. But in central North Carolina, natural hiding places were not so easy to find; men evading conscription had to create their own.[20] Working in small groups or with family members, local farmers burrowed holes into the sides of hills, six or eight feet deep, taking care to remove any leftover soil that might give away the recent excavation. Then they boarded up the open face of the cave, covering the slope with dirt and hanging vines to give it a natural, undisturbed look. For a hidden entrance, they dug a shaft in the roof, leading to a trapdoor covered by branches or a carefully placed log. Cave dwellers often added amenities, such as a carpet of pine needles, a bed of pine boughs laid across a crude bed frame, and perhaps even a cupboard carved out of one of the burrow's walls. In another wall, they dug out a recess for a fireplace, attaching a flue that emerged outside. They kept their fires small and their fuel dry, trying to create as little smoke as possible. Sometimes they placed their flue outlets near a charred stump, so that anyone noticing a bit of smoke would assume it came from a tree left smoldering by lightning or a hunter who had smoked out a possum.

Cave dwellers expended no little ingenuity in disguising their hide-outs, in case conscription gangs came out to scour the woods. One man placed his trapdoor entrance near the end of a fallen tree that stretched across a narrow gorge with a brook below. When home guards came look-ing for him, they found tracks that ended near the fallen tree. They searched the area, thinking he might have gone upstream or down, never guessing that their quarry had done an acrobat's walk along the horizontal tree trunk to a concealed entrance on the other side of the ravine. On an-other occasion, three mossbacks had the entry to their cave covered so art-fully by a massive log that the local militia, sent out to find them, stopped for a leisurely lunch, sitting on the very log placed there by the men the home guards were seeking. The cave dwellers couldn't enjoy the irony much, sitting silently in the dark, hardly daring to breathe for fear of giving themselves away to the armed men only a few feet above their heads.

One enterprising North Carolinian dug his cave underneath the henhouse on his own property, right next to his homestead. He channeled the smoke from his hideout underneath the floor of his house and out the fireplace, so that smoke drifting out the chimney would not create any suspicion. Others relied on their wives and families to keep them out of harm's way. In some families, a certain quilt hung out on the line meant it was safe to come in for dinner while another meant home guards were somewhere nearby. For other families, different kinds of hog calls were used for the same two messages.

Some cave dwellers claimed it took more courage to be a mossback than to be a soldier. Apart from the tension of constant vigilance and the very real dangers of being arrested or shot, there were also frequent false alarms. On one occasion, a cave dweller heard the sounds of voices above his hideout, and then came a thumping on the trapdoor above his head. When the door was flung open, he looked up at two cocked muskets and heard a perempt-tory order to surrender. As he climbed out with hands held high, blinking in the sunlight, he recognized two of his neighbors and fellow mossbacks, who had gotten bored and decided to come over and "arrest" him as a prank.

Not all cave dwellers confined themselves to evading conscription. Some participated in more active forms of resistance. Many belonged to a clandestine organization called the Heroes of America, which was centered in North Carolina but included several adjoining states. Also called the Red

Strings because of the identification token they wore—a red string on the lapel—the heroes boasted a membership of ten thousand men in the Tar Heel State and claimed as well that even Abraham Lincoln and Ulysses S. Grant had secretly joined their cabal. The heroes had their own initiation rituals, secret signs, code words, and a well-developed underground railroad for returning escaped Federal soldiers to Union lines.[21]

In the last few months of the war, some of the North Carolina cave dwellers felt safe enough to come out by daylight and do some hunting in the woods. One such group, armed with muskets and fowling pieces, came into a clearing and stumbled onto a squad of Confederate soldiers. After a moment of panic and a near clash of arms, the mossbacks recognized the others as deserters from Lee's army in Virginia. Having found each other out, there was a certain somber camaraderie among the men headed for home and those who had never left.

THE FREE STATE OF WINSTON, ALABAMA

It was a recurring pattern throughout the southern highlands: when leaders in a state capital called for it to secede from the Union, small farmers in the mountains wanted to secede from the state. In northern Alabama, the upcountry people were closer, geographically and culturally, to east Tennessee than to the cotton-growing counties of their own state. They had rail connections to Memphis and Chattanooga but no direct line to Selma or Montgomery, which were several days' journey away. Like the upland people in Virginia and Tennessee, northern Alabamans talked about forming a new state, joining perhaps with several counties in east Tennessee and north Georgia to form Nickajack, after the lake of that name near the border of the three states.[22]

The contrast between "black belts" and other parts of the state was nowhere more evident than in Alabama. In 1860, Winston County, in the upland north, included only 3.4 percent slaves. Most of the adjacent counties in the mountains also had less than 10 percent slaves. By contrast, in the cotton-belt counties across the middle of the state (Dallas, Greene, Marengo, Sumter, and Wilcox), the percentage of slaves ran from 75 to 80 percent.[23] When Alabama called its secession convention in January 1861, only one northern county (Calhoun) sent a secessionist representative and only one southern county (Conecuh) sent a "cooperationist."[24]

Though there was never much doubt as to which way the state would go, Alabama's secession convention held at Montgomery on January 7–11, 1861, was a tempestuous affair. There was plenty of oratory, sometimes violent in tone, on both sides. One northern delegate, Robert Jemison of Tuscaloosa, said he thought it would be unfortunate if the state withdrew from the Union, risking war, based on a convention majority of only one. At that, William L. Yancey of Montgomery, known throughout the country as the "Prince of Fire-eaters," replied that even if an ordinance of secession passed by only one vote, it would still legally represent "the fullness, and the power, and the majesty of the sovereign people of Alabama." He added that the state would "expect and demand, and secure unlimited and unquestioned obedience to that Ordinance," and that those who refused would be treated as traitors and "enemies of the State."[25] The short, sturdily built Yancey concluded: "In this great contest there are but two sides—a Northern and a Southern; and when our Ordinance of Secession shall be passed, the citizens of the State will ally themselves with the South. The misguided, deluded, wicked men in our midst, if any such there be, who shall oppose it, will be in alignment with the abolition power of the federal government, and as our safety demands, must be looked upon and dealt with as public enemies."[26]

At the conclusion of these ominous words, there was a commotion in the hall, and northern Alabama delegates jumped to their feet in reply. A representative from Huntsville declared that the counties in the north would "resist the invasion of their rights by a tyrant at home as readily as from abroad."[27] Jemison, the delegate who had first raised the possibility of a majority-of-one vote for secession, replied to Yancey bitterly and at length. He asked how Yancey planned to deal with "great popular masses" in parts of the state if they resisted the ordinance of secession: "Will the Gentleman go into those sections of the state and hang all those who are opposed to Secession? Will he hang them by families, by neighborhoods, by towns, by counties, by Congressional Districts? Who, sir, will give the bloody order? Who will be your executioner? Is this the spirit of Southern chivalry? Are these to be the first fruits of the Southern republic? Is this the bloody charity of a party who seeks to deliver our own beloved sunny South from the galling yoke of a fanatical and puritanical abolition majority?"[28]

Despite the deep divisions evident in the speeches from the floor of the convention, the vote to secede passed by a clear majority. At that, the cooperationists moved to have the ordinance submitted to a popular referendum, a motion that was voted down. Once it was clear they would not prevail, twenty-one delegates, nearly all from northern counties, drafted and signed a minority report, denying any responsibility for the secession ordinance passed by the majority.[29] Probably the most vociferous of the cooperationist delegates was twenty-two-year-old Christopher Sheets (also spelled Sheats) of Winston County, who continued to protest loudly that people from his part of the state would not abide an ordinance to secede. Refusing to be silenced, Sheets was wrestled to the floor by a dozen other delegates, dragged outside to a waiting carriage, and hauled off to jail, without charges, for the remainder of the convention. Before the assembly adjourned after four tumultuous days, most of the cooperationist delegates decided to bow to the inevitable. They withdrew their minority report and signed the ordinance of secession.[30]

But if the north Alabama delegates eventually submitted to the majority, many of the people who had sent them to Montgomery did not. The northern counties felt betrayed by their own delegates. They believed that the delegates, except for Christopher Sheets, had collapsed under pressure and had not faithfully represented their point of view. It was reported that the Stars and Stripes continued to fly over the courthouses in Athens and Huntsville after the ordinance of secession had been announced.[31] A month after the convention, William Yancey was burned in effigy in Limestone County on the northern border of the state.[32] In the weeks after the convention, northern Alabamians were quoted as saying they would "secede from Yancey rather than from the Union."[33]

After a series of smaller protests scattered around the northern counties that spring, it was decided to have a mass meeting on July 4, 1861, at Looney's Tavern in Winston County. In the month before the meeting, six volunteers rode out in six directions for six days to announce the upcoming Independence Day assembly.[34] On the appointed day, more than twenty-five hundred people gathered, coming from a dozen counties in northern Alabama and from as far away as Georgia, Mississippi, and Tennessee.[35] The informal assembly passed a resolution commending Christopher Sheets for "loyalty and fidelity to the people . . . in voting against secession, first, last, and all of the time."[36] A second resolution proclaimed that a state could not legally secede from the Union, but that if it could, a county could, by the same logic, secede from the state.[37] At the reading of this resolution, a Confederate sympathizer in the crowd shouted out in sarcastic disbelief, "The

Free State of Winston!" Though he was mocking the idea, the name caught on and was used in the county for a century or more after the Civil War.[38] A third resolution declared, "We think our neighbors in the South made a mistake . . . when they attempted to secede and set up a new government. We, however, do not desire to see our neighbors in the South suffer wrong, and, therefore, we are not going to take up arms against them; but on the other hand, we are not going to shoot at the flag of our fathers, Old Glory, the flag of Washington, Jefferson, and Jackson. Therefore, we ask the Confederacy on the one hand and the Union on the other, to leave us alone, unmolested, that we may work out our own political and financial destiny here in these hills and mountains of North Alabama."[39]

Though nothing like an independent state of Winston was ever close to becoming a reality, Unionists in the northern counties continued to meet throughout the war, openly displaying U.S. flags at their gatherings. Called "home-made Yankees" or "Alabama Yankees," upland farmers assembled in meetings of up to four hundred men to provide mutual support, to exchange information, and sometimes to arrange contacts with nearby Federal armies.[40] Christopher Sheets was a frequent speaker at these clandestine gatherings, a man who had become a local hero and leader while still in his early twenties. Sheets remained a shadowy figure throughout the war. The scanty records available suggest that he acted as a liaison between local Unionists and the Federal army and that he spent at least part of the war in a Southern prison. After the war, he edited a local newspaper, the *North Alabamian*, served a term in Congress (1872–74), and filled a variety of other government posts at both the state and national level before his death in 1904.

In the first year of the war, loyalists (those loyal to the Confederate state of Alabama) and tories (those still supporting the Union) opposed each other mainly through verbal threats and local boycotts. But when the Conscription Act passed in April 1862, the conflict came into the open and turned more violent. Like the mountain farmers in other states, many in north Alabama wanted to sit out the war, to stay home and look after their families and property. But when the "conscription cavalry" came looking for recruits, one had to join the Confederacy or oppose it. Southern enrollment officers were thorough and energetic in their work. As one draftee said, they "burned the woods and sifted the ashes for conscripts." Another unwilling recruit complained that the Confederate army would take any man who had not been dead for more than two days.[41]

In September 1862, Confederate Gen. Gideon Pillow complained to his superiors that there were eight to ten thousand tories hiding in the hills of northern Alabama, adding that they were "vicious as copperheads."[42] Though it seemed unlikely at the time, Pillow also passed on reports that some of the "home-made Yankees" were riding out of the mountains to become blue-clad Yankees in the Federal army. In this, he was correct. Two months earlier, 40 men, dodging Confederate patrols, had traveled to Decatur to join the Union army. Encouraged by this, Union Col. Abel Streight took a small force into the mountains and spread the word that he was seeking recruits. He brought back another 150 men almost overnight. These, plus the 40 who had just enlisted, made up the first two companies of the First Alabama Cavalry (USA). By December 1862, there were enough men on hand to organize the Alabama cavalry into two regiments, with headquarters in Glendale, Mississippi. By the end of the war, 2,066 men would serve in the First Alabama Cavalry (USA).[43]

The cavalry regiments of "home-grown Yankees" saw limited action, and their duties consisted mostly of recruiting and raiding in northern Alabama, guarding prisoners, or serving as guides in the remote mountain terrain. Sometimes they were called upon to fight fellow Alabamians, as on April 17, 1863, when they were ordered to charge the Fourth Alabama Cavalry (CSA), under Col. Philip Roddy. Their own commander, Col. Florence M. Cornyn, complained later that the charge was made without heart and that the men of the First Alabama should have captured a piece of horse artillery, which they allowed the Confederates to carry away. He didn't explain that he had ordered the Alabamians to make the charge with their carbines *unloaded*. And, according to local historian Wesley S. Thompson, the First Alabama and Roddy's Cavalry recognized each other and had a tacit agreement not to engage in anything more than perfunctory maneuvers against their fellow Alabamians.[44]

Two companies of the First Alabama served as guides on Col. Abel Streight's ill-fated (or ill-planned) expedition across northern Alabama in April 1863. Streight's idea was to lead a "flying column" out of northern Mississippi, travel behind enemy lines through the mountains of Alabama, and isolate Chattanooga by tearing up railroad tracks west and south of the city. But Streight's force was hardly a "flying" column. Many of his men could barely ride, and most of them were mounted on mules. Pursued by a smaller but better-trained and better-mounted force led by Confederate Gen. Nathan Bedford Forrest, Streight's men engaged in a three-day running fight before the entire Federal troop surrendered to the "Wizard of the

Saddle" and his men. Most of the Union troopers, including the Alabamians, went to the military prison near Andersonville, Georgia. Some of the officers, including Streight, were sent east, to Libby Prison in Richmond.

More fortunate were elements of the First Alabama who served as Gen. William T. Sherman's headquarters escort on his famous, or infamous, March to the Sea, cutting a broad swath of destruction across the state of Georgia from Atlanta to Savannah. These same Alabamians accompanied Sherman on his march through South Carolina and North Carolina, and they took part in his triumphal procession through Washington, D.C., after the fall of the Richmond regime. They returned to their homes in northern Alabama after the war, often to find their lives more in danger from ongoing partisan violence there than they had been while in uniform.

As in western Virginia and eastern Tennessee, mountain folk in Alabama had to endure not only the depredations and hard-handed requisitions from soldiers in both blue and gray, they also suffered at the hands of local militia from both sides or from plunderers whose only side was their own. Unionist guerrillas calling themselves "Destroying Angels" or "Prowling Brigades" raided the homes of Confederate sympathizers, burned cotton gins, and carried off cattle, money, even blankets and bedsheets.[45] The names of Confederate bands did not find their way into the history books, but they must also have been a troublesome lot. On December 12, 1863, Alabama governor Thomas Watts wrote first to the Confederate secretary of war and then to Jefferson Davis himself, asking for help in controlling, not Unionist rangers operating in the mountains, but *Confederate* irregulars.[46]

After the war, families on both sides acted on longstanding grudges and settled old scores. Barn burning and bushwhacking plagued the northern counties throughout the 1860s. Andrew B. Moore, governor of Alabama from 1857 to 1863 and later the state's historian, summarized the situation in the northern mountains by saying that "toward the end of the war the struggle degenerated into one of revolting butchery."[47] Once civil war becomes a ceaseless, remorseless feud among neighbors, the distinction between right and wrong is blurred by a much more primal distinction between "us" and "them."

THE REPUBLIC OF JONES

ON JULY 12, 1864, the *Natchez Courier* reported that Jones County, Mississippi, in the southeastern corner of the state, had seceded from the Confederacy.

According to the article, the new Republic of Jones was already a going concern, with a commander in chief, a secretary of war, foreign ministers, a legislative assembly, and an army and a navy. It had also fought and defeated a Confederate column sent up from Mobile, under "Colonel Mowry," and had issued paroles to prisoners on pieces of birch bark. The *Courier's* story came complete with a copy of a battlefield dispatch from Maj. R. Robinson, announcing his complete rout of Confederate forces, including a copy of a prisoner's certificate of parole.[48]

If there were oddities about this story, they were overlooked at the time. Jones County is sixty-five miles inland, so it is not clear what use it might have for a navy. And most of Jones County's able-bodied men were on duty in the Confederate army in 1864, so it would seem unlikely that this remote district with a total population of 3,323 could find the personnel for a national government with its own armed forces.[49] The dates on the war dispatch (January 27, 1864) and parole papers (February 2, 1864) were also suspect, as there were no Confederate operations in Jones County until March 1864.

All these details, as well as the birch-bark paper (probably a satirical swipe at the backwardness of the Piney Woods people), suggest that the unsigned *Courier* article was a hoax. Yet there was a germ of truth in the tale. In February 1864, Union Gen. William T. Sherman, reporting to Washington on operations in Meridian, Mississippi, about thirty-five miles north of Jones County, included a document that he identified as a "declaration of independence by certain people who are trying to avoid the Southern conscription, and lie out [the war] in the swamps." Sherman added that he had replied to the separatists that he supported their efforts and encouraged them to organize for their mutual defense.[50] The document Sherman enclosed has been lost, so it is not known if he was referring to dissenters in Jones County. It is known, however, that two Confederate columns, one under Col. Henry Maury and one led by Col. Robert Lowry, were both sent to Jones County in March and April 1864 to disperse guerrilla bands and round up deserters. Those two names together sound like the *Courier's* Colonel Mowry, but neither of the expeditions was by any means routed. Between the two of them, Maury and Lowry returned hundreds of men to Confederate service, hanged a dozen more, burned down the home of one suspected troublemaker, and took horses, cattle, and household goods from local residents.

Whatever the *Courier* article's mixture of history and hoax, the story of the Republic of Jones quickly took on a life of its own. The piece was reprinted in Union-oriented newspapers from New Orleans to New York. In 1886, army historian G. Norton Galloway treated the journalistic flight of fancy as sober fact in his article "A Confederacy Within a Confederacy," published in the *Magazine of American History*. Galloway repeated the *Courier* yarn with a straight face, explaining that the republic's actual name was the Jones County Confederacy, that its president was Nathan "Nate" Knight, that it had a population of twenty thousand (mostly "refugees from the Davis government"), as well as a well-equipped army of ten thousand. Five years later, Harvard historian Albert Bushnell Hart cited Galloway's article in *New England Magazine* as an example of civil discord within the Confederacy. Hart's essay was hotly disputed by historians in the South, and the existence of the Republic of Jones became the subject of national debate.[51]

In 1893, Eli Lilly (founder of the pharmaceutical company still known by his name) offered first-hand testimony to bring some clarity and perspective to the issue. Lilly had been a major in the Indiana cavalry during the war and was captured and held prisoner at Enterprise, Mississippi, in Clarke County. Speaking at a veterans reunion in Indianapolis, Lilly explained that in November 1864 an elderly black man had come up to the prisoners and told them ominously that the Republic of Jones was going to rob and murder them if they were carrying any valuables. Lilly said that, upon investigating this odd warning, he found out that there was indeed a group calling itself the Republic of Jones about thirty miles southwest of the POW camp, a paramilitary outfit that "held supreme control over Jones County and the surrounding country." As Lilly was informed, "They had their President, Vice-president, Cabinet, and an army of several hundred men, banded together for mutual protection, general plunder, and to keep out the Confederate army." Lilly said this guerrilla band in Jones County was powerful enough to wipe out small groups of Confederates sent to conscript them, but it was compact enough to "take to the swamps and pine barrens" if pursued by a larger military force.[52] Lilly's recollection was later confirmed by another former prisoner of war held at Enterprise, who added that the group's leader was named Newton "Newt" Knight.

Though the "thousands" became "hundreds," and the republic began to look more like a guerrilla band, the legend of the Jones County Confederacy became a permanent part of American folklore. Newt Knight granted an interview to the *New Orleans Item* in 1921 to get his version of events on the record before his death the following year. Knight's son, Thomas Jefferson Knight, published a memoir in 1935, in which he portrayed his father as a Robin Hood of the Civil War, defending the poor folk of Jones County from the depredations of Confederate soldiers. Newt's grandniece, Ethyl Knight, took the opposite approach in *The Echo of the Black Horn* (1951), depicting her famous ancestor as the black sheep in an otherwise genteel and respectable Southern family. Journalist James Street produced a fictionalized account of the Republic of Jones in *Tap Roots* (1943), which was made into a popular film of the same name in 1948, starring Van Heflin and Susan Hayward.

Beneath all the layers of legend and propaganda, Jones County and its Unionist guerrilla bands do typify many common elements of Southern dissent during the war. Jones County had about 12 percent of its population enslaved, the lowest proportion of any county in the state of Mississippi.[53] The region consisted mainly of small farmers who raised corn and hogs amid the virgin pines, grassy slopes, and boggy lowlands of the Piney Woods district. The whole of Jones County raised less cotton than any single good-sized plantation along the Mississippi River, and farmers in the area had no ready access to rail lines or commercial markets.

When the state convention met at Jackson on January 9, 1861, to decide on the issue of secession, Jones County sent a cooperationist delegate, John H. Powell. In keeping with his antisecession mandate, Powell voted in favor of a motion that Mississippi should not secede on its own but should act in concert with other Deep South states, Florida, Georgia, and Louisiana. He also voted for a motion that the ordinance of secession should be ratified by a popular referendum. When both of these motions were defeated, he thought it best to make a show of solidarity and vote with the majority in favor of secession.

Back in Jones County, a good many residents felt that Powell had not served their interests well. As Newt Knight later explained it: "There's one story that after Jones County seceded from the Union she seceded from the Confederacy and started a Free State of Jones. That ain't so. Fact is, Jones County never seceded from the Union into the Confederacy. Her delegate seceded."[54] Whatever their feelings about secession, most able-bodied men in Jones County served in the Confederate army. Newt Knight himself enlisted in July 1861, though his house burned down soon afterward, and he did not report for duty until the following year. Born in 1830 and married to a local woman, Serena Turner, in 1849, Newt was thirty-one when the war began, a tall, wiry man with prominent, steely eyes and dark curly hair and a full beard.

Knight's private war with the Confederacy began soon after the April 1862 Conscription Act became law. Though he joined the army the following month, he never seemed to acknowledge the fact that conscription, by definition, was not voluntary. As Knight later explained: "The next thing we knew, they were conscripting us. The rebels passed a law conscripting everybody between 18 and 35. They just came around with a squad of soldiers [and] took you. If they had a right to conscript me when I didn't want to fight the Union, I had the right to quit when I got ready."[55]

In May 1862, the same month he joined the army, Knight received a letter from his wife, Serena, saying that his brother-in-law, Bill Morgan, had been whipping Newt and Serena's three young sons. Morgan was also cooperating with local Confederate authorities and had turned over to them the one horse the family needed to keep their little farm going. Knight was furious. He went back to the family homestead in Jones County, where Morgan and his wife, Newt's teenaged sister Martha, were also staying. It became clear right away that there was one too many men trying to head the household. Knight became obsessed that Morgan would either bushwhack him or turn him in to Confederate authorities as a deserter. (Perhaps calling in a favor, Morgan had obtained an exemption from military duty, since he was a blacksmith.) One night in June 1862, when Morgan was sitting on the front porch of the Knight family home, he was shot in the head and died. Many assumed the murder was Knight's doing, but Morgan had been known locally as a "desperado" and "a regular outlaw," so the case was never investigated.[56]

By August 1862, Newton Knight had rejoined his unit, the Seventh Battalion Mississippi Volunteers, stationed in the northeast corner of the state. Sickness was rife throughout the army that summer and fall, with up to four in ten Confederate soldiers too ill to report for duty. Despite its weakened condition, Knight's regiment participated in two sharp engagements, the battle of Iuka in September and the battle of Corinth in October, both of which ended in Confederate retreats. By the last week of October, Knight's unit from Jones County (Company F) had fifteen men fit for duty, with thirty-eight in the hospital, five killed or wounded in battle, and six dead from illness.[57] Knight was promoted to corporal and then sergeant that fall, perhaps because of natural leadership ability, perhaps because he was one of the handful of soldiers in Company F still standing, less than one quarter of those who had mustered in the previous May.

That same October 1862, the Richmond government passed the Twenty Negro Law, exempting slaveholders with at least twenty slaves from military service. For Newt Knight and others from Jones County, this was the last straw. One of Knight's closest friends, Jasper Collins, promptly deserted from the army, then stationed at Holly Springs, Mississippi, never to return to military service. Collins went home, dismissing the struggle for Southern independence as "a rich man's war and a poor man's fight."[58] (Some authorities consider Collins to be the source of this oft-repeated phrase among the plain people of the Confederacy. Other scholars believe the phrase originated in northern Alabama.)[59] Knight stayed with the army one more month, then he decided to follow Collins back to Jones County. Although he considered himself done with army life, Knight was arrested as a deserter, roughly handled, and returned to the ranks as a private in February 1863.[60] Knight deserted again in May 1863, this time for good. On returning to Piney Woods the second time, he did not go home but joined a hundred or so other deserters who were "lying out" in the swamps of Jones County.[61]

The number of AWOL soldiers in the Jones County bayou swelled during the summer of 1863. The Seventh Battalion of Mississippi Volunteers was among those trapped in Vicksburg during its six-week siege by Union forces under Ulysses S. Grant. Enduring constant bombardment and facing starvation, Vicksburg's defenders, as well as civilians pinned up in the city, were reduced to eating rats and to drinking soup made from boiled leather shoestrings.[62] On July 3, 1863, the twenty-nine-thousand-man garrison led by Pennsylvania-born John C. Pemberton surrendered. A few of them joined the Federal army, but most went home with certificates of parole. When conscription officials later tried to round up these men and return them to the army, many insisted that, as a matter of honor, they were disqualified from any further military service.

In mid-August 1863, Maj. Amos McLemore of the Confederate Volunteer and Conscript Bureau arrived in Jones County with orders to persuade or compel deserters to return to the ranks. Many of those he was seeking had military training, were well armed, and knew exactly what kind of life awaited them if they returned to their units. McLemore brought four dozen bloodhounds with him to sniff out the men hiding in the woods, but he soon discovered that he was facing not simply several hundred treasonous men but whole communities in rebellion against the Confederacy. Wives and kinfolk hid deserters in their cellars and corncribs, and they rang bells to warn of the approach of the "conscript cavalry." Slaves who had been involved in the Underground Railroad taught local women how to use skunk musk or red pepper to throw bloodhounds off the scent. Eventually, most of the dogs took sick and died, apparently poisoned. Women also took provisions out to the deserters' dens, sometimes holding baskets of food over their heads and swimming their horses to reach men in the most remote spots of the mazy quagmire.[63]

McLemore was a native of Jones County himself and a prosperous local businessman before the war. He did his job well, returning more than a hundred men to army service in his first six weeks in the Piney Woods district. To Newt Knight and others out in the swamps, McLemore was a dire threat. He had the scouts, local informants, and bloodhounds to track down the deserters, and he had the troops to force the absentees back into service.

On the evening of October 5, 1863, McLemore relaxed at a fireside with several Confederate officers at the home of Amos Deason, a Mississippi state representative. Suddenly a door swung open, shots were fired, and McLemore fell out of his chair, dead in a pool of blood on the parlor floor. The murder of McLemore eventually became as much a part of Jones County folklore as the Republic of Jones itself. The site of the bushwhacking, the Amos Deason home, is now a local museum and a haunted one at that. It is said that, on rainy days, McLemore's blood rises through the wood of the floorboards, no matter how many times it is scrubbed clean. According to local legend, every year on the anniversary of McLemore's death, at precisely 11:00 p.m. on October 5, the door to the house opens and closes, as if moved by an invisible hand.[64]

As with Bill Morgan, the obvious suspect in the slaying of Amos McLemore was Newt Knight.[65] By allegedly killing a Confederate officer, Knight and his gang moved from passive resistance to active, from layouts to outlaws (though desertion itself was punishable by death, according to the articles of war.) The week after McLemore's murder, a squad of Confederate provost guards rode into the woods, probably to arrest Newt Knight. They were greeted with a hail of rifle fire and had to deploy in what developed into a small-scale firefight. In the next fifteen months, Knight's company engaged in more than a dozen such shootouts with Confederate cavalry sent to arrest or disperse them.[66]

In the early months of 1864, "Captain Knight," as he was now called, and his guerrillas undertook offensive operations as well as defensive, raiding the homes of Confederate sympathizers and attacking anyone who symbolized Richmond's attempts to establish its authority in Jones County. They drove conscription officer John H. Powell out of the county, never to return, even after the war.[67] This was the same John H. Powell who had been the antisecession delegate who had voted for secession back in 1861. (Ironically, Powell's daughter was married to Jasper Collins, one of the county's most outspoken Unionists and Newt Knight's executive officer.) In February 1864, Sherman reported receiving that "declaration of independence," which most likely originated in Jones County, as the guerrillas there were actively seeking contact with Union forces. In March, Knight's men raided a tax-in-kind warehouse in Paulding, distributing corn to some of the town's unfortunates and carrying off five more wagonloads.[68] (Richmond's tax-in-kind law required farmers to contribute 10 percent of their grain, cattle, or other goods to support the troops. Along with the Conscription Act and the Twenty Negro Act, this policy did much to alienate the plain folk of the Confederacy.)

In March 1864, Knight proclaimed Jones County to be the Free State of Jones, with no sheriff, conscription officers, or tax collectors.[69] Realizing that the home front in the Piney Woods was on the verge of becoming a new battle front, Confederate area commanders sent two well-appointed military expeditions into Jones County that same spring. On March 2, Col. Henry Maury marched up from Mobile with 200 mounted troopers, a battalion of sharpshooters, and a half-dozen pieces of horse artillery, 500 men in all. He spent a week scouring the pine barrens in the southern part of the county, estimating that his men engaged at least 150 armed deserters, capturing all but 20 of them, hanging a few and sending the rest to prison or back into the army. None of Maury's dispatches mention Newt Knight as a guerrilla leader, and none of Knight's later recollections ever mention Maury. It is likely that Maury's operation in the lower half of Jones County engaged a different set of armed deserters who may also have taken to calling themselves the Republic of Jones or some other name suggesting their separateness from the Confederacy.

In late March, Col. Robert Lowry arrived in the northern half of the county from Demopolis, Alabama, with two regiments of infantry, accompanied by cavalry. Lowry's detachment spent a month flushing deserters out of that part of the Piney Woods, hanging nine of Knight's men, sometimes without the benefit of even a drumhead court-martial. Lowry reported that his operations in Jones County were entirely successful and that organized resistance in Jones County was at an end. In some respects, he was right, as the number of deserters lying out in Jones County in the summer of 1864 was only a fraction of what it had been a year earlier. Yet, historically, regular army officers almost always overestimate their success in wiping out guerrilla bands, as the latter usually melt into the woods rather than accept a pitched battle. By November 1864, Jones County guerrillas were strong enough to ambush and capture twenty-one Confederate horsemen, who rode into Piney Woods but walked out, carrying little of value except the paroles they received from Knight. The last known skirmish between Knight's men and Confederate regulars occurred on January 10, 1865.[70]

In examining the activities of Civil War guerrillas on both sides, the question arises if they are entitled to be called irregulars or if they are mere bandits using the chaos of war as an excuse for murder and plunder. In Texas, Gen. Henry McCulloch complained that the partisan rangers in his command waged war "like savages," and they were "but one shade better than highwaymen."[71] In the Florida swamps, several bands of freebooters indiscriminately raided plantations and farms, carrying off cattle, slaves, and whiskey. A gang in the Florida panhandle led by William Strickland called itself "Union Rangers," a rather more respectable name than the "Destroying Angels" or "Prowling Brigades" of north Alabama. But Strickland's men provided food and information to the Federals not out of loyalty to the United States but in exchange for guns and ammunition. In southwestern Louisiana, marauders were so rampant in 1865 that authorities from both sides, North and South, cooperated in their efforts to restore order in the bayou country.[72]

Though Newt Knight was probably a murderer and some of his men were certainly plunderers, the Jones County guerrillas still had a better claim to be called Unionist partisans than the gangs roaming around the hinterlands of Florida or Louisiana. Knight always called himself a "Union man," and two of his chief lieutenants, Jasper Collins and his brother Riley, were known for their pro-Union, antislavery views before and during the war.[73] In January 1861, after the vote of the state convention at Jackson was announced, Riley Collins called a meeting at the local church and gave a passionate speech on the folly of secession. He told the men assembled, one listener later recalled, "not to fight against the Union, but if they had to fight, to stay at home and fight for a cause in which they believed."[74] Riley was a widower and was exempted from conscription because he was the sole support for his children. But this did not stop him from joining his brother Jasper in hiding out with Newt Knight in the swamps. The password to gain entry to Knight's "deserters' den" was "I am of the Red, White, and Blue."[75]

Federal soldiers were sometimes spotted among Knight's company in the pine barrens, though it is not known why they were there. It is known that Knight tried several times to contact Union commanders. He sent Jasper Collins to both Memphis and Vicksburg, seeking to cross into Yankee lines, but Collins couldn't get past the Confederate pickets. After the devastating Lowry raids of April 1864, ten of Knight's guerrillas took a flatboat down the Mississippi River to New Orleans, where they enlisted in the Union army, the First Regiment of New Orleans Infantry.[76]

Knight and the Collins brothers stayed behind, remaining in the Jones County bayou until the war was over. When they came out of hiding, they returned to their families and farms and did not seem to engage in the sort of postwar vendettas that plagued east Tennessee and north Alabama. All three lived to see the twentieth century. In this war, the most ornery men sometimes seemed to live the longest, and Newt Knight lasted until 1922, dying at the age of ninety-two. He is buried in Jasper County, Mississippi, under a headstone that reads, "He lived for the other side."[77]

A BATTLE AND A MASSACRE IN TEXAS

IN TEXAS, resistance to the Richmond government emerged along the borders, the regions farthest from the cotton fields and closest to the Indians. In the 1860s, only the eastern half of the state was truly settled, as there were frontiers facing hostile Kiowas and Comanches to the north (below what is now the southern border of Oklahoma) and to the west (what is now central Texas, around Austin and San Antonio). Texas's cotton-growing plantations and its slave population were concentrated in its eastern river valleys and Gulf Coast counties. Most of the residents in this part of the state had come from the Deep South. In the north, along the Red and the Trinity rivers, newer settlers, many from the Midwest or Upper South, raised cattle, corn, and wheat. The state's thirty thousand German immigrants were concentrated in the counties north and west of San Antonio, and many of these objected to both slavery and secession.[78]

In other Southern states, Unionists lived mainly in outlying regions, such as the mountains of east Tennessee and north Alabama or the pine barrens of Mississippi. During the secession crisis of 1861, Texas had a Unionist residing in a much more prominent place: the governor's mansion. Sam Houston (1793–1863) had been the hero of San Jacinto in 1836, decisively defeating Mexico's Gen. Antonio López de Santa Anna and winning independence for Texas. He had twice served as president of the Lone Star Republic, then as a senator from Texas when the state was annexed in 1845. He was elected governor in 1859 but was out of step with most of the state's leaders in 1861. Houston had described slavery as "evil" and disunion as "an abomination," and he refused to call a secession convention in January 1861.[79] Other state leaders called the convention in his stead, which met in Austin and overwhelmingly approved an ordinance of secession, a vote ratified by popular referendum on February 23,1861. Houston refused to take an oath of loyalty to the Confederacy, and he was replaced by Lt. Gov. Edward Clark as governor in March.

Sam Houston publicly acquiesced once it became clear that Texas had joined the Confederacy (though he privately referred to its president as "Jeffy" Davis and commented dryly that Davis would have preferred to be emperor.)[80] But there were others in the state who continued to oppose secession after it became an accomplished fact. Among the German immigrants, there were a few firebrands who proposed to capture some artillery and occupy Austin and San Antonio, holding out till Federal forces arrived.[81] Such a plan was never pursued, but throughout the war, German dissidents remained a continuing problem for Confederate authorities.

Actually, Texas Germans did not vote or act as a bloc. Those who arrived before the German revolution of 1848 were called the "grays." They wanted to blend with their adopted New World culture and accepted many of its attitudes. In the referendum of 1861, first-wave German immigrants strongly supported secession. For example, the gray settlers in Comal County, just north of San Antonio, voted for secession 398–16. By contrast, the Germans who came to the United States after 1848, fleeing political upheaval in their home country, were called "greens" or "Forty-Eighters." Many of them had tried unsuccessfully to introduce democratic reforms in

Sam Houston

Germany. They came to Texas frustrated by the failure of their homeland to consolidate into a unified country. They also championed liberty and human rights and were disappointed to find states' rights in their adopted country held in higher regard than individual rights.[82] Friedrich Kapp typified the attitude of many of the greens: "The problem of slavery is not a problem of the Negro. It is the eternal conflict between a small, privileged class and the great mass of the non-privileged, the eternal struggle between aristocracy and democracy."[83]

Apart from ideology, the German pioneers on the western fringe of Texas also shared a more immediate concern: Indians. The U.S. government had established a line of forts along the borders, with Texas Rangers on the lookout for raiding parties of Kiowas or Comanches. The Germans felt that the government in Washington had been providing no more than basic protection; they wondered if the new government in Richmond could do even that well. They also felt that they needed their able-bodied young men to serve as home guards on the frontier, not to leave the state to fight in what they called "the American war."[84] When it came time to vote on secession, the frontier Germans of Gillespie County voted against it, 396–16.

Tensions between Confederate authorities and German settlers out west escalated in August 1861, when the Richmond legislature passed the Alien Enemies Act (sometimes called the Banishment Act). This statute declared that all people living within the borders of the Confederacy, fourteen years of age or older, must declare an oath of loyalty or else leave the country within forty days. Some Germans decided to move to Mexico, creating a community of exiles in Matamoros, just across the border from the southern tip of the state. Other greens didn't understand why they were being forced to choose between pledging to a cause they didn't believe in or else abandoning the lives and livelihoods they had worked so hard to build on the windswept prairies.

With the Conscription Act of April 1862, resentment flamed into open revolt. German settlers attacked enrollment officers sent out to the frontier counties, and it was rumored that they raided the homes of Confederate sympathizers as well. In July 1862, five hundred men from three western counties met in Bear Creek, in Gillespie County, to organize what they called the Union Loyal League. In their charter, they explained that the association was founded to provide protection from bands of marauding Indians and "to take such peaceable action as would prevent the forced enlistment of Union sympathizers in the Confederate army."[85]The name of the league was not chosen to placate state authorities. Nor was it clear how they planned to resist military force through "peaceable action."

That summer, Brig. Gen. Paul O. Hébert, commanding the military district of Texas and Louisiana, declared martial law, first in the western counties, then throughout the whole state. In the spring and summer of 1862, Confederate cavalry patrolled the hill country around Fredericksburg, hunting for draft evaders. In late July, another four hundred troopers rode out to Gillespie County, which was considered to be in open rebellion. On arriving in Fredericksburg, a Texas horseman noted that the town consisted of about eight hundred people "almost all of them Germans, and Unionists to a man."[86]

Capt. James M. Duff was in charge of the conscription cavalry. Though Scottish-born himself, he was one of many Texans who resented "the foreign element" who seemed to be taking over parts of the state. When Duff's men went out into the hills looking for German draft evaders, Duff was as likely to execute the Germans as to recruit them. On his scouting missions, he deliberately left behind troopers who were not American-born or who thought the Germans were being treated with excessive brutality.[87] That summer, one Texas trooper confided that he had seen seven men hanged from one tree limb. Another wrote home that in the counties on the Indian frontier, "Hanging is getting to be as common as hunting."[88] Apart from Duff's men, German Unionists also suffered at the hands of a clandestine organization called the Knights of the Golden Circle, local vigilantes who terrorized suspected disloyalists, sometimes slitting their throats or dragging them out of bed for midnight lynchings.

As the violence became more widespread, more and more immigrants decided the time had come to leave the country. On August 1, 1862, a company of sixty-one men, led by Fritz Tegener, left from a secret rendezvous point northwest of San Antonio and headed for the nearest crossing of the Rio Grande into Mexico. The party, including one Mexican, eleven Anglo-Americans, and the rest Germans, was lightly armed, in case they encountered Indian raiders, but they were not expecting any trouble from Confederates. For one thing, their starting point and their route of travel had been kept secret, so they believed they were leaving the country unobserved. Unknown to them, a spy in their midst had already passed this information on to Duff. They also believed the Confederate authorities would be glad to be rid of them, that they were leaving the country as provided for in the Banishment Act passed the year before. To Duff, however, this was a group of armed men moving in secrecy for an unknown purpose, most likely to cross into Mexico and then enlist in the Union army.

Tegener saw his little band as refugees fleeing persecution; Duff saw them as armed guerrillas. The Confederate commander sent a detachment of ninety-four Texas cavalrymen, led by Lt. Colin D. McRae, to intercept the party. One of the Americans in Tegener's party, a veteran scout named John W. Sansom, worried that they were being tracked. He repeatedly asked the inexperienced Tegener to speed up the march and to post a rear guard. But Tegener insisted they were in no danger, and he continued to move through the sunbaked hills by easy stages. He didn't post guards at their night encampments, except for two men to keep an eye on the horses. When they reached the Nueces River on August 9, one day's march from the border, Sansom advised Tegener to push on through and not take a chance of being brought to bay so near their destination. Tegener again disagreed, telling the men to make camp a few hundred yards from the river, in an open meadow surrounded by cedar brakes.

On the night of August 9, the Texas troopers caught up with Tegener's party. Dividing his men into two groups, McRae told them to hide behind the stands of cedar and wait for a gunshot to signal a surprise attack at first light. By chance, one of the German sentinels discovered the dismounted horsemen concealed behind the trees. He was shot dead. Sansom pleaded with Tegener to move to higher, more defensible ground before daylight, but Tegener again discounted his advice. Though the Germans and their companions put up a spirited fight, they were surrounded and had no cover, so the result of the battle was foregone.

A few hours after daybreak, Tegener and about half his party fought their way to the horses and escaped south toward the Mexican border. They left behind nineteen dead and nine wounded. The Texas cavalry suffered two killed and eighteen wounded, including McRae, who turned his command over to the ranking officer, a Northern-born man named Luck. Initially, some of the Texas troopers bandaged the wounded Germans and gave them water. But as most of them were out rounding up the horses or tending to their own wounded, Luck and a small party shot the nine wounded members of Tegener's party, leaving their bodies to rot in the sun. When some of the other Texans loudly objected to the massacre of unarmed men, Luck singled

John W. Sansom

them out to carry their own wounded, the ones too badly injured to ride, on hand litters to the nearest wagon road. Luck left thirty-two men behind to carry eight litters on foot over the scorched prairie under a searing August sun. He told them they would be relieved in three hours. The men on horseback soon disappeared from sight, and the others toiled on under the blazing sun. Three hours passed, then four, then five. When the sun was well past overhead, the litter-bearers ran out of water. Still no one came. Parched, foot-sore, and realizing they had been abandoned, several of the men said they couldn't go on. But others pointed to the wounded men groaning on the blood-stained litters and insisted that they must all keep moving.

Resting whenever they could find shade and searching out prickly pears to keep from dying of thirst, the thirty-two men trudged all afternoon until after sundown. Eventually, they reached the wagon road after carrying the wounded men thirty miles. Finally, wagons met them five miles from the fort, taking the wounded off their hands and giving them all the water they could drink. Luck later explained unconvincingly that he had gone in search of a water hole and had gotten lost before he could send back a relief party.

In his report on the battle of Nueces River, McRae explained that Tegener's party "offered the most determined resistance and fought with desperation, asking no quarter whatever; hence I have no prisoners to report."[89] McRae was severely wounded in the gun battle, and it is possible he didn't know what had occurred after the skirmish had ended. Historians still argue about whether the action at the Nueces River should be called a battle or a massacre. It seems the day's events included something of both. As for the Germans who continued south, six were shot trying to cross the Rio Grande into Mexico. Of the two dozen men who made it safely across, Tegener decided he'd seen enough of war and headed west to California. Eleven other survivors went the other direction: they traveled east to the Gulf Coast, sailed to New Orleans, and enlisted in the Federal army. They served for the duration of the war in a new regiment of cavalry organized by Gen. Benjamin F. Butler: the First Texas Cavalry (USA), composed mainly of Germans.[90] John Sansom served as a scout in the First Texas; he made three more trips back to

Gillespie and the surrounding counties, successfully leading ninety-three men out of Texas and into the Union army. He ended the war as an officer in the Federal cavalry.

Tensions remained high on the Texas frontiers, both the western frontier where most of the German immigrants lived and the northeastern frontier, below what is now Oklahoma. In October 1862, only two months after the Nueces River incident, Brig. Gen. Paul O. Hébert allowed an informal vigilance committee in Gainesville, south of the Red River, to arrest more than two hundred members of an informal peace party in the region. Forty-two of these were hanged or shot on charges of conspiracy, some receiving rudimentary trials, but most simply lynched by a mob. In November 1862, John B. Magruder replaced Hébert as district commander and demonstrated much more finesse in handling dissenters. Magruder continued conscription on the frontiers, but he allowed men to perform their duty on border patrols near home or to serve as wagon drivers. Though there continued to be flare-ups along the Texas borders during and after the war, Magruder's more conciliatory policies generally brought an end to open rebellion on the edges of the Confederacy nearest to Indian Territory.

It was not until after the war that the twenty-eight bodies of Tegener's men killed at Nueces received a proper burial. After lying in the sun for three years until there was nothing left but bleached bones, the remains were gathered up by friends and kinfolk in 1865 and laid to rest in Comfort, Texas. At the burial site today stands a memorial stone engraved with the words, "Treuer der Union," Loyal to the Union.

6

"THE WOLF HAS COME"
THE BATTLE FOR
INDIAN TERRITORY

THE SCENE was one that became all too familiar in the years between 1861 and 1865. An armed force had taken a defensive posture, more than a thousand men crouching or lying prone behind corncribs, fence rails, or hastily excavated earthworks. The other force, infantry in the center and cavalry on the flanks, advanced warily against glinting rifles aimed by soldiers who had already proven they could shoot with deadly accuracy. Though the scene was highly typical in some respects, it was actually one of the most unusual battles of the Civil War. This confrontation did not take place in any of the states, North or South, but in Indian Territory. The defenders in the December 9, 1861, battle of Chusto-Talasah were mostly Union-loyal Creeks; the attackers included a large proportion of pro-Confederate Cherokees, Chickasaws, and Choctaws.

When the war for Southern independence erupted in the spring of 1861, the indigenous tribes of North America might have been expected to dismiss it as a white man's war and stay well out of it. But history, culture, and military necessity made it inevitable that there would be no neutrals in this war, only those who fought and those who suffered the consequences of fighting. Indian Territory, with roughly the same boundaries as present-day Oklahoma, formed a shield for the trans-Mississippi states of the Confederacy. If the Indian nations could be persuaded to join the Rebel cause and to treat Union troops as invaders to be repelled, the South would have a wide buffer protecting Arkansas, Louisiana, and Texas from incursions launched from the newly created Union state of Kansas.

In May 1861, with the guns of Fort Sumter barely cooled, a Confederate delegation led by Albert Pike set out from Fort Smith, Arkansas, to secure treaties with tribal leaders scattered throughout Indian Territory. At the war's outset, the Cherokee nation occupied what was roughly the upper third of present-day Oklahoma; Seminoles and Creeks populated the central portion of the territory; and the lower third was further divided, with Choctaws in the southeast, Chickasaws in the south-central region, and smaller groups in the southwestern corner. Pike's small party traveled to the major tribal centers, mostly in the eastern half of the territory, seeking the influential chiefs' allegiance to the Confederacy.

Albert Pike

Originally from New England, Pike had established a successful law practice in Arkansas before the war, often representing claims of the Indian nations against the federal government and sometimes winning settlements for them in millions of dollars. Having already earned the trust and respect of numerous tribal leaders, Pike rode into Indian Territory with other powerful inducements to secure their cooperation and support. Washington had suspended its sizable annuity payments owed to the tribes for the eastern lands they had ceded, but Pike promised that the Richmond government would resume these payments in full. He also explained that tribal warriors who agreed to fight Yankees were to be paid the same as regular Confederate soldiers, but they would not be required to leave Indian Territory.

Besides these incentives, Pike had other factors working in his favor. Most of the Indian agents who disbursed funds to the tribes in Indian Territory were Southerners. When the Confederacy was proclaimed, these men usually followed their states out of the Union. New commissioners sent out from Washington were not yet able to reach their posts, so the tribes heard only the Southern perspective. Meanwhile, rumors abounded. Some said that Lincoln had already died. Others said that the United States had ceased to exist, thus all earlier treaties were null and void. Still others claimed the federal government planned to confiscate all Indian lands, perhaps for the settlement of blacks.

The government in Washington had neither words nor deeds to counter Confederate promises or prophecies. In accordance with its pre-war treaties, the U.S. government had established a line of forts in Indian

Territory to help keep the peace. In May 1861, however, Forts Arbuckle, Cobb, and Washita were all vacated. At that time, the Union did not have enough soldiers to protect its capital, much less three small outposts in remote Indian Territory. So the blue-clad soldiers in these three forts quietly rode north to Kansas, and Confederate troops occupied the posts without firing a shot. Furthermore, the federal government felt it made no sense to send money to Southern Indian agents if the funds were going to fall into Confederate hands. So the payments that the Indian nations relied on were abruptly suspended, a violation of longstanding treaties. From his post in Kansas, Federal Indian agent C. H. Carruth lamented, "The wonder is not that the Indians should have seceded, but that any remained true."[1]

Albert Pike spent much of the summer of 1861 going about his diplomatic mission with energy and tact. He was able to secure Confederate treaties with the Chickasaws, Choctaws, Osages, Senecas, Shawnees, and several smaller tribes. He also signed pacts with key leaders among the Cherokees, Creeks, and Seminoles, though important factions of these three tribes were not swayed by Pike's blandishments. They wanted no part of the white man's war, and they steadfastly refused to align themselves with the South. These factions were led by three great chiefs: the Cherokee John Ross, the Creek Opothle Yahola, and the Seminole Halek Tustenuggee. These three knew that choosing the wrong side in this war could be disastrous for their tribes, both during the period of armed conflict and afterward, when the victors divided up the spoils. Each of them had opposed the federal government in the past, and each had seen his tribe stripped of vast tracts of land as a result. So they resisted an alliance with the Confederates, even though the U.S. government had failed to live up to its obligations. Their strategy, as one of the chiefs expressed it, was "simply to do nothing, to keep quiet, and to comply with our treaties."[2]

THE FIVE CIVILIZED TRIBES

By July 1861, some tribes in Indian Territory had thrown in wholeheartedly with the South. Others were split in their allegiances, with a substantial number simply hoping to stay out of harm's way. In choosing sides, the tribes in Indian Territory cared little about states' rights or preserving the Union. The Indian nations had never been states of the Union, so the issues that fueled fiery debates among white men were meaningless to them. Their decisions in the great conflict were rooted in their cultural history, not in the political struggles of European settlers and their descendents.

Hundreds of years before the Confederate States of America was born, there was, in the same region of the continent, the Creek confederacy, an association of Indian tribes. The leading tribe in this alliance was, as the name implies, the Creeks (also called the Muscogee). In addition to the Creeks, the Cherokees, Chickasaws, Choctaws, and Seminoles constituted what white men called the Five Civilized Tribes. They lived in parts of what would later become Alabama, the Carolinas, Florida, Georgia, Kentucky, Mississippi, and Tennessee. Unlike the tribes living on the Atlantic coast, the Five Tribes were not immediately threatened by the English colonies in the early 1600s. To a certain extent, these Native Americans admired European technology. They prized items such as beads, guns, kettles, and needles. It was not uncommon at this time for European traders (primarily British, French, or Spanish) to set up shop in an Indian village and to take Native American wives. Furthermore, European colonists could identify to some extent with the customs of the Five Tribes. These Indians cultivated the soil, raised livestock, and many lived in permanent log homes. For the most part, they were eager to learn European methods of farming and quick to adopt European labor-saving tools.

In time, however, the amicable relations between the colonists and the Five Tribes, especially intermarriage, caused profound social changes. This was particularly true among the Cherokees and the Creeks. The Indian populations closest to the settlers tended to become Europeanized in their language, their genetic makeup, and their way of life. At the same time, portions of the tribes who lived farther away from the coasts tended to retain their traditional beliefs and customs. The Cherokee and Creek nations slowly became divided, like the branches of a tree that steadily grew farther and farther apart. When titanic pressures were later applied to these tribes, the full-blood traditionalists and the mixed-blood Europeanized factions of each tribe tended to react differently.

Initially, the European settlers were few in number and did not have much impact

John Ross

LIBRARY OF CONGRESS

on the indigenous tribes. But the number of whites grew at a prodigious rate, far faster than any other people on the continent. Between 1750 and 1770, the number of colonists doubled from one million to more than two million. This was in an era when most Indian tribes, decimated by wars and Old World diseases, could be counted in the tens of thousands.[3] As the colonists pushed farther north, south, and especially west, the tribes were either assimilated or forced to migrate away from white settlements. This movement often brought them into conflict with other tribes that already resided in the outlying regions.

At first, Europeans settlers and Native Americans tried to live together peacefully. In every part of the country, however, coexistence soon led to friction, friction to abrasion, and abrasion to violence. Among other points of contention, the Indians and colonists had fundamentally different ideas about the land. To the whites, land was an asset like jewelry or livestock that could be bought, held, or traded as financial advantage dictated. But most Indians would no more sell a piece of land than they would barter away a family member. (In later years, when some tribes were forcibly evicted from their lands, the soldiers in charge marveled that the Indians stroked the trees, patted the rocks, and dangled their fingers in the streams by way of saying farewell.)

From very early on, white settlers coveted Indian lands. In 1791, an Indian agent serving the newly formed American government traveled through Creek territory and reported the fertile and pristine lands he rode through "must, in process of time, become a most delectable part of the United States."[4] In the case of the Five Civilized Tribes, ancestral territory was not usually taken away by brute military force. More often the tribes were leveraged out of their lands through treaties that applied a variety of pressures and promises, both legal and extralegal. Unscrupulous deal makers, often representing the U.S. government, did whatever it took—including bribes, one-sided laws, threats, and whiskey—to induce Native Americans to cede title to thousands and thousands of acres.

One technique to accomplish the transfer of Indian lands was dealing with a "treaty

Opothle Yahola

T. L. McKENNEY AND J. HALL, *THE HISTORY OF THE INDIAN TRIBES OF NORTH AMERICA* (1836–44)

chief." Typically, Indian nations were loosely ruled by councils, not by a single man who had the authority to speak for the tribe as a whole. Wily white negotiators, then, instead of treating with a stolid council of chiefs that represented a whole Indian nation, would isolate a single chief or a small group of subchiefs and apply intense pressure until they won the lopsided land-transfer agreement they sought. Over the vehement protests of the majority of Indians who did not want to give up the land, the white authorities would then enforce the dubious new treaty, by military force if necessary, as if it were lawfully agreed upon by all parties.

To combat this practice of making agreements with treaty chiefs, several Indian nations, including the Cherokees and the Creeks, instituted a "blood law." This law provided the death penalty to any Indian who sold land to the whites without the approval of the full council of chiefs. The blood law was a desperate measure enacted to counteract the alarmingly rapid loss of huge tracts of Indian land.

By the 1820s, the most momentous issue among the Five Civilized Tribes was whether or not to cooperate with white authorities and relocate west of the Mississippi River. The two factions of the Cherokee and the Creek tribes, representing the full-blood traditionalists and the mixed-blood accommodationists, were divided on this issue. Virtually none of the tribe members wanted to relocate, but those of mixed ancestry tended to be more pragmatic. They saw that removal from their eastern lands, voluntarily or by force, was inevitable. Their goal was to negotiate as favorable a deal as possible. By contrast, the full-blood Indians had no interest in negotiating. They would not sell or trade their lands for any price and would not leave their homes unless physically dragged away.

In this turbulent era, forceful new leaders arose among the Five Tribes. Among the Creeks, one of the principal spokesmen for the full-blood faction was Opothle Yahola. Although he could neither read nor write, Opothle Yahola was eloquent in speech, a tall and imposing man with strong, regular features. He was bitterly opposed to those who would sell the Creeks' birthright, even for large, fertile tracts of land to the west. And while he was known for his powers of expression, he could also be blunt. In the heated debates between the opposing Creek factions, Opothle Yahola once reminded an adversary, a leader of the mixed bloods with the decidedly un-Creek name of William McIntosh, that the penalty for the unauthorized sale of Indian lands to whites was death.

McIntosh, however, did not heed this grim warning. Succumbing to pressures and promises from white negotiators, and acting contrary to the wishes of a vast majority of Creeks, McIntosh acted as a treaty chief and signed an agreement in February 1825 that ceded a huge tract of Creek ancestral land. A few months later, after a meeting of the governing council, a hundred Creek warriors went to McIntosh's house and executed him. It became clear that day that the Indian tribes were deadly serious about their blood laws. The rift between the full-blood traditionalists and the mixed-blood accommodationists had widened into a great chasm. It was much more than a political feud. Blood had been spilled. This was more like a declaration of war.

Among the Cherokees, the leader of the traditionalist, nonremoval faction was John Ross. He stood in contrast to Opothle Yahola in almost every way. Ross was only one-eighth Cherokee. He was baby-faced, with blue eyes, educated in eastern schools, and he could only speak a rudimentary form of the Cherokee language. But he shared with Opothle Yahola a passion for the well-being of his people. And unlike most of the mixed bloods in his tribe, Ross had a fierce determination that the Cherokees would not give up one more acre of land.

In 1828, the struggle of the Creek Opothle Yahola and the Cherokee John Ross to hold on to their tribal lands suffered a mortal setback. Andrew Jackson was elected president, the first chief executive of the United States who had been born in humble circumstances. Jackson had been elected in part for his reputation as an Indian fighter. He believed that white men and Native Americans could never live in harmony. He thought the only solution was to move the tribes far away. In his inaugural address, he announced that one of his top priorities was the relocation of Indians. And he kept his word. With Jackson's support, the Indian Removal Act was passed by Congress in 1830. This gave the government full authority to trade lands west of the Mississippi River for Indian lands in the East.

With the Indian Removal Act, the fate of the Five Tribes was sealed. Whether voluntarily or by force, the Five Tribes would go to the region west of Arkansas, the newly created Indian Territory. In the 1830s, the Five Tribes (as well as other tribes around the country) were relocated. The Chickasaws and the Choctaws went first, and they did not greatly resist. The removal of the Cherokees and the Creeks came at the end of the decade and was much more traumatic. In the summer of 1838, a glum Gen.

Winfield Scott with seven thousand troops marched into the Cherokee nation to force the Indians out. Those who refused to cooperate were chained and forced to march west under guard. Tens of thousands were forcibly "removed" to Indian Territory. Many died along the way of disease and exposure, including John Ross's wife, Elizabeth. The forced relocation of the Cherokees to Indian Territory, known as the Trail of Tears, is a well-known and tragic episode in American history. But the phrase should be plural, because many tribes besides the Cherokees were moved by force, and they traveled to Indian Territory by numerous highways, rivers, roads, and trails, all of them drenched in tears.

Even after the Cherokees were settled in Indian Territory, the tribe's blood law remained in effect. Because John Ross would not negotiate with Federal authorities, government agents had approached other, more amenable, mixed-blood tribe members. Among these were Major Ridge, who had once fought with U.S. forces against hostile Creeks; John Ridge, his son; and Elias Boudinot, the editor of the Cherokee-language newspaper the *Phoenix*. These apparently well-intentioned men believed relocation was inevitable, and they negotiated what they thought was a favorable agreement. The vast majority of Cherokees disagreed. Shortly after the Cherokee nation was relocated to Indian Territory, on the night of June 22, 1839, Major Ridge, John Ridge, and Elias Boudinot were assassinated. To Cherokee traditionalists, this was the death penalty carried out according to well-known tribal law. But to the surviving family members, this was the cold-blooded murder of political rivals. Among the grieving and outraged relatives was Stand Watie, Boudinot's brother, who would later become a brigadier general in the Confederate army.

In the Cherokee and Creek tribes, relations between the full-blood traditionalists and the mixed-blood accommodationists could hardly have been worse. The enmity between them was every bit as intense as it was between the most vehement abolitionist and the most diehard secessionist. Blood had been shed more than once. And now the two factions of each tribe were crowded together in unfamiliar new lands. This was a formula for tension and bloodshed that would plague the Indian Territory for decades.

When the Civil War broke out in 1861, Opothle Yahola was still a senior leader of the Creeks, and John Ross was still a principal chief of the Cherokees. Daniel and Chilly McIntosh, sons of the man who was executed for signing away Creek lands, were now prominent leaders of the mixed-blood Creeks. And Stand Watie, related to all three men who had been executed under the Cherokee blood law, was now a leading member of the prosperous mixed-bloods of that tribe. The challenge that lay before Confederate negotiator Albert Pike was to unite these diverse men into a coherent force that would be willing to fight against the United States. As Pike was soon to discover, this would be an almost impossible task.

OPOTHLE YAHOLA HEADS NORTH

IN EARLY July 1861, the full-blood factions of the Cherokee, Creek, and Seminole tribes were still clinging to their neutrality. That summer, however, the accelerating momentum of the Civil War forced all those in Indian Territory to choose one side or the other. On July 12, John Ross's archrival, Stand Watie, was commissioned a colonel in the Confederate army and given a regiment, the Second Cherokee Mounted Rifles. On July 21, Rebel armies routed Union forces under Gen. Irvin McDowell at Manassas, Virginia. This greatly enhanced the credibility of the Confederacy in the eyes of many Indians. A few weeks later, in early August, Southern forces prevailed at Wilson's Creek in southwestern Missouri, not far from the border of Indian Territory. Although Stand Watie did not fight in this battle, some of his troopers did, and they earned a flurry of favorable publicity in the Southern press. Some even gave the Indians credit for turning the tide of the battle.

Albert Pike warned Chief Ross that the Confederate government would not accept Cherokee neutrality. If Ross refused to align with the South, Pike threatened to go to the mixed-bloods under Stand Watie and negotiate with them. This was Ross's worst fear, and in August 1861, it seemed close to becoming a reality. Ross had been principal chief of the Cherokee for more than three decades, and he did not want to be forced out now, especially not with his nation on the verge of war. Earlier in the year, when the Southern states were seceding one by one, Ross had written coolly, "I regret most deeply the excitement which has arisen among our white brethren: yet by us it can only be regarded as a family misunderstanding among themselves."[5] But

Stand Watie

AUTHOR'S COLLECTION

now Ross was in turmoil. He said he felt like a drowning man in a flood who would grab onto any floating log that came along in the desperate hope of surviving the deluge. In the first summer of the war, the drowning man was the Cherokee nation, and the log seemed to be the Confederacy. Ross had little concern for the Union or states' rights. He was trying to follow the path that seemed safest for his people.

Ross wrote to Opothle Yahola, saying he had decided to support the South and urging the Creek leader to do the same. Opothle Yahola was astonished and incredulous. Thinking the letter might be a forgery, he sent it back to Ross, asking if it was authentic. Ross assured him that it was. On that day, John Ross and Opothle Yahola parted ways. Instead of joining Ross and the Cherokees, Opothle Yahola turned in the opposite direction. In mid-August, he and another Creek chief, Oktarharsars Harjo (called "Sands" by the whites), wrote to Lincoln and requested the military protection they had been promised in their treaties: "Now the wolf has come. Men who are strangers tread our soil. Our children are frightened, and mothers cannot sleep for fear. This is our situation now. When we made our treaty at Washington you assured us that our children should laugh around our houses without fear, and we believed you."[6] The following month, Opothle Yahola received a reply from C. H. Carruth, the U.S. Indian agent in Barnsville, Kansas. Carruth assured the Creeks that Lincoln had not forgotten them and that, as soon as the necessary preparations had been completed, Federal troops would return to Indian Territory to expel the Rebels. Unfortunately for the Union-loyal Indians, it would take the U.S. government nearly a full year to make good on Carruth's promise.

With events in Indian Territory building to a crisis, Opothle Yahola and his Creek followers retired to his two-thousand-acre plantation near North Fork Town, about fifty miles west of the Arkansas border. Opothle Yahola hoped to gather together all Indians who were opposed to the Confederacy and either wait for Federal protection or simply ride out the storm in peace. From all over Indian Territory, Unionist refugees flowed to North Fork Town. The camp swelled with Chickasaws, Choctaws, Comanches, Delawares, Kickapoos, Shawnees, and Wichitas. Although Opothle Yahola was a slaveholder, free blacks also came, as well as runaway slaves who considered North Fork Town a possible gateway to freedom. Though about fifteen hundred of these refugees were armed men, the other twenty-five hundred were women, children, and the elderly who brought with them wagonloads of food and household goods as well as horses, cattle, sheep, oxen, and dogs.[7]

As the number of refugees soared, the problem of feeding all these people and their livestock became more difficult with each passing day. The old Creek chief could see no evidence that Union troops were coming to their rescue, and he sensed that Rebel forces nearby were daily becoming more hostile. To the Confederates, Opothle Yahola's motley throng was not a band of fugitives but rather a potential military threat. In early November 1861, the Creek leader decided to take his people north. He knew they could find fresh forage for the livestock in that direction. And he hoped to add to his strength by passing through Cherokee territory, since many of that tribe still favored the Union, despite Ross's alliance with the Confederacy. That route would also bring them closer to possible aid, both military and commissary, from Kansas. On November 5, Opothle Yahola and his four thousand followers pulled up stakes and headed toward the Kansas border.

At about the same time, Daniel and Chilly McIntosh, leaders of the pro-Confederate Creeks and sons of the slain treaty chief, wrote to Rebel authorities asking for military assistance to deal with Opothle Yahola and his followers. This request went to Col. Douglas Cooper, the Confederate officer in charge of Indian Territory while Albert Pike was in Richmond getting his treaties ratified. Cooper was a Mississippian and an old friend of Jefferson Davis, who had appointed him to be an agent to the Chickasaw and Choctaw nations before the war. The colonel agreed with the McIntosh brothers that Opothle Yahola's force constituted a potential menace, and he vowed to either "compel submission" on the part of the Union-loyal chief or else to drive him out of Indian Territory.[8]

SKIRMISH AT ROUND MOUNTAIN

AT FORT GIBSON, in the Cherokee nation near the Arkansas border, Col. Douglas Cooper amassed a considerable force to accomplish this task. His fourteen hundred mounted soldiers were made up of six companies of pro-Confederate Chickasaw and Choctaw infantry, a Creek cavalry regiment, a battalion of Seminoles, and a battalion of the Ninth Texas Cavalry under Lt. Col. William Quayle. In early November 1861, Cooper's mounted troops rode southwest from Fort Gibson to Opothle Yahola's plantation near North Fork Town. When they arrived on November 15, however, they discovered that the large party of Union-loyal Indians were no longer there, that Opothle Yahola's "army" had been gone for quite some time.

Cooper, fearing the Unionist Indians might escape to Kansas without a fight, quickened the pace of his pursuit. Following the trail left by Opothle Yahola's wagons and livestock, Cooper's men headed northwest. After three days of hard riding, Cooper caught up with the slow-moving Indian band not far from the confluence of the Cimarron and Arkansas rivers in the north-

Douglas H. Cooper

ern part of Creek territory. Late on the afternoon of November 19, Cooper's advance scouts spotted smoke from myriad campfires on the horizon and reported that a large company had passed this way just a few hours earlier.

Though it was midafternoon, Cooper, not wanting to waste a minute, called up Quayle and his Texans and ordered them to charge into the camp of the Union-loyal Indians. Without hesitation, Quayle's battalion charged off in the direction of the wafting strings of smoke. All they found, however, was an empty camp with a few smoldering fires. They spotted two Indians in the distance, though, who dug their heels into their horses' flanks and rode off at a gallop. Quayle ordered his troopers to pursue the scouts, hoping they would lead his men to Opothle Yahola's main camp. The Confederate detachment chased the Indians for about four miles, until the scouts disappeared into a large stand of trees. As the Texans tried to follow, the dense woods in their front suddenly erupted in a deadly hail of bullets. Several of the cavalrymen toppled from their horses. Quayle instantly realized he was facing a thousand or more rifles and ordered his men to retreat.

Far in the rear, Cooper heard the shots and ordered the rest of his brigade to come to the Texans' support. Cooper's men rode hard, and when they arrived, they found confused fighting in the fast-approaching darkness. On the Confederate right, some prairie grass had caught fire, adding to the chaos. Cooper and his aide dismounted and walked closer to a clump of trees. Seeing silhouettes moving about in the woods, they called out, asking if they were Texans. The elusive shadows answered with a heavy volley of rifle fire. Cooper ordered his men to return the fire, which they did, but it was now too dark for either side to see their targets. As night came, the firing on both sides died down. This first skirmish in Indian Territory, later called the battle of Round Mountain, was over.

At that point, Opothle Yahola was content simply to fend off his pursuers. He knew he faced a tenacious foe, better trained and more heavily armed. Besides, Cooper's legion was not burdened with thousands of women and children and countless wagons loaded with household goods. During the night, a sympathetic Cherokee came to Opothle Yahola and invited him and his large company to cross into Cherokee territory to rest and regroup. Opothle Yahola readily accepted the offer. Under the cover of darkness, his mixed party of soldiers and refugees slipped quietly away, fording the Arkansas River and seeking shelter in Cherokee lands. As they departed, they set fire to the prairie grass between them and the Confederates. At about 1:00 a.m., sleeping Rebel horsemen were startled awake by frantic cries of "Fire! Fire!" They hastily assembled and quickly retreated from the flames that were about to overtake their supply train.

At first light, Cooper discovered that Opothle Yahola and his followers were gone. In their haste and their need to travel light, the Union-loyal Indians had left behind scores of horses and cows, as well as twelve wagons loaded with flour, sugar, coffee, and salt. This time Cooper was not so swift to pursue. His men and their mounts were fatigued by three days of hard riding followed by a confused skirmish and a middle-of-the-night prairie fire. Most of the forage in the area had now been eaten or burned off. As Cooper pondered his next move, he received a message from Brig. Gen. Benjamin McCulloch in nearby Arkansas. McCulloch feared Union Maj. Gen. John C. Frémont was massing troops in Missouri for a major south-

Benjamin McCulloch

ward campaign. McCulloch ordered Cooper to break off the pursuit of Opothle Yahola and make his troops available for the defense of Arkansas.

Obeying his orders, Cooper led his troopers southward to Concharta, where he had arranged to have a supply train meet him. In his battle report, Cooper listed his Round Mountain casualties as 6 killed, 4 wounded, and 1 missing. He estimated he had killed or wounded 110 of the Unionist Indians, but most historians consider this number inflated.[9] (Since Opothle Yahola's force was not a regular Union army outfit, he filed no reports.) It took Cooper and his mounted regiments four days to reach Concharta. When he arrived, he learned the threatened Federal attack on Arkansas had been a false alarm. Union troops in Missouri were actually pulling back. Cooper was free to resume his original mission of dealing with Opothle Yahola's armed fugitives.

THE BATTLE OF CHUSTO-TALASAH

By NOVEMBER 29, Cooper's men were rested, resupplied, and ready to tangle again with the tough Creek chief who was known in Indian Territory as "Old Gouge." This time Cooper's strategy was to split his command and attack the Unionist Indians from two sides. He would lead the first column himself and pursue Opothle Yahola as before. The other column, under Col. William Sims, would slip behind the fleeing Indians and cut off their retreat.

In addition, Cooper was expecting aid from a third fighting unit, the First Cherokee Mounted Rifles. These Cherokee troopers were not regular Confederate cavalry. They were originally home guards of the Cherokee nation and had only joined the Southern cause a month earlier when their chief, John Ross, pledged to support the Confederacy. They were led by Ross's nephew, Col. John Drew. Virtually all of Drew's men were "Pin Cherokees." The Pins were full-blood Cherokees who belonged to a secret fraternal organization called the Keetoowah, which means "Chosen Ones."[10] The Keetoowah were opposed to the mixed-blood faction of the Cherokee nation who had signed away their tribal lands, and they also objected to slavery. They wanted to preserve ancient Cherokee rituals and revive the traditional Cherokee values of liberty, equality, and community. As a sign of their Keetoowah membership, they wore a distinctive emblem of crossed pins on their shirts. Hence, they became known as Pins. In the curious eddies and crosscurrents of the Civil War, here was a regiment opposed to slavery but fighting for the Confederacy and about to attack the slaveholder Opothle Yahola, who was steadfastly loyal to the Union.

As Cooper's horsemen rode northward in early December, they received a report that Opothle Yahola planned to attack them en route. Cooper abandoned his strategy of a pincer movement and ordered Sims's and Drew's forces to join him at a rendezvous a few miles away from Opothle Yahola's sprawling camp in Cherokee country. Late on the night of December 8, Drew discovered that more than four hundred of his Pin Cherokee troops had slipped away in the darkness. These Keetoowah soldiers knew the commitment of their chief, John Ross, to the Confederacy was halfhearted at best. They had been willing to destroy Yankee invaders, but not fleeing women and children, and not their Creek brothers to whom many Cherokee were related by marriage. So when the opportunity arose, most of the Pin Cherokees quietly mounted their horses and rode out of camp.

On the morning of December 9, 1861, Cooper was unsure what to make of the situation. He was deeply troubled by the desertion of the Pin Cherokees, if for no other reason than it greatly lengthened his odds. Days before, he had left orders for reinforcements to join him, but he was not sure when they would arrive. Deciding to play it safe, Cooper and his men broke camp, forded Bird Creek, and rode in a southerly direction closer to his expected reinforcements. They had gone about five miles when gunfire erupted. About two hundred Creeks on horseback were falling on the rear of his column. Cooper reacted quickly. First, he detailed one hundred men to protect the supply train. He then deployed his men for battle: the Chickasaw and Choctaw Mounted Rifles on the right, the Ninth Texas Cavalry and Drew's sixty or so remaining Pin Cherokees in the center, and the Creek Mounted Rifles on the left. Once the troops were in position, he ordered them to counterattack. The two hundred Unionist Indians then turned and galloped toward the river, with Cooper's men close on their heels. When the Creek horsemen reached the woods at the water's edge, they dismounted and melted into the bushes and trees. When Cooper's men tried to follow, they were again surprised by a sudden volley of bullets. For the second time in three weeks, they had charged into an ambush.

The Creeks had taken up a defensive position in a long, looping bend of the Bird River, a place the Cherokees called Chusto-Talasah, which means "Caving Banks." In this horseshoe bend was a farmhouse, a corncrib, and a long rail fence, all of which provided cover. The river also had high banks, which Opothle Yahola's men used as a natural parapet. Standard tactical manuals of the day discouraged an army from engaging the enemy with a rushing river immediately in its rear, but Opothle Yahola had scouted the river beforehand and had found some hidden fords. This was a traditional Creek battle tactic. In the firefight that ensued, Cooper's cavalry tried to attack the Union-loyal Indians from the flanks and rear, but they couldn't find a place to ford the river.

Cooper dismounted his men and detailed every fifth man to watch the horses while the others marched through the woods to confront their entrenched foe. With both sides now in position, the woods crackled with heavy small-arms fire. At one point, the leader of the Texans, Quayle, spotted some Pin Cherokees firing at his troopers. He assumed these were the sixty Keetoowah who had not deserted the night before, and he ordered them to stop firing on their allies. As the sniping continued, he realized these were not the sixty Pins who had stayed with Drew, but rather the four hundred who had stolen away in the night. They had not only deserted the Confederacy but had taken their rifles and joined Opothle Yahola.

In the battle of Chusto-Talasah, both sides had plenty of cover, so neither side could get the upper hand. At one point, pro-Confederate Chickasaws and Choctaws were able to press forward and capture the farmhouse. Their advance was unsupported, however, and they had to fall back. Then it was the Unionist Indians' turn to try to break the stalemate, as a detachment dashed out to attack the troopers holding the horses. This daring assault was also repulsed. Both sides kept up the firing until darkness began to fall. As at Round Mountain, the sounds of battle died away with the coming of night, with neither side able to claim victory.

Cooper ordered his men to pull back, regroup, and prepare for the resumption of battle at daybreak. When morning dawned, however, the Confederates awoke to discover Opothle Yahola's forces had used the hidden fords to make their escape. In his official report, Cooper described Opothle Yahola's forces as "disappearing almost as if by magic."[11] Cooper listed his casualties as fifteen killed and thirty-seven wounded. He estimated his men had inflicted five hundred casualties, but again this figure seems high, since there were only twenty-seven of Opothle Yahola's dead left on the field.[12]

The Confederates might well have claimed victory at both Round Mountain and Chusto-Talasah. After both battles, they held the field when the smoke had cleared. And twice they reported inflicting losses much heavier than they had suffered. But the morning after Chusto-Talasah, Cooper was in no mood to celebrate. He was having much more trouble than expected bringing Opothle Yahola's party to bay. And it was unnerving to have so many of his Pin Cherokees change sides the night before the battle.

Over the next few days the news for the Confederates in Indian Territory only got worse. A hundred more Pin Cherokees stationed at Fort Gibson deserted their posts and joined Opothle Yahola. The Confederate flag flying over the fort had been taken down. Cooper was becoming increasingly anxious about the disintegrating state of affairs in the Cherokee nation. On December 11, he wrote to the Confederate post at Van Buren, Arkansas, urgently requesting ammunition, supplies, and reinforcements, saying that, without forceful action, "we shall lose Indian Territory."[13]

THE DECISIVE CONFRONTATION AT CHUSTENAHLAH

WHEN COOPER'S dispatch reached the garrison at Van Buren, the Arkansas and Texas cavalry units there were commanded by thirty-three-year-old Col. James McQueen McIntosh. McIntosh was an 1849 graduate of West Point who had resigned his commission in May 1861 to join the Rebel army. (James's younger brother, John Baillie McIntosh, wore Union blue and would eventually rise to the rank of major general in the Federal army.) James McIntosh (no relation to the mixed-blood Creek leaders with the same surname) immediately realized the gravity of Cooper's situation. He called his men out of winter quarters and ordered that supplies and ammunition be sent to Cooper without delay. As disturbing reports continued to trickle in from Indian Territory, McIntosh decided to take matters into his own hands. He would lead the Arkansas and Texas cavalry units himself.

Within a few days of receiving Cooper's plea for assistance, McIntosh rode out of the Confederate camp in Arkansas, leading sixteen hundred well-rested and well-equipped men. During the three days' journey to join Cooper at Fort Gibson, the unseasonably mild weather suddenly turned cold. An icy front swept in, freezing the roads and the Confederate troopers alike. When the weary and cold Arkansas and Texas reinforcements arrived at Fort Gibson on December 19, Cooper was surprised to see McIntosh at their front. He had asked for fresh troops, not realizing he would get their commander as well.

The newly arrived cavalrymen rested at Fort Gibson for two days while McIntosh and Cooper studied maps and outlined a plan, as McIntosh phrased it, "to settle matters in the nation."[14] They decided upon another pincer movement, with McIntosh striking Opothle Yahola with overwhelming force from the west while Cooper slipped behind him to cut off his retreat to Kansas. About midday on a bitterly cold December 22, McIntosh's troops set out. They headed northwest along the Verdigris River, toward Opothle Yahola's last known position. For four days they rode, battling the cold, without any sign of their foes. Late on Christmas Day, however, as they were setting up tents in the twilight, about two hundred Indians appeared, as one Texan recalled it, "as if they had emerged from the bosom of the earth."[15] McIntosh's men were eager to pursue these Indian riders, but he refused to take the bait. Smoke from a large encampment had been spotted in the distance, and McIntosh wanted to wait for daylight.

During the night, a messenger from Fort Gibson reached McIntosh with news that Cooper's column had been delayed. Cooper's wagon drivers had deserted him, and he was several days behind schedule. If McIntosh was going to engage Opothle Yahola the next day, he was going to be on his own. The following morning, McIntosh's men broke camp early and rode slowly and warily in the direction of the smoky haze they had spotted the day before. Late in the morning, as they crossed ice-encrusted Shoal Creek, the clatter of rifle fire rang out from the woods in their front. Before them lay Shoal Creek and a steep, rocky slope with thick stands of trees to their right and left. Opothle Yahola had chosen his ground well. He had arrayed his Seminole troops under Halek Tustenuggee on both sides of the hill, from which they could fire into the Rebel flanks. At the crest of the hill were mounted Creek warriors to contest the Confederate advance if they somehow progressed that far. For the Union-loyal Indians this was a desperate last stand, because they were running low on ammunition.

McIntosh's brigade could not stay where it was without being chewed to pieces. He must either retreat or advance, and the decision must be made quickly. An officer looking at his watch noticed it was just about noon when the bugler sounded "Charge." The Confederate horsemen obeyed the command, and as they advanced up the slope, the Union-loyal Creeks and their allies intensified their rifle fire. To the Indians' surprise and consternation, McIntosh's men did not halt or even slow down. Some on horseback and some scrambling on all fours, they clambered up the slope and soon reached the crest. The fighting there was hand-to-hand, but the Rebels were better trained and more heavily armed. Before long, most of the Indians broke ranks and ran. In his official report, McIntosh wrote that his Third Texas Battalion had assaulted the hill "with the irresistible force of a tornado, and swept everything before it."[16]

While most of Opothle Yahola's militia retreated, many stood firm against impossible odds. One Texan recalled an old Creek warrior who was holding off eight to ten cavalrymen by himself. The Rebels did not want to kill the man and begged him to surrender, but he refused. At that point, as the Texan recounted, "his admiring foes were compelled to dash out his brave old life."[17]

After securing the hill, McIntosh's men remounted and pursued the fleeing Indians. A running battle ensued, with Opothle Yahola's men trying in vain to form new defensive lines. The pro-Union Indians regrouped over and over again, firing from behind boulders and digging in on a series of ridges. At each point of resistance, however, the Arkansans and Texans were able to punch through and continue the pursuit. Whooping and shouting, the Confederate horsemen chased Opothle Yahola's routed band for about three miles. About half an hour before sunset on that short, cold December day, McIntosh called for his men to regroup. He was more than satisfied with what they had accomplished.

Late that afternoon, three hundred Confederate Cherokee reinforcements under Col. Stand Watie reached the scene of the struggle. The battle was over for the day, however, and Watie's men joined McIntosh's in camp. McIntosh reported 3 of his men killed and 32 wounded. He estimated he had killed at least 250 of Opothle Yahola's men and captured 180 women, children, and blacks, as well as hundreds of oxen, horses, and sheep. Among the articles the fleeing Creeks left behind was a silver medal commemorating a peace treaty concluded between the Creeks and the British in 1694.[18]

The next morning, McIntosh's and Watie's men were up before daybreak to continue the pursuit. They rode about twenty miles before catching up with Opothle Yahola's slow-moving train. Watie's men were fresh and eager to get in on the kill. One officer reported they hounded the Union-loyal forces with "utmost enthusiasm and with irresistible impetuosity."[19] Watie and his men had been waiting a long time to settle some old scores. On December 27, the enthusiastic Confederate pursuers killed eleven more pro-Union men and captured another seventy-five women and children without suffering any casualties of their own.[20] That brought an end to the battle of Chustenahlah (also called the battle of Patriot Hills).

McIntosh was highly pleased with the results of his short campaign. On December 28, he turned his column to the south and headed back toward winter quarters. They had not ridden far when they encountered Cooper's column, which was eager to pitch into battle. Opothle Yahola's band had fled out of reach, however, so there was not much left for Cooper's men to do. McIntosh and his troopers continued on south, but Cooper decided to scour the region for stragglers from Opothle Yahola's party and other pro-Union

Indians. Over the next few days, Cooper's men found a few scattered Indians here and there, often in groups of only 3 or 4. They killed 6 Indians, whom they assumed to be Unionists, and captured about 150 more. This was a grim foreshadowing of the coming months in Indian Territory, when bands of armed men would roam the countryside, killing and burning with no clear military objective.

The weather grew even colder in the last week of 1861. Sleet fell, and one of Cooper's men froze to death. Content that he had done everything he could to sweep the area free of Union-loyal Indians, Cooper turned his column around and followed McIntosh south. Meanwhile, it took two days for the remnant of Opothle Yahola's party to reach the Kansas line. Most had fled without food or warm clothing. Some had lost their shoes. Federal authorities in Kansas were not prepared to receive the thousands of refugees who suddenly poured across the border. That bitterly cold January 1862, there was almost no food or shelter for the displaced Indians. To make matters worse, thousands more Unionist Cherokees and Seminoles flowed into Kansas as the situation in Indian Territory descended into anarchy. Of those who had survived the arduous journey, hundreds died in camp, including Opothle Yahola's daughter. A physician arrived at the scene in February 1862 and reported having to amputate more than one hundred frozen limbs. He also counted seven children who were entirely naked. Describing the condition of the refugees in southern Kansas, the Federal agent for the Creeks, George Cutler, reported, "Their suffering was immense and beyond description."[21]

Col. James McQueen McIntosh did not concern himself with the fate of Opothle Yahola's party after it crossed into Kansas. His mission was to drive them out of Indian Territory, and this he had done. In his battle report, he noted with pride that the Unionists had been expelled from Indian Territory and that John Ross and his Cherokee followers had been intimidated into standing by the Confederacy. All in all, he believed that his troopers, after their long, circuitous ride through Indian Territory, had accomplished their mission in full. Col. Douglas Cooper's report on the campaign was less enthusiastic. He complained that if McIntosh had waited a few days for Cooper's column to catch up, the two columns together might have rounded up Opothle Yahola's entire company, not allowing any to escape.

Fortunately for McIntosh, the authorities in Richmond did not share Cooper's disappointment. Within weeks, McIntosh was promoted to brigadier general. He did not have much time, though, to savor his victory over Opothle Yahola or to bask in his promotion. The next month, at the battle of Pea Ridge, Arkansas, a bullet found his heart, and he was left among the dead on the field as the defeated Confederates were forced to pull back.

ONGOING VIOLENCE IN INDIAN TERRITORY

IN THE summer of 1862, a half year after the rout of Unionist Indians at Chustenahlah, the Federal army in Kansas finally completed its preparations and sent an expedition south into Indian Territory. The column, led by Col. William Weer, consisted of two thousand men, including three companies from Opothle Yahola's surviving Creeks. Weer's force accomplished little other than the capture of Cherokee chief John Ross. Once in Federal hands, Ross declared his loyalty to the North and denounced the Confederacy. He was sent to Washington, D.C., where he became a spectator for the rest of the war, though he had three sons who all served in the Federal army. At about the same time, Opothle Yahola, still living with his displaced people in Kansas, vowed to lead Creek regiments back into Indian Territory. This hope was never to be realized, however. In the spring of 1863, the old warrior fell ill and died. He was buried next to his daughter near Belmont, Kansas.

A few months after Opothle Yahola's death, a second, more substantial Union force, led by Maj. Gen. James G. Blunt, left Kansas and plunged deep into Indian Territory. The climax of this campaign came in July 1863, when Blunt engaged and soundly defeated five thousand troops under Douglas Cooper, now a brigadier general, at Honey Springs in the Creek nation. After this Union victory, major clashes between regular army units diminished, but violence in Indian Territory became even more widespread. After the summer of 1863, lawlessness prevailed as armed partisans from both sides roamed the countryside and indiscriminately killed and burned. Few structures escaped the torch, and hundreds of thousands of cattle, the Indians' main source of wealth, were either killed or driven off. By the time Robert

James G. Blunt

E. Lee surrendered at Appomattox Court House in April 1865, almost the whole of Indian Territory lay barren and destitute.

Before he died, Opothle Yahola expressed his hope that the treaties of the Creek nation with the U.S. government would remain in force. He and thousands of his followers had remained loyal to the Union and had fulfilled their treaty obligations. When accounts were settled after the war, however, Opothle Yahola and his steadfast loyalty to the Union were little remembered. U.S. government negotiators took the position that the treaties with the Five Civilized Tribes were void because some of their members had supported the Confederacy. Back in the 1830s, when the Creeks were forced to give up their homes in the east, a government official had promised them that their new lands in Oklahoma would be theirs in perpetuity, for "as long as the grass grows and the rivers run."[22] But now, three decades later, in the aftermath of the Civil War, the Creeks were forced to surrender about half of their remaining land in Indian Territory. Among Indians who fought on both sides in the great conflict, their Lost Cause began long before the Civil War and continued long afterward.

7

SOUTHERN SLAVES TURNED UNION SOLDIERS

CONFEDERATE FORCES PULLED OUT of Charleston, South Carolina, on February 17, 1865, two months before the war's end. When a column of Federal soldiers marched into the city the next day, throngs of local slaves crowded the streets, laughing and crying and shouting that the "year of Jubilee" had come at last. Regimental bands played "The Battle Cry of Freedom," and the soldiers sang as they marched, shaking hands with well-wishers as they continued on toward the city center. These self-possessed men in blue, carrying rifles and marching with well-drilled precision, were members of the Twenty-first U.S. Colored Troops. Most of them had been slaves themselves when the war began in this city less than four years earlier.[1]

The acclaimed 1989 film *Glory* vividly portrays the dedication and daring of the Massachusetts Fifty-fourth, the regiment composed mostly of free blacks (with white officers) from all over the North. The Fifty-fourth's valiant but unsuccessful assault on Fort Wagner, one of the garrisons guarding Charleston Harbor, in July 1863 forever put to rest the question of whether black men would make good soldiers. The Fifty-fourth Massachusetts, led by Bostonian Robert Gould Shaw, is certainly the best known of African American fighting units in the Civil War. But three-quarters of the 180,000 black soldiers who served in the Federal army from 1862 to 1865 were from Confederate states, and most of these were freed slaves.[2]

When the war began in the spring of 1861, the Confederacy's three and a half million blacks were among its greatest assets—literally. In April 1861, the value of slaves in the eleven seceding states exceeded the value of

Southern railroads, real estate, and bank deposits combined. Southern blacks made up the bulk of the Confederate labor force. Besides their role in growing and harvesting cotton, tobacco, and food crops, they maintained roads and rail lines, erected fortifications, mined salt and lead, built bridges, and worked as mechanics, teamsters, dockworkers, cooks, and personal servants. Blacks also helped supply the sinews of war. More than half of those who manned the rolling mills, foundries, and machine shops of the massive Tredegar Iron Works in Richmond were black, as were three-fourths of the workers in the naval ordnance factory in Selma, Alabama.[3] And, of course, every black laborer performing vital work behind the battle lines allowed a white man to serve in the ranks.

In other slaveholding societies in the New World, such as Surinam and Cuba, there was never a pretense that slavery was anything other than forced labor. But in the American South, there evolved what historian William W. Freehling calls the "domestic charade of Massa and Cuffee," the notion that both races, master and slave, consented to the social order. Benign white masters claimed to be looking after a less-gifted race, and blacks were thought to be a loyal laboring class that was grateful to be cared for by their betters.[4] Most slaves found it in their best interest to go along with the charade, to be as obedient, servile, and nonthreatening as they could. Yet, even while living out the stereotypes thrust upon them, slaves would sing among themselves, "Got one mind for white folks to see, / 'Nuther for what I know is me; / He don't know, he don't know my mind."[5]

Despite the carefully cultivated fiction that both races consented to a slave-labor society, there were also a good many safeguards to ensure that blacks played the role assigned to them. Besides overseers and plantation guards, there were also pervasive curfews and night patrols, required passports for slaves on the road or in town, and vigorous enforcement of fugitive slave laws, including brutal punishment for those captured and returned to their owners. Yet even with their well-organized policing system, their vast superiority of arms and resources, and the outwardly compliant behavior of the most slaves, Southern whites could never overcome persistent fears of a widespread slave revolt—a sudden, bloody uprising that would overturn their whole social order. After all, there had been dozens of violent insurrections in Cuba and Brazil. In Haiti, the slaves had overthrown their French masters and established their own nation in 1803. And it certainly didn't help matters to have Northern abolitionists stridently condemning slavery as a moral cancer, practically encouraging slaves to rise up in the night and murder their masters in bed.

Slaves in the American South did attempt to revolt on several occasions, but never with much success. From the colonial period to the Civil War, there were more than a hundred conspiracies among slaves to rebel or run away en masse.[6] But most of these were uncovered in the early stages, usually by informants who were rewarded for betraying the plans of their fellow slaves.[7] In the two centuries before the Civil War, there were less than a dozen revolts or mass escapes in which slaves succeeded to the point of arming themselves and threatening nearby communities. The most famous of these was the Nat Turner rebellion, which erupted in Southampton County, Virginia, in 1831 (see page 44). But there were notable uprisings before and after Nat Turner's. In 1739, fifty slaves in Stono, South Carolina, ransacked and burned a local armory, slaughtered two dozen local whites, and marched south, hoping to pass through Georgia and take refuge in an abandoned Spanish fort in Florida. The Stono rebels were intercepted by mounted militia, and all were shot down or captured.[8] In 1826, seventy-seven slaves aboard a Mississippi steamboat overpowered the ship's crew, killing five whites, and then made their escape to Indiana. In the 1840s, there were three incidents in the Border States (Kentucky, Maryland, and Missouri) in which bands of black fugitives, numbering in the dozens, armed themselves and tried to fight their way into a free-labor state. In all three instances, the slaves willingly accepted open battle with companies of local militia before being violently subdued.[9]

With the coming of the Civil War, there were intensified anxieties about what the slaves would do. With tens of thousands of white Southerners marching off to faraway battlefields, would there be enough men left at home to control local slaves? Blacks comprised one-third to one-half of the population in most Confederate states, and they outnumbered whites four or five to one in many cotton- or rice-growing counties. Would there be a bloody race war at home while Southern men were fighting Yankees hundreds of miles away?

Though there were isolated incidents of rebellion, there was no widespread uprising.[10] Slaves did not take up arms directly against their masters; rather they took to their feet whenever they heard that Yankee troops were nearby. Thousands of slaves did not wait for Lincoln's Emancipation Proclamation, which took effect on January 1, 1863. Rather, they emancipated themselves whenever they thought they had a fair chance of reaching Federal lines before their owners or overseers caught up with them. At least five hundred thousand slaves ran away during the course of the war, about one in seven in the Confederate states. (Some authorities estimate the number to be twice that high.) Besides the more than one hundred thousand who joined in the Federal army, another twenty-nine thousand freedmen (most of whom freed themselves) served in the navy.[11] Another two hundred thousand fugitive slaves served in the North as cooks, scouts, carpenters, blacksmiths, teamsters, or farmhands.[12] In general terms, at least a half million blacks who were working for the Confederacy at the beginning of the war were performing equally valuable services for the North by the war's end.

However dramatic that change sounds in retrospect, at the time it came more as an evolution than a revolution. Slaves had been running away from their masters at a rate of about five thousand a year in the 1850s, and that rate didn't change much with the opening of hostilities.[13] But as blue armies made more and more incursions into Confederate states, there began a trickle of refugees toward Federal lines in the summer of 1861, a steady stream in 1862, and then a veritable flood in succeeding years. The Northern response to this torrent of runaways also evolved during the four years of war. In the first year, Federal commanders continued to enforce the Fugitive Slave Act, trying to make it clear to slave owners everywhere, especially in the Border States, that this was a war for union, not for abolition. But the slaves themselves did not see it that way. However much leaders in Richmond might talk about states' rights and those in Washington about preserving the Union, slaves throughout the South believed early on that this war was about their liberation. With the war less than a month old, slaves began what one Southern newspaper headlined a "Stampede from the Patriarchal Relation."[14]

On May 23, 1861, about five weeks after the war began, three runaway slaves walked up to the picket guards at Fort Monroe, the Federal stronghold at the tip of the York-James Peninsula in Virginia. When interviewed by the commanding general, Benjamin F. Butler, they said they had been sent to help construct a Confederate battery on the other side of Chesapeake Bay. At an opportune moment, they had taken a small boat and paddled across the water in hopes of gaining their freedom. Before the war, Butler had been known as one of the wiliest lawyers in the state of Massachusetts, and in this instance, he once again showed his skill in making the law serve his purposes. When a Confederate officer, Maj. John B. Cary,

On May 23, 1861, three slaves sought asylum at Fort Monroe. In response to demands for their return, Federal commander Benjamin F. Butler replied that the fugitives had been confiscated as "contraband of war." In doing so, Federal policy changed dramatically in terms of runaway slaves.

BATTLES AND LEADERS

came to Fort Monroe to reclaim the runaways under the provisions of the Fugitive Slave Act, Butler pointed out that Virginia had seceded and was now a foreign country, so U.S. laws no longer applied. Cary reminded Butler that the federal government had declared secession unconstitutional, insisting that the laws of the United States were still in effect throughout the South. Butler nimbly changed his position and argued that the property of those in armed rebellion could be confiscated as contraband of war. He said that if the Confederate officer who owned the slaves would present himself and take an oath of loyalty to the United States, his slaves would be returned to him. Otherwise, they would be retained as contraband.[15]

Butler may not have been the first to apply the word *contraband* to runaway slaves, but he certainly made the term popular. Two days after Butler declared the first three fugitives to be contrabands who need not be returned to their masters, another eight runaways appeared at the gates of Fort Monroe and declared themselves to be Rebel property, ready and willing to be confiscated. The next day sixty more slaves arrived at what blacks were calling "the freedom fort."[16] Once word was passed along the "grapevine telegraph," there were hundreds of fugitives seeking the safety of Federal lines. Many of those on the coast did not wait for Union armies to arrive but made their way out to Federal ships on blockade duty outside key Confederate ports. Some slaves stole fishing boats and sailed out to the Federal blockaders. Others made canoes of hollowed-out logs and paddled out to sea. Some made crude rafts of plaited strips of grass and rope and tried to steer them into open water. Not all made it out to the ships, and some perished in the attempt.

As one of Butler's aides later expressed it, "An epigram abolished slavery in the United States."[17] The precedent set at Fort Monroe in May 1861 was applied throughout the war whenever Federal armies pushed their way into Confederate territory. Many Southerners were truly shocked that their slaves proved so surprisingly disloyal. Complaining about all the runaways, a planter near Selma, Alabama, concluded bitterly that blacks were "the most treacherous, brutal, and ungrateful race on the globe."[18] Southerners were also surprised

Benjamin F. Butler

to see that it was not just unruly field hands and chronic troublemakers who were running off but some of their most trusted and beloved personal servants. When his slaves began sneaking away to nearby Yankee camps, a Vicksburg planter asked the "patriarch" of his slaves, Silas, if the elderly man and his wife were planning their escape as well. Oh no, "Uncle Si" reassured his owner, they were too old for that and they were going to stay right where they were. That night all the remaining slaves on the plantation slipped away, including the aged couple. When the planter rode out after them the next day, he found Uncle Si in the woods, bending over the lifeless body of his wife. The planter asked, not unsympathetically, why the old man would subject her to such a strenuous journey, one she clearly was not strong enough to endure. Silas replied simply that it couldn't be helped, adding pensively, "But then, you see, she died free."[19]

Even when they did not run away, slaves displayed a marked difference of demeanor toward their owners or overseers once they heard that Federal armies were near. Sensing that their owners' power over them was slipping away, blacks became more openly independent and insubordinate. In Virginia, an elderly coachman who had encountered Yankee horsemen on the road went home to his master's closet, put on the finest suit of clothes he could find, completing his attire with a handsome walking stick. Then he presented himself to his owner, sitting in the parlor, and explained that from thenceforth his master could drive his own coach.[20] Under similar circumstances, a black house servant in Mississippi announced to her mistress one day that "answering bells is played out."[21] Some slaves rose up in open revolt, overpowering their overseers, looting plantation houses and carrying off livestock, occasionally firing upon Confederate home guards. But most blacks could "scent freedom in the air," as Southern diarist Mary Boykin Chesnut put it, and they didn't expect to have to fight for it. A common attitude was expressed in a reported conversation between two slaves whose plantation was near Federal lines. When one brought up the idea of taking up arms, the other asked, hadn't he ever seen two dogs fighting over a bone? The first said that, of course, he had, but he didn't see what that had to do with anything. The second answered that it is the dogs who do all the fighting, not the bone.[22]

Planters and local authorities tried everything to stem the tide of fleeing slaves. They doubled picket lines, increased night patrols, and enforced a strict passport system whereby any slave found off the plantation had to show a written permission slip signed by an owner or overseer. Runaway slaves who were captured or caught were stripped, flogged, and sometimes executed as a warning to others. One hundred fifty thousand slaves were marched off to Texas, considered to be out of reach of Federal incursions.[23] Others were fettered or placed in jail cells as a precaution. Search parties randomly inspected slave cabins in search of books or maps, and groups of black men were not allowed to congregate beyond the hearing of an overseer or local deputy.[24] Despite the best efforts of slave owners and local leaders, blacks continued to throng into Yankee lines. As early as August 1862, a Confederate general in North Carolina estimated that planters in his district were losing one million dollars a week in the value of fugitive slaves.[25]

As the war progressed, runaway slaves proved to be as much a gain to the North as they were a loss to the South. For one thing, freedmen provided valuable service to the Federal army as spies, guides, and local informants. William H. Seward, Lincoln's secretary of state, noted in an official dispatch that "everywhere the American general receives his most useful and reliable information from the negro, who hails his coming as the harbinger of freedom."[26] Allan Pinkerton, the head of the Federal secret service in the first two years of the war, concurred, explaining that he gained a great deal of important information from contrabands about Confederate fortifications and harbor defenses, as the slaves themselves had been the main labor force used to construct these works. Pinkerton particularly commended a former slave, John Scobell, who traveled around northern Virginia in the guise of a personal servant, playing the part of an unlettered, happy-go-lucky slave. Putting others off their guard with his easygoing manner and beautiful singing voice, Scobell obtained a wealth of information from seemingly casual conversations or from local newspapers and documents left within view of someone others assumed was illiterate.[27]

Blacks who were still slaves also supplied crucial assistance to hundreds of escaped Union soldiers trying to make their way to the nearest Federal lines. Using the same Underground Railroad system they had developed to smuggle runaway slaves north, blacks provided food and shelter for escaped prisoners, hid them in their cabins or in the woods, and guided them to their next safe station on the trek to freedom. One such fugitive prisoner explained after the war, "It would have been impossible for our men, held as prisoners in the South, to make an escape without the aid of Negroes."[28] Another escapee, observing how freely the slaves shared their own meager fare and endangered their own lives for the sake of strangers, wrote in his journal, "If such kindness will not make one an Abolitionist, then his heart must be made of stone."[29]

Throughout the war, when Union forces entered a Southern city, they were welcomed as liberators by cheering throngs of blacks. When Federal ships sailed into New Orleans in May 1862, the few whites to be seen along the wharves were sullen and silent, but the African Americans shouted, waved their hats, and cried "Praise the Lord!" There were similar demonstrations in Virginia in 1862, Tennessee in 1863, Georgia in 1864, and South Carolina in 1865. As they marched into one Southern port city, Federal troops heard a jubilant black man shouting over and over, "Lord bless these damned Yankees! Lord bless these damned Yankees!" Since that was how he had always heard Northerners referred to, he seemed to think the adjective and noun went together automatically.[30]

FROM FREEDMEN TO FEDERAL SOLDIERS

Within days of Lincoln's call in April 1861 for seventy-five thousand volunteers to put down the rebellion, free blacks over all the North, and even Canada, began meeting and organizing, with the intention of volunteering for the United States army. Companies began forming and drilling in Boston, Cleveland, Detroit, New York, Providence, and even Baltimore, in slave-state Maryland. In Philadelphia, free blacks vowed to raise and equip five regiments (five thousand men) for the Federal army.[31] In all cases, local and national authorities declined to accept black recruits, and in some instances, blacks were told that any further meetings of a military nature would be forcibly broken up by police.[32]

Clearly, the time had not yet come for the Union to consider accepting African Americans, from North or South, into military service. Lincoln himself summed up the two most common objections to enrolling blacks in the army. In August 1862, when the state of Indiana offered to supply two regiments of blacks for the Federal hosts, Lincoln turned down the proposal, explain-

Frederick Douglass

ing, "To arm the negroes would turn 50,000 bayonets from the loyal Border States against us that were for us." Two months later Lincoln commented, "If we were to arm them [blacks], I fear that in a few weeks the arms would be in the hands of the rebels."[33] In the first half of the war, Lincoln felt he couldn't afford to alienate whites in the four slave states that had remained in the Union—Delaware, Kentucky, Maryland, and Missouri. Like many other Northerners, he also doubted the fighting qualities of men who had been trained from birth to be acquiescent and servile.

To those who questioned the fighting spirit of blacks, Frederick Douglass pointed out that African Americans had fought ably (on both sides) in the Revolutionary War and that free blacks in Louisiana had participated in Andrew Jackson's celebrated victory over the British at New Orleans in 1815. As Douglass put the case dryly, "Colored men were good enough to fight under Washington. They are not good enough to fight under McClellan. They were good enough to fight under Andrew Jackson. They are not good enough to fight under General Halleck."[34] Douglass might have also pointed out that black men had been fighting, killing, and dying in "Bleeding Kansas" all during the undeclared civil war that raged out in Kansas Territory from 1854 onward.

Despite the official policy announced in Washington, it was in Kansas (added as a new Union state in January 1861) that blacks first began fighting in organized military units. In August 1862, James H. Lane, the U.S. senator from Kansas who had made his name as a leading "Jayhawker" (abolitionist guerrilla) before the war, began raising the First Kansas (Colored) Volunteer Infantry, consisting of free blacks from Kansas and escaped

James H. Lane

slaves from Missouri. Lane claimed he had been given informal permission by Lincoln himself to recruit blacks in the West, even after he was given explicit instructions to the contrary by Secretary of War Edwin M. Stanton. Lane's black volunteers were not acknowledged in Washington, and they were drilled in secret in Kansas, away from whites who might be outraged at the sight. And many of the black soldiers weren't exactly volunteers either. Lane, aptly nicknamed the "Grim Chieftain" before the war, explained to his new recruits, some of whom were more abductees than inductees: "We don't want to threaten, but we have been saying that you would fight, and if you don't fight we will make you."[35]

The First Kansas (Colored) did fight, and they fought well. Still not acknowledged by Washington, the regiment's first engagement came in October 1862, when about 250 black infantrymen under white officers left Fort Lincoln, in eastern Kansas, and established an outpost near the Missouri border that they called Fort Africa. The Kansas troops were on the lookout for Confederate guerrillas operating in the Osage River basin, and it didn't take long to find them. On October 29, the First Kansas clashed with several dozen Confederate horsemen, a brief but fierce skirmish at Island Mound, Missouri, that left 8 Union men dead, including a white officer, and 11 wounded. Among the fallen was a Cherokee black named John Six Killer, who shot 2 of the enemy off their horses, jabbed another with his bayonet, and clubbed a fourth with the butt of his rifle before falling himself, mortally wounded.

Suffering at least thirty casualties, the mounted Rebels withdrew eastward, starting a prairie fire behind them to discourage pursuit. After this first military engagement of the war in which black soldiers took part, the greatest tribute to those who fought at Island Mound came from one of the Confederate militiamen, who wrote, "The black devils fought like tigers. . . . Not one would surrender."[36] In January 1863, the First Kansas (Colored) was officially enrolled in the Union army, participating in a dozen battles in Kansas and Arkansas as well as innumerable minor skirmishes. By the time they were mustered out in 1865, the First Kansas had proven their mettle in terms of what veterans called the "butcher's bill," having one of the highest rates of dead and wounded of any Union regiment in the war.[37]

While slaves were being turned into soldiers at a western outpost of the Union, a similar experiment was under way at another isolated outpost: the Sea Island region of South Carolina. Apparently, such recruiting was most likely in districts where the need for soldiers was great and the distance from Washington was also great. In November 1861, a combined army-navy expedition captured the Port Royal region on the South Carolina coast about forty miles south of Charleston. In March 1862, Gen. David Hunter was named area commander, heading the "Department of the South," a grandiose name for what was essentially a Federal toehold on the South Carolina coastline, to be used as an anchorage and coaling station for the Federal blockading squadron.

The sixty-year-old Hunter started out the war as a by-the-book commander. In the early months of 1862, Hunter served as Gen. Jim Lane's nominal commander in the Department of the West, and he objected to the Grim Chieftain's high-handed tactics. But once Hunter arrived in South Carolina, he took a page out of Lane's book, not Lincoln's. Short on troops and seeing a wealth of available manpower—slaves whose masters had fled when Federal troops arrived—Hunter began enrolling and training former slaves as soldiers. Like Lane, Hunter often used forceful enlistment methods that sometimes resembled kidnapping more than recruitment. For example, Hunter's enrolling agents might enter a Sunday-morning church service and begin rounding up all the able-bodied black men for military service, except for those who escaped by jumping out the windows. Hunter's methods were so heavy-handed that some local African Americans thought that what they had been told was true, that Federal troops intended to capture Southern slaves and ship them off to Cuba.[38] The new "volunteers" were issued uniforms (dark blue coats and red trousers) and organized in April 1862 as the First South Carolina Volunteer Regiment. The next month, Hunter declared all slaves in his department free, a decree that was quickly disavowed by Lincoln, who still wanted to avoid alienating congressmen

David Hunter

LIBRARY OF CONGRESS

from Union-loyal slave states. But they were not so easily mollified. In June 1862, an irate Kentucky legislator asked Hunter if it was true he had formed a regiment composed of fugitive slaves against the explicit orders of Washington. Hunter sardonically replied that he had not raised a regiment of "fugitive slaves" in South Carolina, but that he had organized "a fine regiment of persons whose late masters are 'fugitive rebels.'"[39]

However much Hunter's vigorous initiatives and mordant wit pleased Northern radicals, he had never received permission to turn former slaves into soldiers, and Congress refused to fund his new regiment. In August 1862, Hunter was forced to disband all but one company of the First Carolina, mainly for lack of money to pay and equip his new recruits. His idea would ripen in time, but his approach had been clumsy from beginning to end. He had not secured proper authorization from Washington, had been too high-handed in his recruiting tactics, and he had alienated his own officer corps as well as powerful members of Congress. David Hunter was one of many Civil War generals whose ideas and ambitions outpaced his abilities.

Nonetheless, as 1862 progressed, the unorthodox views of Federal generals like James Lane and David Hunter moved more and more to the center, eventually becoming the national government's official policy. In March of that year, Congress officially decreed that fugitive slaves should not be returned to their owners. In April, the national legislature outlawed slavery in Washington, D.C. In July, it gave the president discretionary powers to enroll blacks into the army. In August 1862, the same month Hunter disbanded all but one company of the First South Carolina, Secretary of War Edwin M. Stanton approved the request of another Union general in South Carolina, Rufus Saxton, to train and equip up to five thousand former slaves. This action suggests that Hunter's problem was not so much his philosophy as his personality.

On September 22, 1862, Lincoln himself announced his preliminary Emancipation Proclamation: as of January 1, 1863, all slaves in states, or parts of states, still in rebellion would be "then, thenceforward, and forever free." When the proclamation became law at the beginning of 1863, it included the notable addition that freed slaves were eligible for service in the armed forces of the United States. Though they would not officially become a part of the Union army until the turn of the year, black units in the Federal army were already seeing action in the fall of 1862. Apart from the skirmish at Island Mound, Missouri, in October, Saxton's newly authorized black regiments in South Carolina began coastal raids in Georgia and Florida the following month.

Conducting a reconnaissance in force the first week of November, companies from the First Carolina pushed back Confederate pickets at several coastal garrisons, killed or captured a dozen gray-clad soldiers, freed 150 slaves, and destroyed property worth twenty thousand dollars.[40] Throughout this and several other forays along the rivers and many-islanded coasts of the southeastern seaboard, the First Carolina's white officers were consistently impressed by their soldiers' bravery, discipline, and eagerness to come to grips with the enemy. Thomas Wentworth Higginson, a colonel who had been an outspoken abolitionist before the war and a personal friend of John Brown, filed a report in January 1863 that glowed with praise for the black soldiers under his command: "The men have been repeatedly under fire; have had infantry, cavalry, and artillery arrayed against them, and have in every instance come off not only with unblemished honor, but with undisputed triumph."[41] Higginson went on to explain why contraband soldiers were particularly well suited for the work: "No officer in this regiment now doubts that the key to the successful prosecution of this war lies in the unlimited employment of black troops. Their superiority lies simply in the fact that they know the country, while white troops do not. . . . Instead of leaving their homes and families to fight, they are fighting for their homes and families, and they show the resolution and the sagacity which a personal purpose gives. It would have been madness to attempt, with the bravest white troops, what I have successfully accomplished with black ones."[42]

After two black regiments captured Jacksonville, Florida, in March 1863, Gen. David Hunter, still commanding the Department of the South, sent to Washington an equally enthusiastic dispatch: "I am happy to announce to you my complete and eminent satisfaction with the results of the organization of negro regiments in this department. . . . In the field, these regiments, so far as tried, have proved brave, active, docile, and energetic. . . . I find the colored regiments hardy, generous, temperate, strictly obedient, [and] possessing remarkable aptitude for military training. . . . They are imbued with a burning faith that now is the time appointed by God, in His All-wise providence, for the deliverance of their race." Hunter also reported that doubts among whites about the value of African American soldiers were rapidly receding, as the latter were consistently demonstrating their qualities in training and on the battlefield.[43]

ROBERT SMALLS AND THE CASE
OF THE STOLEN STEAMSHIP

IN THE early morning hours of March 13, 1862, the Confederate steamship *Planter* slipped away from a dock in Charleston Harbor and steered toward open water. A sentry standing on the shore fifty yards away noticed the *Planter* cast off its moorings, but he sensed nothing unusual about a Confederate transport running early morning errands in the inner harbor. Yet what he saw was unusual in the extreme: the crew of the *Planter* that morning intended to deliver its cargo of artillery and ammunition not to a nearby island battery, as supposed, but rather to Federal ships patrolling off the Carolina coast. On that memorable day, the captain, crew, and passengers of the *Planter* were all runaway slaves.

The leader of this bold company was twenty-two-year-old Robert Smalls, who had been assigned to the *Planter* the previous year. Smalls was born in 1839 in Beaufort, South Carolina, thirty miles down the coast from Charleston. His mother, Lydia, was the cook and housekeeper for John McKee, a Sea Island planter who is generally assumed to be Robert's father. When the elder McKee died in 1848, his thirty-seven-year-old son Henry McKee inherited Lydia and nine-year-old Robert. Three years later, Henry moved to Charleston, leaving Lydia in Beaufort but taking Robert with him to act as a manservant. Sturdily built but short in stature, Robert was known as Robert Small, a name he later changed to Robert Smalls.

When he arrived in Charleston, Robert first came into contact with free blacks working a wide variety of occupations, including masons, carpenters, cooks, blacksmiths, and sailors. Always independent-minded, Robert worked out an agreement with Henry McKee whereby he would find his own jobs in and around Charleston, paying his master fifteen dollars a month out of his earnings. From the start, Smalls was drawn to the waterfront, working first as a stevedore on the Charleston docks, then as a sailmaker and rigger, and then finally a sailor. When he was eighteen, Robert married another slave, Hannah Jones, who gave birth to a daughter, Elizabeth Lydia Smalls, the following year. While still in his teens, Robert contracted with Hannah's owner to buy her time for seven dollars a month, planning eventually to pay eight hundred dollars for the freedom of his wife and daughter. In the meantime, Robert learned everything he could about sailing, piloting, and navigation.

Robert was pressed into service in 1861 and assigned to the *Planter*, a highly service-able ship with up-to-date machinery. Built of live oak and red cedar, she was 150 feet long, 30 feet wide at the beam, and drew 3 feet 9 inches of water. A side-wheeler with a wood-burning engine, the *Planter* was used as a cotton steamer before the war, capable of carrying fourteen hundred bales. She was chartered by the Confederate government late in 1861, fitted with a 32-pounder pivot gun on the foredeck and a howitzer on the

Robert Smalls

afterdeck, and used as a troop transport, dispatch carrier, and mine layer. The *Planter* had a crew of eleven, including three white officers (a captain, mate, and engineer), plus eight slaves. Already recognized locally as an accomplished steersman, Smalls was assigned to the *Planter* as the ship's pilot. (At the time, he was called the wheelman, the title of pilot being reserved for whites.)

When the Federal army and navy occupied the Sea Island region in November 1861, Smalls learned that his mother had decided to stay behind, and he feared for her safety. But he soon received word that she was living comfortably in the McKee household in Beaufort, earning good wages as a cook for Union officers. Though he was, of course, relieved to hear of her good fortune, it made it all the harder for him to hear that his mother was suddenly free, something she'd longed for all her life, while he and his young family continued on as slaves only forty miles up the coast. Smalls also heard that Federal commanders in the area were welcoming contrabands, treating them kindly, and even teaching them to read and write.

When one of Smalls's fellow crewmen joked that the slaves on the *Planter* could manage the ship on their own and didn't need their white officers, Smalls immediately latched on to the idea and told his fellow sailors to not mention it again, except among themselves. He laid careful plans over the next several days, alerting his family that they should be ready to leave on short notice, making sure he knew all the proper signals between ships and the forts ringing Charleston Harbor, and awaiting an opportune moment.

That moment came in the early morning hours of March 13, 1862. The *Planter* had been loaded with an especially valuable cargo that day—four heavy cannon and two hundred pounds of ammunition—to be delivered to Forts Ripley and Sumter the next morning. When the three white officers decided to spend the night on shore (against standing orders), Smalls put his plan into action. He had his wife and daughter rowed out to the *Planter*, along with family members of several of his co-conspirators. Smalls broke into the captain's cabin and put on that officer's white coat and straw hat, which fit well since the two men were of similar build. Smalls had even been practicing the captain's distinctive gait, so that he wouldn't create any undue suspicion among the sentinels in the forts looking out at the vessel as she sailed by.

Hoisting the ship's two flags, the Confederate Stars and Bars and the state's Palmetto flag, the crew of the *Planter* pulled away from the wharf and set out for open water at the leisurely speed of a dispatch ship running errands, not the scurrying pace of fugitive slaves making a dash for freedom. (The crew had decided in advance that, if they were detected, they would blow up the ship with all aboard, including women and children, rather than be taken alive.) At each of the island batteries they passed in Charleston Harbor—Castle Pinckney, Fort Ripley, and Fort Sumter—Smalls gave the expected signal, a coded series of whistles and hisses that he had learned in his many trips piloting the ship in and out of the harbor. All went exactly as planned: the *Planter* was duly observed by the sentinels, but there was nothing unusual in this, and the ship's passing was routinely noted in logbooks.

The greatest danger of the night came not from Confederate batteries but from the Federal warships blockading the harbor mouth. As soon as the *Planter* was beyond range of Sumter's guns, she quickened her pace and

The three-hundred-ton side-wheel steamer *Planter* served the Confederate army as a transport and dispatch vessel in Charleston Harbor. On May 13, 1862, ship's pilot Robert Smalls steered the vessel past numerous Confederate outposts and surrendered it to a Union blockader.

U.S. NAVAL HISTORICAL CENTER

lowered her flags. Smalls ordered a white bedsheet run up the flagpole as an ensign of surrender, which he hoped the Federal lookouts could see by starlight. The nearest Union ship, the USS *Onward*, commanded by Capt. F. J. Nichols, came about and prepared to fire a broadside at the oncoming ship, assuming the *Planter* had been sent out to ram one of the blockaders. With the *Onward's* guns loaded and lanyards pulled taut, a watchman cried that he saw a white flag on the mast of the ship steaming toward them. Nichols belayed the order to fire, and soon the Union crew could see a crowd of runaway slaves on the deck, including five women and three children, all laughing, and waving, and clapping their hands. Smalls welcomed a boarding party onto the deck of the runaway steamer, introducing himself and explaining, as he reported later, "I thought the *Planter* might be of some use to Uncle Abe."[44]

Smalls's successful escape with the *Planter* and its crew created a national sensation, and he became an instant celebrity. Within two weeks, Congress voted to award the *Planter's* crew seven thousand dollars in prize money, including fifteen hundred dollars for Smalls. All the major newspapers reported the story, Northern newspapers with elation, Southern papers with indignation. The *Philadelphia Inquirer* noted that, as valuable as the steamship was for use in Southern coastal waters, "the accession of Smalls is deemed of more importance than the heavy guns of the *Planter*, as Smalls is thoroughly acquainted with all the intricacies of navigation in that region."[45] The *Charleston Courier*, by contrast, reported, "Our community was intensely agitated Tuesday morning by the intelligence that the steamer 'Planter' had been taken possession of by her colored crew, steamed up and run out to the blockaders. The news was not at first credited."[46] Voicing outrage over the negligence of the ship's white officers, the *Columbia Guardian*, published in the South Carolina state capital, expressed its hope that "recreant parties will be brought to speedy justice, and the prompt penalty of the halter [noose] speedily enforced."[47] From Richmond, Gen. Robert E. Lee sent a message stating that all necessary precautions should be taken "to prevent the repetition of a like misfortune."[48]

In August 1862, Robert Smalls traveled from South Carolina to Washington, D.C., accompanied by a white Methodist chaplain of the Federal army. He met several times with President Lincoln and Secretary of War Edwin M. Stanton, recounting the story of his dramatic escape and urging the enlistment of South Carolina contrabands for military service. Smalls personally carried a letter from Stanton to Gen. Rufus Saxton in South Carolina, authorizing him to raise and equip up to five thousand former slaves as Federal soldiers.

Upon his return, Smalls continued to act as pilot for the *Planter*, transporting troops, destroying railroad bridges on coastal rivers, and neutralizing torpedoes (underwater mines) that he himself had helped install as part of his work for the Confederate navy. Smalls participated in seventeen naval battles in the next three years. In December 1864, while steaming up the Stono River, south of Charleston, the *Planter* encountered heavy plunging fire from the surrounding bluffs, damaging its smokestack and lookout tower, one shell making a direct hit on the pilothouse where Smalls and the ship's captain were sitting. The captain ordered the ship beached in order to surrender, but Smalls refused, explaining that he and other black crewmen could expect no mercy, as they were escaped slaves who had taken up arms against their former masters. The captain left the wheelhouse in a panic, and Smalls steered the ship under full steam through a gauntlet of artillery fire back to open water, beyond the reach of the guns. For his bravery and coolness under fire, Smalls was promoted to ship's captain, commanding the same craft on which he had served two years earlier as a slave crewman. Smalls's exploits were recounted over and over in reports by the secretary of the navy, speeches of U.S. congressmen, editorials by Frederick Douglass, even in songs and poems published in the North.[49] In the Sea Islands region, Smalls grew into a living legend. As the oft-repeated story went, one naysayer had muttered, "Smalls ain't God." To which came the reply: "That's true. But he's young yet."[50]

After the war, Smalls was elected a South Carolina state representative in 1868 and state senator in 1870. He served three terms in the national Congress during the turbulent Reconstruction era, then spent his last years as a customs collector in his hometown of Beaufort, buying the same house where he had grown up as a slave. Feeling that he and his mother had always been treated kindly by their former masters, Smalls also purchased a farm for the McKee family, whose fortune had been entirely wiped out by the war.[51] Smalls died quietly in 1915, a half century after the end of the war that had so transformed his life. From slave to ship's captain, contraband to congressman, Smalls's career seems to bear out his own observation made in 1895: "My race needs no special defense, for their past history in this country proves them to be the equal of any people anywhere. All they need is an equal chance in the battle of life."[52]

PRIDE, PREJUDICE, AND PERSEVERANCE

By March 1863, the month African American troops occupied Jacksonville, Florida, Lincoln's own reservations about using former slaves as soldiers were completely abolished, and he hoped that similar units could be raised up and down the Mississippi River. That same month he wrote to Andrew Johnson, the governor of Union-occupied Tennessee, "The colored population is the great *available* yet *unavailed of* force for restoring the Union. The bare sight of 50,000 armed and drilled black soldiers upon the banks of the Mississippi would end the rebellion at once."[53] Though Lincoln overstated his case about fifty thousand black troops in the western theater winning the war, he was in earnest about trying to raise that many recruits among former slaves in the Mississippi Valley. In March 1863, he sent Adj. Gen. Lorenzo Thomas to Louisiana to raise and train as many black regiments as he could. By the end of the summer, there were fourteen regiments of freedmen ready for service and another twenty-four regiments in the process of being trained and equipped.[54]

Apart from former slaves, the Federal army was also strengthened by the addition of three regiments of Louisiana Native Guards, free blacks from the New Orleans area who had begun the war as Confederate soldiers. Led by well-to-do Creoles of color, fluent in both French and English, the Louisiana Native Guards, sometimes called the Corps D'Afrique, originally enlisted as home guards to help defend the Crescent City. But they were never issued weapons, and when the Confederate defenders evacuated New Orleans in April 1862, the Native Guards were not given orders, so they decided to stay behind to test their fortune with the Yankees. Gen. Benjamin F. Butler, the same Union commander who had redefined runaway slaves as contrabands the previous year, was then commanding the New Orleans occupation troops, and after some initial hesitation, he was persuaded that the Native Guards could defend their homes and families just as well in blue uniforms as they had in gray.

The Native Guards, like other African Americans in the Federal army, soon learned that racial attitudes among Northern whites differed very little from those in the South. Blacks who had served as officers in the Native

Guards from the beginning were asked to resign their commissions, since many white soldiers refused to obey their orders. On one occasion, the Native Guards were subjected to deliberate friendly fire from white artillerymen who didn't think they should have to serve alongside African Americans.[55] Black soldiers also received less pay than whites until the last year of the war, and they were more often assigned to heavy labor or fatigue duty. They were also sent to the hottest and most disease-ridden areas under Union occupation, because many believed that they were more resistant to malaria and other fatal diseases. This theory was disproved by the statistics. Of the 180,000 blacks who served in the Union army, more than one-fifth (37,300) died during the four years of war, more than 95 percent from disease, a mortality rate three times higher than in white regiments.[56]

Apart from their concern about offending slave owners in the Border States, officials in Washington were slow to recruit blacks because of widespread racial prejudice in the other Northern states as well. As one Wisconsin brigadier explained to Lincoln the prevailing attitude among his officers, "They hate the Negro more than they love the union."[57] In August 1863, Lincoln publicly admonished those who resisted his policy of turning former slaves into Federal soldiers: "You say you will not fight to free negroes. Some of them seem willing to fight for you. . . . There will be some black men who can remember that, with silent tongue, and clenched teeth, and steady eye, and well-poised bayonet, they have helped mankind on to this great consummation; while I fear there will be some white ones unable to forget that, with malignant heart and deceitful speech, they strove to hinder it."[58]

As in Kansas and South Carolina, black soldiers in the Mississippi Valley were called upon to prove themselves in battle. In May 1863, two regiments of the Louisiana Native Guards participated in the Federal assault on Port Hudson, Louisiana, the Confederate stronghold on the Mississippi River, about twenty-five miles above Baton Rouge. Like Vicksburg, 240 winding miles upriver, Port Hudson was strategically placed on a bluff high above the river. Together the twin citadels closed off the Mississippi to Northern shipping and kept open a vital corridor connecting the trans-Mississippi with the rest of the Confederacy.

In mid-May 1863, Gen. Nathaniel Banks took thirty thousand men to Port Hudson to storm its defenses. Banks was granted high rank because of his political clout, not his military ability, and his assault on the river city was one of many occasions on which the valor of Union soldiers was wasted by the ineptness of their commanders. Built on a bluff eighty feet above the river, the citadel could not be assailed from any direction without having to climb a steep slope in full view of well-placed infantry behind a twenty-foot-thick parapet, backed by siege guns and field artillery pieces. Two regiments of the Native Guards were placed on the extreme right of the attacking army. This gave them a narrow corridor for advancing, but they were hemmed in on the right by swampy backwater from the big river, on the left by Confederate rifle pits, and straight ahead by steep slopes covered with entrenched sharpshooters and presighted artillery. Nevertheless, the men of the Native Guards saw this as their chance to answer once and for all the question, "Will they fight?" So when the order came for them to advance at about 10:00 a.m. on May 27, 1863, fifteen companies, just over a thousand men, stepped briskly ahead, taking heavy losses as soon as they came out of the willow trees and into the open. They charged three times amid murderous fire, their officers shouting orders and words of encouragement in both English and French. Some of the Creole soldiers tried to wade neck-deep through the swamp in order to grapple with the enemy, only to be shot down as soon as they emerged from the water. Others were wounded and carried back to have their wounds dressed, but they refused to retire and went back wrapped in blood-soaked bandages to join their comrades. At the end of the day, the thousand men of the Native Guards who had made the impossible assault on the Confederate left flank suffered more than three hundred casualties; their rate of killed, wounded, and missing was the second highest of any regiments who joined in Banks's piecemeal assault.

The Federal army would eventually settle down to a siege of Port Hudson, and the strongpoint finally surrendered on July 9, 1863, five days after the fall of Vicksburg. But if the direct assault of May 27 achieved little else, it won for the Native Guards the respect they had been seeking. Banks wrote in his official report about the qualities of the black troops engaged: "The history of this day proves conclusively to those who were in a condition to observe the conduct of these regiments, that the government will find in this class of troops effective supporters and defenders. The severe test to

Nathaniel Banks

LIBRARY OF CONGRESS

The Louisiana Native Guards, composed of free blacks from New Orleans, began the war as a Confederate home guard unit but joined the Federal army after the occupation of the Crescent City.

LIBRARY OF CONGRESS

which they were subjected, and the determined manner in which they encountered the enemy, leaves upon my mind no doubt of their ultimate success." A white officer who watched the assault agreed, writing that his "prejudices with regard to negro troops have been dispelled by the battle the other day." He went on to explain that "the brigade of negroes behaved magnificently and fought splendidly; could not have done better. They are far superior in discipline to the white troops, and just as brave."[59]

Within two weeks of the assault on Fort Hudson, black troops would again get a chance to show their fighting qualities, this time as defenders. While Ulysses S. Grant was maneuvering south of Vicksburg in the summer of 1863, trying to approach the fortified city from its landward side, one of his key supply depots, Milliken's Bend, was placed just along the west bank of the river. The Rebels, hoping to cut Grant's supply line and make him abandon his campaign, attacked the supply base at Milliken's Bend on June 7 with fifteen hundred men, including a regiment of cavalry, led by Gen. Henry McCulloch. The Federals numbered about eleven hundred men, mostly from newly formed companies of former slaves, some with less than three weeks' training. The Federals fought from behind a sloping six-foot-high levee, with additional cover from broken lines of hedgerows. In several places, the Confederate horsemen broke through, and there was hand-to-hand fighting along the top of the levee. Eventually, the Union gunboat *Choctaw* began lobbing shells into the fray, hitting soldiers from both sides in the fight but convincing McCulloch that the depot could not be taken and that he should withdraw. After the battle, among the dozens of dead bodies in both blue and gray, there were found eight broken bayonets, a tes-

The initial Federal assault on the Confederate stronghold at Port Hudson, Louisiana, on May 27, 1863, marked the first large-scale use of black troops in combat. Two regiments of the Louisiana Native Guards charged the Confederates three times and suffered the second highest Union casualty rate of the war.

LIBRARY OF CONGRESS

tament to the ferocity of the fighting. Though they held their position, the defenders at Milliken's Bend suffered nearly 40 percent casualties in killed, wounded, and missing.

As at Port Hudson, the determination and bravery of the African American soldiers who fought at Milliken's Bend transformed many white officers from doubters to believers. In his report on the engagement, Grant wrote, "In this battle most of the troops engaged were Africans, who had but little experience in the use of fire-arms. Their conduct is said, however, to have been most gallant, and I doubt not but with good officers they will make good troops."[60] Adm. David Dixon Porter stated more simply in his report that the black recruits "stood at their posts like men."[61] Two weeks after the action at Milliken's Bend, Gen. Lorenzo Thomas reported that the prejudice against black troops was nearly universal among whites at first, but that "finally it was overcome, and the blacks themselves subsequently by their coolness and determination in battle fought themselves into their present high standing as soldiers."[62]

Some of these dispatches sound more like recommendations than battle reports. And it is clear that Union generals like David Hunter and Lorenzo Thomas wanted their experiment to succeed, so they took every opportunity to praise the performance of African American soldiers in their command. But reports such as these can be supplemented by the observations of line officers who were simply writing home, with no thought of the propaganda value their words might have. After Port Hudson and Milliken's Bend, one Wisconsin officer wrote that he had previously had a low opinion of blacks as combat soldiers. But when he saw them in action, he had to admit, "By Jasus, they're hell in fighting."[63] Another white officer who had his doubts about recruiting African Americans concluded simply, "They seem to have behaved just as well and as badly as the rest and to have suffered more severely."[64]

Amid the high praise of some officers and the ongoing doubts and prejudices of many others, blacks continued to join the Federal army in ever increasing numbers. By the end of October 1863, there were fifty-eight black regiments in the Union army, comprising more than thirty-seven thousand men, including their white officers.[65] A year later, that number had nearly tripled. In the last year of the war, African American troops participated in every major campaign except for Sherman's march across Georgia.[66] Among their other marching songs, such as "John Brown's Body" and "The Battle Hymn of the Republic," black soldiers in Federal blue had another song of their own:

> So rally, boys, rally, let us never mind the past;
> We had a hard road to travel, but our day is coming fast,
> For God is for the right, and we have no need to fear—
> The Union must be saved by the colored volunteer.[67]

By the war's end, nearly 180,000 blacks had served in the Union army, one-tenth of its total strength, and another 29,000 in the navy, more than one-fourth of its number. African Americans served in 449 engagements, including 39 major battles. More than 37,000 blacks died while serving in the Union army and navy. Twenty-one black soldiers and sailors received Medals of Honor for exceptional valor.[68] When asked brusquely who he thought he was to wear a Federal uniform, a private in the First South Carolina Volunteers spoke for many of his fellow slaves turned soldiers. He stood at attention and replied, "When God made me, I wasn't much, but I's a man now."[69]

8

THE DISTAFF SIDE
OF DISSENT

Early in 1863 an elderly woman from northern Alabama came into the Federal lines around Decatur and asked to speak to Col. Abel Streight, who was recruiting local Unionists for the Northern army. When taken to see the cavalry commander, she said her name was Anna Campbell and she knew where the Federals could pick up at least two dozen new troopers. Streight was interested, but he didn't know the mountain country and didn't have the men to spare to go out on an expedition to find Campbell's potential enlistees. (Then, too, there was an outside chance this could be a ruse, designed to ambush Federal riders miles away from the nearest Union lines.) Sensing Streight's hesitation, Campbell volunteered to ride thirty-five miles each way over the mountainous terrain to guide the new recruits herself to the Federal camp. She was as good as her word. Within a day and a half of her interview with Streight, Campbell rode back into camp with thirty young Alabamians, all ready to be mustered into the Federal army. She had made a round trip of seventy miles through rough hill country in thirty-six hours in order to deliver thirty new riders for the First Alabama Cavalry (USA).[1]

As Campbell's remarkable ride shows, dissent in the war for a Southern Confederacy was not a male prerogative alone. The most visible resistance came from men, as they were the ones who evaded the draft, deserted, or took up arms against their fellow Southerners. But more often than not, these individuals did not go out on their own. They had wives, mothers, sisters, and sympathetic neighbors giving them food and shelter, places to hide, and warnings of danger. Women often provided the moral, emotional, and logistical support that allowed a husband, son, or brother to march to a different drummer than the one heard by the great majority of Southern soldiers.

In general, women in the South reflected and reinforced attitudes of the males of their families. Wives and daughters of wealthy planters generally supported the war as staunchly as the men they sent off to battle. But women in western Virginia, eastern Tennessee, and other regions with fewer slaves and slaveholders were just as likely as their men to wonder how much they should be expected to sacrifice for a cause they did not consider their own.

The diaries, letters, conversations (and sometimes mass meetings) of Southern women provide valuable clues as to the state of overall Confederate morale during the protracted conflict. In the first year of the war, men and women were caught up equally in what the French called *rage militaire,* the first frenzied outburst of patriotic zeal to defend hearth and homeland and strike down the contemptible foe. Young ladies in Texas taunted able-bodied men who were slow to enlist by sending them hoopskirts and bonnets.[2] A letter signed "Many Sewers" in a Rome, Georgia, newspaper chided local men for seeking political exemptions instead of answering the call of duty. The patriotic seamstresses offered to sew free uniforms for the faint-hearted stay-at-homes if they would join the army.[3]

By the winter of 1861–62, however, it was becoming increasingly clear that this was not going to be a short and glorious war in which "God wore the gray." The casualty lists continued to grow, as did prices. Women were called upon to take up what had been considered man's work: tilling fields, harvesting crops, supervising slaves, working in factories. More and more women became teachers and nurses, two more jobs that had previously been considered outside the feminine sphere.[4] In 1862, newspapers began running editorials with titles such as "Don't Write Gloomy Letters" warning women on the home front that their plaintive letters to the men in the ranks were undermining morale and contributing to desertion.

In July 1863, the twin blows of Gettysburg and Vicksburg cast a shadow over the whole Confederacy, causing some to realize for the first time that this war might not be won. The numbers of men dying, more often from disease than battlefield wounds, represented a far higher percentage of able-bodied white males in the South than in the North. Luxuries had already disappeared from store windows, and necessities were getting harder and harder to come by. A factory-made dress that had cost $9 in the fall of 1861 went for $195 two years later. Sugar, salt, and flour were increasingly scarce. Twenty dollars would buy a family only enough groceries for one day.[5]

On April 2, 1863, Mary Jackson, whose son was serving in the army, led a group of angry, threadbare women to the capitol in Richmond to demand relief. Armed with a pistol and a knife, Jackson and her followers marched down the street shouting, "Bread or blood." Governor John Letcher tried ineffectually to calm the mob, which swelled to more than a thousand, but they ignored his pleas and broke into twenty local stores, taking bread, bacon, and shoes, but also stealing luxury items such as jewelry and embroidered dresses. They also ransacked the offices of Jewish and German merchants, believing they were hoarding goods in order to drive up prices. Eventually, Jefferson Davis himself came outside and appealed to the women's patriotism, saying he sympathized with their plight as he took some coins out of his pocket and flung them into the crowd. But the women did not disperse until armed troops arrived and began making arrests. Although Southern newspapers were instructed not to report on the Richmond bread riots of 1863, there were similar outbreaks on a smaller scale that year in Atlanta, Georgia, and Mobile, Alabama, as well as half a dozen other cities and towns from the Atlantic coast to the Appalachian highlands.[6]

In 1864, more and more women didn't just write gloomy letters to the men in the rank; they openly pleaded with them to leave the army and come home. Farms and shops were deserted; homes were left unprotected from Yankee troops and marauding bands; children were starving. Mary Boykin Chesnut, the wife of a wealthy South Carolina planter, described in her diary a vivid scene in which a frantic young woman in a "cracker bonnet" yelled at her husband as they dragged him away to return to the ranks, "You desert again, quick as you kin. Come back to your wife and children. Desert, Jake! Desert agin, Jake!"[7] Such scenes must have been all too common, as one Confederate official candidly explained, "Desertion takes place because desertion is encouraged. . . . And though the ladies may not be

On April 2, 1863, a group of women and children staged a march from Richmond's Capitol Square to the business district. Their number soon swelled to more than a thousand, and what began as an orderly plea for bread turned into a riot. Only the threat of military force dispersed the crowd.

LIBRARY OF CONGRESS

willing to concede the fact, they are nevertheless responsible for the desertion in the army and the dissipation in the country."[8]

In surveying civilian morale over the course of the war, historian Drew
Gilpin Faust suggests that "by early 1865, countless women of all classes
had in effect deserted the ranks. Refusing to accept the economic depriva-
tion further military struggle would have required [and] resisting additional
military service by their husbands and sons, . . . they directly subverted the
South's economic and military effectiveness."[9] Explaining how the demands
of modern warfare burdened Southern women more and more grievously
as the war progressed, Faust concludes, "Historians have wondered in recent years why the Confederacy did not endure longer. In considerable
measure, . . . it was because so many women did not want it to."[10]

ELIZABETH VAN LEW

APART FROM the broad outlines that can be discerned in Southern women's
declining morale, there are individuals who stand out for their distinct
voices or their unusually bold actions in resisting Confederate authority. Besides Anna Campbell, whose rugged ride helped bring new Alabama recruits into Union lines, and Mary Jackson, who led a historic women's
rally-turned-riot in Richmond, there were other notables such as Harriet
Tubman and Rebecca Wright. Tubman is famous as the runaway slave
turned Underground Railroad guide who made nineteen trips into the
South before the war, leading three hundred slaves back across the Mason-
Dixon Line. During the war, Tubman, then in her sixties, worked as a Union
scout, helping recruit slaves in the Sea Island region of South Carolina for
the Federal army. Another well-known female Southern dissident is Rebecca Wright, a Quaker schoolteacher in Winchester, Virginia, who aided
Union Gen. Philip H. Sheridan in his 1864 Shenandoah Valley campaign.
In September 1864, Wright sent a note to Sheridan, wrapped in tin foil and
hidden in the mouth of an elderly slave, in which she described Confederate troop strengths in and around the city. Using that information in con-
junction with what he learned from his own scouts, Sheridan launched the
battle of Third Winchester on September 19, a victory that gave the Federals control of the town for the remainder of the war.

One of the Union's most valuable and accomplished spymasters during
the war was certainly not among the usual suspects: she was a native-born

Virginian, a wealthy, middle-aged socialite named Elizabeth Van Lew. Apart from giving aid and comfort to Federal soldiers in Richmond prisons, Van Lew developed a complex spy network in the Confederate capital, with operatives in local prisons, in government offices, and even in the home of President Jefferson Davis. Van Lew supplied useful information first to Union Gen. Benjamin F. Butler and then to George Gordon Meade. In the last few months of the war, when U. S. Grant's army was laying siege to the Confederate capital, he received the latest Richmond newspapers in time for breakfast every day, courtesy of Miss Van Lew—as well as fresh-cut flowers from her garden.

Elizabeth Van Lew

Born in 1818, Elizabeth Van Lew was the eldest daughter of John and Eliza Van Lew. Elizabeth's father was a prominent Virginia businessman who lived in one of the most resplendent homes in all Richmond. Situated on Church Hill, the highest point in the city, the Van Lew mansion was a spacious three-story structure with a broad portico in front supported by six imposing columns. In back was a splendid piazza with luxuriant, terraced gardens and a panoramic view of the city below.

Though they were transplanted Northerners (John was of colonial New York Dutch stock, and Eliza was from Philadelphia), the Van Lews moved in the highest social circles in Virginia. They counted Chief Justice John Marshall as a personal friend and entertained the best Richmond families—Lees, Cabels, Carringtons—in their Church Hill residence. Jenny Lind, "the Swedish Nightingale," sang in their parlor during her tour of America, and Edgar Allan Poe recited his poem "The Raven" there.

In her early teens, Elizabeth was sent to school in Philadelphia. Her Quaker governess there had strong convictions about the evils of slavery, and her words struck a responsive chord in the young Elizabeth. She had never forgotten hearing as a child about an African American woman who literally dropped dead from grief upon learning that her infant child had been sold to another master. When John Van Lew died in 1843, twenty-five-year-old Elizabeth persuaded her mother to change the status of the family's nine slaves to that of paid household servants.

This was not a popular thing to do in Virginia in the 1840s. Though Elizabeth was described as a "pleasing, pale blond" by one visitor and as "lovely in appearance" by another, she had few suitors, and the family became increasingly isolated. Though she was intelligent, well-schooled, and well-mannered, Elizabeth was also outspoken in her views about slavery. One friend recalled a time when she and Elizabeth sat in a carriage outside a large tobacco factory, listening to slaves sing hymns as they worked. Though the visitor was mainly impressed by their untutored harmonies, she looked over to see Elizabeth weeping.

When the war came in 1861, Elizabeth was forty-two years old, living with her mother and her younger brother John at the Church Hill residence. Others said the war was about democracy or states' rights, but Elizabeth set down her feelings plainly in her journal. She felt that the root cause of the trouble was slavery: "Slave power crushes the freedom of labor. Slave power is arrogant, is jealous and intrusive, is cruel, is despotic, not only over the slave, but over the community, the State."[11]

One need not wonder how such opinions, if spoken aloud, would be received by others in Virginia during the Civil War. Elizabeth wrote vividly in her journal about the war fever that swept Richmond in the spring of 1861—rallies and torchlight parades, women and even little girls learning to shoot pistols, men saying they wanted Abe Lincoln's ear as a memento once the Yankees had been whipped. Outspoken as ever, Van Lew declared she was still for the Union. Such remarks were met with scowls and muttered oaths, fingers wagged in her face, even threats to kill her or burn down her house. She confided to her journal: "One day I could speak for

The stately mansion on Richmond's Church Hill was the center of Elizabeth Van Lew's Union spy network. Beginning early in the war, Van Lew became the Union's most reliable source of information on the situation in the Confederate capital.

my country; the next I was threatened with death. . . . Loyalty was now called treason, and cursed."[12]

Fort Sumter surrendered on April 13, and the Virginia legislature voted to secede four days later. One of the earliest clashes of the war was at Big Bethel, near the Virginia seacoast, on June 10. The first trickle of Union prisoners began arriving in Richmond a few days later. When Elizabeth heard about the hardships of the captives, she went to Ligon Prison, a makeshift facility that a few months earlier had been Ligon's Tobacco Factory and Warehouse. There she spoke to Lt. David H. Todd, the prison overseer, and asked to be assigned as a hospital nurse. Though Todd was the half brother of Mary Todd Lincoln, Abraham Lincoln's wife, he showed no sympathy whatsoever for Elizabeth's request. He answered that he knew a good many people who would rather shoot the Yankees than look after them, adding that she was the only woman who applied for such a job.

After Todd flatly refused her offer, Van Lew took her case to Christopher Memminger, the Confederate secretary of the treasury. At first, Memminger also refused, explaining sternly that such a class of men were not fit company for a lady. But Van Lew was as quick-witted as she was persistent, and she answered that she had once heard Memminger preach beautifully on the subject of love. When Memminger's expression brightened, Van Lew added that if they wanted "our cause" to succeed, shouldn't they seek God's favor by helping even the thankless and unworthy? Memminger hesitantly agreed and gave her a note of introduction to Gen. John Winder, provost marshal in charge of all the city's prisons, who wrote out a prison pass for her.

From that time on, Elizabeth, sometimes accompanied by her mother, made regular visits to several of the buildings in town where Federal prisoners were being held. They took them home-cooked food, medicine, blankets, and books to read. They changed bandages, wrote letters, and consulted with doctors about those who needed special care. On many days Elizabeth was seen going into one of the prisons first thing in the morning and not returning home till twilight. It seems she was the opposite of Tennessee Williams's Southern lady: strangers could always depend on her kindness.

Photographs of Elizabeth from the Civil War period depict a small, frail-looking woman with a pointed nose and chin. However, several prisoners left sketches of her in their journals or memoirs, portraits of a woman with kind eyes and a generous smile. There is no record that these were ever shown to Van Lew to flatter her vanity. It seems fitting that prisoners would

Union prisoner portrait of Van Lew

remember their tireless, selfless helper not as a stooped, sharp-featured woman in her middle years, but as a blooming belle.

War came to Richmond in earnest after the battle of First Bull Run (July 21, 1861). While the city's hospitals were overwhelmed with Confederate wounded, the city's prisons were overwhelmed with Yankee captives. This included six hundred soldiers taken at Manassas, as well as Washington officials who had gone out to watch what they supposed would be a Union victory. When the Van Lews visited the new group of prisoners, they found one of the captive civilians gravely ill and arranged to have him transferred from the prison's hospital ward to their home on Church Hill. Despite their best efforts, the young man died soon afterward and was buried in the local cemetery.

The Van Lews' attentions to the Northern prisoners did not go unnoticed. Ten days after First Bull Run, an article appeared in the *Richmond Enquirer* that noted "every true woman in the community" was tending to sick and wounded sons of the South. It went on to explain that "two ladies, mother and daughter, living on Church Hill . . . have been expending their opulent means in aiding and giving comfort to the miscreants who have invaded our soil, bent on raping and murder, the desolation of our homes and sacred places, and the ruin and dishonour of our families." The article concluded that such an open show of sympathy for the enemy could be interpreted as nothing other than an endorsement of the "cause and conduct of the Northern vandals."[13]

Elizabeth's reaction to this harsh public rebuke was typical: she cut out the notice and saved it, intent nonetheless on doing the same things she had been doing. But once again her natural kindness was complemented by natural shrewdness. Having taken one of the Northern prisoners into their home, the Van Lews now invited a Southern prison warden to stay with them. Decent housing was hard to find in the overcrowded city, and so Elizabeth invited Capt. George Gibb, head of Harwood Prison, to bring his family and live on Church Hill. The Gibbs took them up on their offer, with an understanding that the Van Lews would be permitted to continue visiting Federal prisoners. From that time until the end of the war, both women, but especially Elizabeth, became familiar sights around the city's prisons and hospitals, doing whatever they could (including spending a great of their own money) to alleviate the suffering, privation, or just plain boredom of prison life.

There is no record of when Elizabeth's job description expanded from comforter to undercover agent, but it probably occurred in the spring of 1862. In March, Libby Prison was opened in Richmond, a special facility for officers and high-ranking civilians. Libby was a large warehouse fronting the James River that was leased by Luther Libby, ship's chandler and grocer, until he was given notice by Confederate authorities to vacate within forty-eight hours. It was a red-brick building, three hundred feel long and three stories high, with a gabled roof. Each of the three floors was divided into three sections, large one-hundred-feet-by-forty-feet spaces originally designed for storing tobacco. The guards' quarters, kitchen, and hospital ward were on the ground floor, with prisoners' rooms above. On the second and third floors, there was hardly any furniture, except for a few scattered cots and packing crates. Prisoners stood, leaned against a wall, or sat on the floor to eat, play cards, or read. Most of them slept on the floor at night, many without blankets. The windows had no panes but iron grates, and there was a "dead line" around each window. Any man who stood in front of the window, in plain sight of the guards outside, was liable to be shot.

In her visits with the officers at Libby, Elizabeth became increasingly aware that what they knew—where they had been captured, gun emplacements they had seen during the trip to Richmond, unguarded words by their captors—could by very useful to the Federal commanders at Fort Monroe on the lower Chesapeake. She was too closely watched by the guards to engage in open conversation with the prisoners about military

Libby Prison was at the foot of the hill on which the Van Lew mansion stood. Thus it was natural that Elizabeth and her mother devoted a great deal of their time to the well-being of Union prisoners, which included providing a safe house for escapees seeking to return to Federal lines.

LIBRARY OF CONGRESS

matters, so she had to devise other ways to exchange information. Sometimes she hid coded messages on slips of paper tucked into the spines of books. At other times she carried a chafing dish with a false bottom to smuggle in contraband items such as greenbacks so that prisoners could buy extra food or bribe a guard.

Sensing the danger of trying to sneak anything in or out under the close scrutiny of the guards, Elizabeth developed more ingenious methods for exchanging information. She regularly brought in new books for the prisoners to read, which were duly inspected by the guards. But she began putting pinpricks over certain letters on each page, spelling out questions, which could be answered by pinholes made on another page. Even the most suspicious guards never noticed anything out of the ordinary in the books Elizabeth carried in or out.

As George B. McClellan's ponderous army edged toward Richmond in the spring of 1862, Van Lew was typically blunt. She told her neighbors she had readied a room for McClellan in case he wanted to use her home as his headquarters. After the Seven Days' battles, in which Lee's smaller force pushed McClellan all the way back to the protection of his gunboats on the lower James, Elizabeth sensed that she was in danger. General Winder considered revoking her prison pass and placing her under arrest. And she found a crudely scrawled note pinned to the front door of her home. With a skull and crossbones on top and a house on fire at the bottom, it said, "Look out. Look out. Look out. Your house is going at last. FIRE." It was signed "White Caps," apparently a forerunner of the Ku Klux Klan.

Most people would decide the time had come to lay low, but that simply wasn't a part of Van Lew's nature. Rather she decided to change tactics. Elizabeth knew that she was considered a crank or an eccentric throughout Richmond, and she decided to play upon this fact. Instead of the elegant dresses she had formerly worn, she began to go out in a shabby dress and broad-brimmed country bonnet, her hair hanging loosely about her shoulders. She sang or muttered to herself and seemed not to notice when others spoke to her.

Before long, the guards started calling her "Crazy Bet," a name that was soon picked up all over town. Even the children came up with a ditty: "Crazy Bet, Crazy Bet. Lives in a mansion with no rooms to let." But like Hamlet, Van Lew was only "mad north by northwest"—or in this case, north by south. While her fellow Virginians thought she had become deranged, the Yankee prisoners wrote about her "attractive manners" and referred to her as "God's angel." Van Lew confided to her journal, "They call me Crazy Bet, but it helps me in my work."[14]

Despite this ploy, Van Lew realized how closely she was being watched, even seeing Winder's agents sometimes at night peering from behind one of the massive pillars of her front portico. More and more, she recruited others and financed an underground network of Unionists. One of her associates, Thomas McNiven, a local baker code-named Quaker, said that he personally knew of at least three hundred Union sympathizers in Richmond during the war, collecting information, bribing guards, and providing safe houses for escaped prisoners. Eventually, Van Lew placed her operatives in the Confederate Navy Department, War Department, and several other government offices. In 1863, she arranged through a mutual friend to have her own servant, Mary Elizabeth Bowser, placed in the home of Jefferson and Varina Davis. Bowser reported what she overheard and what she read from sensitive documents lying on Davis's desk. (It was assumed at the time that black servants could not read, but Bowser had been educated at the Quaker School for Negroes in Philadelphia at her employer's expense.)

Apart from gathering information, Van Lew's agents were also instrumental in helping escaped prisoners make their way back to Federal lines. Some Richmond prisons, such as the enlisted men's prison on Belle Isle, in the James River, were almost impossible to escape from. The men were kept outdoors where they could always be watched, and there were swift currents on both sides of the island. But Libby was built originally as a tobacco warehouse, not a prison, so there were more opportunities to slip away. Sometimes all that was needed was to bribe the right guard at the right time. Other plans were more inventive. One prisoner bribed a medical orderly to declare him dead; he was removed from Libby in a pine box. Another prisoner had been a tailor in civilian life and was hired by a Confederate officer to alter his coat. The prisoner made the needed alterations, then put the coat on and walked right past the guards.

But escaping Libby was not the same as escaping danger. As one successful Union fugitive put it, "We all regarded the Confederacy as one huge military prison. To get through to our lines we had to have help from someone outside."[15] Sometimes that help came from unexpected directions. Such was the case with Capt. William H. Lounsbury of the Seventy-fourth New York Infantry. One afternoon he was standing at roll call, listening to one of the guards, Sgt. Erasmus Ross, swear at them as he bellowed out their names. Ross was considered one of the most brutal and unfeeling of the guards at Libby, a swaggering young man who liked to brandish two pistols and curse the "Damned Yankees." So Lounsbury was nonplussed when Ross turned to him after roll call and muttered, "Be at my office at 9:30 tonight." The New Yorker did as he was told, whatever his apprehensions. When he arrived, Ross pointed him to a back room, where Lounsbury found a Confederate officer's uniform slung over a chair. Putting the uniform on, he returned to discover that Ross had left him alone. Wondering perhaps if he was dreaming, Lounsbury headed for the front door, where he was not challenged, then toward the gate, where he again was not stopped. Once out on the street, he was met by a black man, who escorted him directly to the Van Lew mansion.

Lounsbury was one of many who made it back to Federal lines safely through the good offices of the "brutal" Erasmus Ross. The Libby sergeant was actually the nephew of one Van Lew's close associates, a Union-minded businessman in Richmond, Franklin Stearns. Ross's assignment to Libby as a guard was another of Van Lew's crafty manipulations of the tangled Richmond bureaucracy.

Even when there was real danger of being arrested or having her house burned down, Van Lew continued to use her mansion as a hideout for escaped prisoners. Many years after the war, Van Lew's niece told about a winter's night in 1863 when she was about ten years old. She awoke in the night and heard the creaking of footsteps outside her bedroom door. Getting up and peering out, she saw her aunt Elizabeth climbing the stairs with a candle in one hand and a bundle in the other. Tiptoeing out into the hall, the little girl watched her aunt go to the top of the stairs and slide back one of the wooden panels. To her amazement, a thin, bearded face appeared in the opening, and Aunt Elizabeth passed the bundle inside. The man behind the wall spotted the little girl and winked at her, putting his finger to his lips to show that she needed to keep mum about what she'd seen.

Though the little girl did keep the soldier's secret, and her aunt's, for many years, it is believed that the empty compartment over that magnificent pillared portico was Van Lew's main hideaway. And it must have been a good one. On at least one occasion, General Winder sent his men to search the Van Lew home after an escape, and they returned empty-handed—even though the escapees were crouched breathlessly behind a wall and could hear the heavy footsteps of the soldiers searching the house.

The "Great Escape" from Libby, perhaps the greatest in the Civil War, was engineered by Col. Thomas E. Rose of the Seventy-seventh Pennsylvania Volunteers in February 1864. Once again, Van Lew was a key to the plan's success, especially in distributing escapees to safe houses all over Richmond.

Rose was a clear-eyed, burly man who had fought in the Mexican War, been taken captive, and tunneled his way out of his prison pen to safety. So when he found himself again a prisoner in this war, he immediately began organizing another tunnel project. Libby had six three-story chimneys that ran from the foundation all the way up the building. Rose, or one of his associates, wondered what he might find if he pried loose a few chimney bricks. Sure enough, he found a cavity between the chimney and the surrounding walls, a natural shaft that dropped all the way to the cellar.

The first problem was how to get down the shaft, a straight drop from the prisoners' floor to the building's foundation. Rose's crew covered up the bricks they pried loose with latrine barrels while they worked on a solution. Then another prisoner supplied what they needed: a hundred-foot rope he had stolen while on work duty outside the prison walls. Using the rope, Rose and his crew lowered themselves into a rat-infested cellar, where they began digging a tunnel toward the James River. After two attempts that failed because the ground was too oozy with seeping sewage, the prisoners found a direction in which the soil was firm enough for digging. They began cutting a horizontal tunnel, really not much more than a large rabbit hole two feet in diameter, toward an empty lot away from the guards' line of sight. The next problem became the tunneling itself. The only implements they had to dig with were a small hand chisel and a case knife. The going was slow, and even the most optimistic of the men wondered if they could dig the fifty feet or so without being discovered. (Rose's work crew of fifteen was so secretive that even most of the other prisoners in Libby, more than a thousand, didn't realize there was an escape plan afoot.)

As the dirt from the digging piled up, Rose and his crew had to figure out how to get the dirt from the far end of the tunnel back out the entrance. They found a wooden spittoon, shaped like a small crate, and attached a piece of rope to both ends. When a

Thomas E. Rose

G. W. CABLE, ED., *FAMOUS ADVENTURES AND PRISON ESCAPES OF THE CIVIL WAR* (1885)

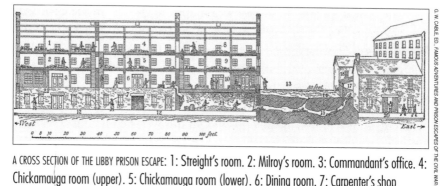

G. W. CABLE, ED. *FAMOUS ADVENTURES AND PRISON ESCAPES OF THE CIVIL WAR* (1895)

A CROSS SECTION OF THE LIBBY PRISON ESCAPE: 1: Streight's room. 2: Milroy's room. 3: Commandant's office. 4: Chickamauga room (upper). 5: Chickamauga room (lower). 6: Dining room. 7: Carpenter's shop (middle cellar). 8: Gettysburg room (upper). 9: Gettysburg room (lower). 10: Hospital room. 11: East or "Rat Hell" cellar. 12: South side Canal Street. 13: North side Carey Street. 14: Open lot. 15: Tunnel. 16: Fence. 17: Shed. 18: Kerr's warehouse. 19: Office James River Towing Co. 20: Gate. 21: Prisoners escaping. 22: West cellar.

digger, or sapper, had filled the box, he would tug on the rope as a signal for the others to pull it out and empty it, then he would pull it back in for another load. The others took the extra dirt and spread it out wherever the guards wouldn't notice it. Fortunately, the floors of the prison wards were already so filthy, so cluttered with mudcakes, straw, and debris that it wasn't very difficult to mix in the new dirt with the old.

Finally, after seventeen nights of digging (and one near miss when they dug upward too soon within sight of a guard station), Rose's workers completed the tunnel, coming up in a vacant lot out of sight of the prison. Some wanted to start climbing out right away, but Rose insisted they get rested up and organized for the next night. So on February 9, 1864, well after dark, the company of fifteen were ready to make their escape. There were thirty in all, as each digger was allowed to choose one companion to make the getaway with him. The hole was so tight that some men had to remove their clothes and push the bundle in front of them in order to squeeze through the narrow space. One of the highest-ranking officers invited to join the escape was Col. Abel Streight, the same officer who had been so successful in recruiting Alabama dissidents for the Union cavalry until he was captured and sent to Richmond in May 1863.

Rose's plan was to crawl through the tunnel in twos, with a few minutes separating each pair, so that men could disperse properly in town without calling too much attention to themselves. But before the last of the original thirty had gotten out of the brick hole, word spread all through the building that a tunnel escape was in progress. Several hundred prisoners crowded around the opening, trying to be the next one down the rope to the tunnel. At first, there was something of an orderly exit, but soon it became clear that not everyone there could get out before the cooks came in to start breakfast at 4:00 a.m. Before long, the crowd turned into a mob, as everyone tried to be the next one through the hole. Officers tried to assert their rank and older men their dignity, but it turned into a scrum in which the strongest man became the first in line.

In the middle of this melee, there was the clank of metal in the darkness across the cavernous room. Two prisoners came up and whispered hoarsely that the guards were coming. The mob pushing toward the escape hole now became a mob rushing away from it, as most headed for the staircase. One witness said the men were so tightly packed that you could lift your feet and still be carried along by the crush of the crowd. But just as everyone cleared away from the escape hole, the same two who had warned about the guards rushed over to the opening and started down the rope. The rascals had made the clanking noises themselves by rattling pots and pans, figuring that was their only chance to get to the front of the line. When the ruse was discovered, the mass of men rushed back over to the top of the ladder and started another free-for-all.

Even with all the commotion, no guards ever came in during the night to investigate. By the time the sky began to lighten, 109 prisoners had crawled through the hole and out into the chilly February air. It wasn't till roll call the next morning that the guards discovered anyone missing, much less 109 men. There was a great deal of confusion during the first count, as men called out "here" more than once, or changed places, or held up hats on sticks in the back row. Finally, the officer in charge made the prisoners walk by him one by one and discovered how many men could not be accounted for.

The guards questioned the remaining prisoners closely, but they couldn't find out from any of them what had happened. Even after a close inspection of the building, inside and out, they weren't able to find either the escape hole behind the latrine barrels or the exit hole in the adjoining lot. Eventually, the tunnel was discovered, and despite themselves, the guards couldn't help but admire what they called "The Great Yankee Wonder." Some of the guards in that ward were thrown into another Richmond prison, Castle Thunder, as Gen. John Winder assumed they must have been bribed to look the other way. (There may be something to this. Though he was not jailed, the officer in charge of counting the prisoners that morning was Erasmus Ross, Van Lew's covert agent.)

It was only after the mass escape that the truth came home that for a Union soldier on the run, all the Confederacy was one huge prison. At least half the escapees tried to head directly for the Federal lines near Williamsburg. But by then search parties were all over the city, and every Rebel soldier in Virginia knew he was supposed to be on the lookout for escaped prisoners. Rose himself made it to within sight of friendly campfires at Williamsburg before being apprehended. Others were picked up trying to wade waist-deep through the freezing waters of the Chickahominy Swamp. In the final tally, of the 109 who escaped on the night of February 9, 59 made it safely to Federal lines, 48 were recaptured, and 2 drowned trying to elude their pursuers.[16]

Once again, it was Van Lew's "underground railroad" that saved many of those who made it back to Federal lines. Soon after the escape, these were directed to hideouts all over the city and kept out of sight for days, sometimes weeks, until they could quietly leave the city. Van Lew's network took care of many of these arrangements, as it had done for so many small-scale escapes in the past. The night after the escape, Van Lew met with Abel Streight at one of the safe houses in Howard's Grove, north of the city. He was a husky, blond-haired man who seemed to her surprisingly robust for someone who had just crawled out of jail. With Streight was Maj. Bedan McDonald of Ohio, who struck her as an "honest, genial man." He showed Elizabeth an old chisel, much worn down from hard-handed use, that had been his digging tool. Van Lew offered to put it somewhere safe for him, but he replied that he'd rather take it along as a keepsake. (Both Streight and McDonald made it safely back to Union lines, and both survived the war. One can only assume that stubby chisel found a place of honor for many years in the McDonald household in Ohio.)[17]

Apart from her work with Union prisoners, Van Lew became an increasingly important source of information for Union generals in the eastern theater of the war. Early on, she established a line of communication between Richmond and the armies at Fort Monroe on the seacoast. She created a five-stage relay of messengers, beginning at her house on Church Hill, out to her family farm south of town, then along the James River, all the way to Federal lines. Coded messages were carried mainly by her servants, who called the least attention to themselves along the country roads. They sometimes carried messages in the hollowed-out soles of their work boots. Other times they carried baskets of eggs, with one egg emptied of its usual contents, containing instead tiny rolls of paper inserted through a small hole.

Having worked with several lower-echelon intelligence officers, Van Lew was contacted directly by Gen. Benjamin F. Butler, commanding the Army of the James, early in 1864. His first letter to her was delivered by one of his civilian spies, William Rowley. Dated January 18, 1864, the letter is addressed to "My Dear Aunt." It complains about Yankees stealing the mail, says that Aunt Mary is feeling much better, adding that Jennie sends her love. It is signed, "Yours affectionately, James Ap. Jones." However, when the letter was rubbed with lemon juice and held next to a candle, another message appeared. It thanked the reader for her patriotism and explained that the person bearing the message would tell her how to create invisible ink and show her to how to read letters that had been so prepared.

From that time on, Butler and Van Lew corresponded regularly. In a letter dated March 4, 1864, Butler becomes "Uncle Thomas," who offers innocuous remarks about Aunt Mary's health and about sisters quarreling over who has the prettiest baby. When lemon juice and heat were applied, a note appeared concerning weightier matters. It asks about ship movements in the Confederate Naval Yard at Richmond, about the possibility of an attack in North Carolina, and whether Van Lew has heard any talk of Richmond being evacuated. It also acknowledges previous information received and says matter-of-factly, "Arrests will be made."

It was a tip from Van Lew to Butler that led to the notorious and ill-fated Kilpatrick-Dahlgren cavalry raid in March 1864. Van Lew informed Butler that the Confederates were planning to send all Yankee prisoners out of Richmond and relocate them in Georgia. She suggested that Butler send a force of forty thousand to rescue the prisoners before they could be carried off. Butler recognized that as an unrealistic plan, thinking that if he could get forty thousand troops into Richmond, he might as well capture the city. Butler forwarded the information to Secretary of War Edwin M. Stanton, who conferred with Lincoln and then authorized a cavalry raid of thirty-five hundred troopers to be led by Gen. H. Judson Kilpatrick and Col. Ulric Dahlgren, the twenty-one-year-old son of Union Adm. John Dahlgren.

Forcing his way past Confederate outposts on the Rapidan River, Kilpatrick led the main body straight toward Richmond while Dahlgren took five hundred horsemen toward Goochland, thirty miles north of the Confederate capital. Kilpatrick reached the outskirts of Richmond but found the fortifications there too strong, and he did not have the element of surprise as he had hoped. (There were at least as many Confederate spies in Washington as there were Unionist spies in Richmond.) Kilpatrick withdrew to Federal lines, but Dahlgren lost contact with the main body, and his troopers were eventually run down by Confederate cavalry. Dahlgren himself was shot and killed in an ambush near King and Queen's Court House, thirty miles east of Richmond.

Already ill-conceived, the Kilpatrick-Dahlgren raid became infamous when Richmond authorities produced papers found on Dahlgren's body that called not only for freeing the prisoners but also for assassinating Jefferson Davis and his cabinet and setting the city ablaze. Union commanders denounced the orders as forgeries, and Dahlgren's father noted that Dahlgren's name was misspelled. (It is still unclear to this day whether the orders were genuine or counterfeit.)

Southern leaders were so outraged by Dahlgren's apparently barbaric intentions that Davis ordered him buried in an unmarked grave. Despite a secret night burial, one of Van Lew's servants was nearby to mark the spot. Perhaps feeling guilty that her message had helped instigate the poorly planned raid, Van Lew led a party herself in the dead of night to disinter Dahlgren's body and rebury it on her farm outside Richmond. She then sent a note through the lines to Admiral Dahlgren, saying, "Your son's body is safe, and will be returned after this unhappy war is over." Later, when tempers had cooled, Confederate officials agreed to return Colonel Dahlgren's body, only to find it had disappeared. Its location was a mystery to them until after the war.

Later in 1864 Van Lew began corresponding with Gen. George Gordon Meade, commanding the Army of the Potomac. Van Lew's code name in their exchange of messages was Babcock. Very little of this correspondence has survived, because, soon after the war, Van Lew asked the War Department to destroy all her dispatches. (She assumed, probably correctly, that her life could be in danger if it were known how extensive her spying activities had been.)

The only surviving specimen of the Van Lew–Meade correspondence, found among her papers, is a message from the general,

Ulric Dahlgren

HARPER'S WEEKLY

addressed to Babcock, asking which roads the Confederates were using to supply their armies around Fredericksburg. Her answer is not known. The choice of Babcock as a code name, though, turned out to be unlucky. Early in 1865 an unfortunate fellow by the name of Lemuel Babcock, a known Union sympathizer, was arrested and thrown into jail. Though he later escaped while being transferred to a prison farther south, Van Lew changed her code name soon afterward to Romona.[18]

When Ulysses S. Grant, general in chief of all Federal armies, established his headquarters at City Point early in 1865, he too established an almost daily correspondence with Van Lew. Using the same five-stage relay system along the James River, she sent him the daily Richmond newspapers in time for his breakfast, often sending along a rose or other fresh flowers from her garden. Van Lew answered whatever questions she could about Confederate gun emplacements, troop movements, ships coming and going, and the location of torpedoes (land and water mines). Grant found her information to be of the highest quality, which is not surprising: her information on troop strengths and movements came directly from her agent in the Confederate War Department and her maps of the Richmond defenses came directly from her agent in their army corps of engineers.

The long Federal siege of Petersburg finally ended in early April 1865. Jefferson Davis was sitting in a Sunday-morning church service on April 2 when he received a telegram from Robert E. Lee saying the Confederate government should evacuate the capital that very day. Davis, his cabinet officials, and the government archives all took trains south to Danville that evening; Lee's army veered to the west. Before evacuating the city, Confederate soldiers set fire to the tobacco warehouses along the waterfront, not wanting all that valuable merchandise to fall into the hands of the Yankees. But a high wind carried the flames toward the city center, engulfing hundreds of downtown buildings. The streets were full of people, some dazed and panic-stricken, others drunk and in the mood for plunder.

From her home on the hill, Van Lew watched the spectacle with horror and fascination. In her journal she wrote: "The constant explosion of shells, the blowing up of the gunboats, and of the powder magazine, seemed to jar the earth and lend a mighty language to the scene. All nature trembled at the work of arbitrary power, the consummation of the wrongs of years."[19]

When Federal soldiers arrived in the city about sunup, they set to work putting out fires and stopping the looters. Van Lew observed the jubilation with which black people welcomed the Northern soldiers: "There were wild bursts of welcome from the negroes. . . . No wonder the walls of our city were swaying, the heart of our city a flaming altar, as this mighty work was done. . . . The wonderful deliverance wrought out for the negro; they feel but cannot tell you; but when eternity shall unknot the record of time, you will see written for them by the Almighty their unpenned stories, then to be read before a listening universe."[20]

While Union forces were still coming into the city, Van Lew went to a hiding place and unpacked a huge flag, nine feet tall and twenty feet long, and ran it up the flagstaff of her home. It was Old Glory, the first U.S. flag to fly over the city of Richmond after its fall. In the city, people could see the Stars and Stripes as it unfurled in the smoky morning light. Some cheered, but others muttered and began to walk up to Church Hill. They jumped over the stone wall and stood amid the manicured gardens, shouting and jeering, demanding that the flag should come down—or else. Out came a little woman dressed all in black. She stared intently at the crowd until they fell silent. Then, in a shrill voice, she told them that whatever they did to her house, the Yankees would do to theirs. Recognizing some faces in the crowd, she pointed a trembling finger. "I know you! And you! And you!" she declared sternly. There was a long silence, then one by one the crowd headed back down the lawn and dispersed.

That same morning a haggard-looking young man arrived at the Van Lew mansion seeking protection. It was Erasmus Ross, the erstwhile prison guard at Libby. The prisoners having been released during the night, he feared he had played his part too well. He was afraid that if any of them saw him on the street, they would hang him or shoot him on the spot. So he stayed close to Van Lew, knowing she could vouch for him and explain it was he who had helped many of the Federal officers get free.

As Grant entered the city, he was aware of the danger to Van Lew and her property. He sent one of his aides, Col. Ely S. Parker, to make sure she was afforded military protection. When a Federal detachment arrived at her home, however, she was not there. Not knowing how much longer the war was going to last, Van Lew had taken her carriage to the burned-out capitol to see what valuable documents had survived the fire.

A few months after the fall of Richmond, Grant and his wife, Julia, paid a personal call on Elizabeth Van Lew at her home. They sat on the piazza and drank lemonade, and Grant told Elizabeth that she supplied the most valuable information he had received from Richmond during the war. He presented her with his calling card, which became one of her most prized possessions down the years.

By war's end, the Union had been preserved, but the Van Lews were ruined. They still owned the house on Church Hill, but the family fortune had all gone to buying supplies for Union prisoners or for financing the spy network. In 1867, Gen. George H. Sharpe, head of the Bureau of Military Information (soon to become the Secret Service), wrote a long, highly commendatory letter about Van Lew, detailing all her services to the Union during the war and requesting that the army repay her fifteen thousand dollars. This request was not acted upon, but when Grant became president in 1868, one of his first official acts was to appoint Elizabeth Van Lew as postmaster general for the city of Richmond. This was probably intended as a sinecure, to ensure her an income of at least twelve hundred dollars a year. But she took the job quite seriously and applied herself every bit as much as she had to her war activities. She served throughout the eight years of Grant's two terms, one of the few women in all of nineteenth-century America to hold that high a position in the civil service.

Van Lew lost the job when Rutherford B. Hayes became president, despite Grant's personal recommendation that she be retained. It is some measure of her administrative ability that even former Confederate Gen. W. C. Wickham wrote her a letter of commendation, saying, "Your management of the Richmond post office has, I believe, been eminently satisfactory to the community here."[21] After several years of clerical jobs, and after selling off the family's silver, china, and other valuables, the Van Lews were again on the verge of financial ruin. Eventually, a group of Union veterans, many of whom remembered her kindness and generosity to them at Libby, established an annuity for Van Lew, guaranteeing her a modest but reliable income.

In general, though, the postwar years were difficult ones for the Van Lews. Their Union sympathies had always been well known, and more and more, her neighbors learned that Elizabeth had done much more during the war than just look after Yankee prisoners. The Van Lews were virtually alone, except for their house servants. Adults shunned Elizabeth, and children called her a "Yankee" and a "witch." But her convictions never wavered. In her journal, she wrote, "From the time I knew right from wrong, it was my sad privilege to differ in many things from the opinions and principles of my locality."[22]

As she had all her life, Elizabeth in her later years still referred to her fellow Virginians as "our people," but she made no apologies for her espionage activities during the war. As she explained in her journal, "A person cannot be called a spy for serving their country within its recognized boundaries. Am I now to be branded a spy by my own country for which I was willing to lay down my life?" In another journal entry, she complained that even Northerners seemed not to understand her: "Here I am called Traitor, farther North a Spy—instead of the honored name of Faithful."[23]

When Elizabeth's mother, Eliza, died in 1875, Elizabeth wrote that there weren't even enough family friends to serve as pallbearers. Her later years were lonely ones, brightened mainly by the presence of her beloved niece, daughter of her brother John (the same little girl who knew how to keep a secret).

Elizabeth died in 1900 at the age of eighty-one, and her death was little noted in Richmond. But even though a generation had passed since the war, there were those in the North who remembered what the Van Lews had done for their husbands, sons, and brothers. Hearing that her grave in Richmond was unmarked, the family of a Union officer, Paul Joseph Revere of Boston, decided to have a monument placed over her burial place.

Revere, great-grandson of the Revolutionary War hero, had been imprisoned in Richmond in 1862 and placed for a while on death row. He remembered vividly how Elizabeth Van Lew had offered him kindness and hope in that grim hour. Revere was exchanged at the end of the year and killed at the battle of Gettysburg the following July. But his family knew perfectly well that soldiers are not the only ones who make terrible sacrifices in wartime. Over Van Lew's grave they placed a marker that can still be seen today in Richmond's Shockoe Cemetery:

ELIZABETH VAN LEW
1818–1900
She risked everything that is dear to man—friends, fortune, comfort,
health, life itself, all for one absorbing desire of her heart—that slavery
might be abolished and the Union preserved.

CONCLUSION

WHO LOST THE CAUSE?

HISTORIANS AGREE THAT THERE were a number of large-scale military engagements in America between 1861 and 1865, as well as widespread civil unrest. But beyond that, the debates begin: What should the conflict be called? What were its chief causes? Why did the North prevail? Most elusive of all, what did it all mean? There have been more than ten thousand books written about the Civil War in the last century and a half, and yet none of these questions has been answered to everyone's satisfaction.

The usual name for the conflict, the Civil War, was the one most commonly used on both sides during the war. This was the term used by Southern generals such as Robert E. Lee and James Longstreet as well as the Richmond newspapers. But this term was later criticized as misleading, since there were not two warring factions seeking to gain control of the nation's government. Rather the war came because one section of the country attempted to create a new republic, and the other section refused to allow one nation to split into two. Some Southerners prefer to call the conflict the War Between the States, as it involved a fairly well-defined struggle of eleven Southern states to withdraw from their union with the remaining twenty-three Northern and Western states. This name has its merits, so long as one acknowledges the truth of William W. Freehling's remark that the conflict could just as aptly be called the War Within the States.[1]

The U.S. government's official name for the conflict is the War of the Rebellion. Of course, this name has little appeal for many Southerners, as it makes the epic struggle sound more like an insurrection, on par with Bacon's Rebellion or the Whiskey Rebellion. (In general, it would seem that successful revolts, such as those in America, France, and Russia, achieve the status of revolutions. Unsuccessful revolts are usually consigned the status of rebellions.) Some Southerners call the conflict the War of Northern Aggression, on the theory that Southern states had a constitutional right to secede and the federal government had no constitutional right to interfere by force. On the other end of the spectrum is a Northern name that includes its own theory, the Slaveholders' Rebellion, a term preferred by abolitionists such as Frederick Douglass.[2] All such names have their particular advocates, but obviously a more value-neutral name, such as the Civil War, is most likely to continue in popular usage.

On a more scholarly level, the perennial question is, why did one side prevail over the other? Even the way one phrases the question is highly significant. In 1960, a number of distinguished historians gave their answers to the question *Why the North Won the Civil War*. In 1986 came another set of answers, offered under a title that created a whole different emphasis: *Why the South Lost the Civil War*. Then came *Why the Confederacy Lost* (1992), a crucial rephrasing to emphasize that the South and the Confederacy are not interchangeable terms. The Confederates certainly lost a war in 1865. But African Americans in the South did not come out of the conflict feeling they had lost a war. Nor did west Virginians, east Tennesseans, or tens of thousands of other mountain folk. Nor did individual Southerners such as George H. Thomas or Elizabeth Van Lew.

That the Confederacy failed is indisputable, but the *reasons* it failed continue to be very much disputed. In his farewell address to his troops after the surrender at Appomattox, Robert E. Lee explained that "The Army of Northern Virginia has been compelled to yield to overwhelming numbers and resources." That theme has often been echoed down the years, summarized effectively by Richard Current in *Why the North Won the Civil War*, where he points out how the Northern states had more than twice the population, three times the railroad mileage, and nine times the industrial output. Current concludes: "Surely, in view of the disparity of resources, it would have taken a miracle . . . to enable the South to win. As usual, God was on the side of the heaviest battalions."[3]

Yet if all it takes to win wars is material superiority, then why did the British fail to prevent American independence and why did America fail to achieve its objectives in Vietnam? Another prominent Civil War general, Joseph E. Johnston, emphatically rejected the notion that the Confederate cause was doomed from the outset. He said that Southerners had *not* been "guilty of the high crime of undertaking a war without the means of waging it successfully."[4] Johnston, along with his colleague P. G. T. Beauregard, suggested that the blame lay more with failures of leadership in the Richmond administration. This view has often been repeated, perhaps most emphatically by David M. Potter in *Why the North Won the Civil War*, where he catalogs Jefferson's many failures as a civilian administrator and military strategist. Contrasting these with Lincoln's "superlative qualities of leadership," Potter goes so far as to say, "If the Union and the Confederacy had exchanged presidents with one another, the Confederacy might have won its independence."[5]

As their title suggests, the authors of *Why the South Lost* (1986) change the emphasis from Northern superiority, in leadership or material resources, to Southern vulnerability, especially the deterioration of its civilian morale. Documenting how declining military fortunes contributed to an even more decisive decline in civilian support for the war, *Why the South Lost* echoes the famous pronouncement of southern historian E. Merton Coulter. In his classic study *The Confederate States of America* (1950), Merton concluded that the South lost the war because its "people did not will hard enough and long enough to win."[6]

More recently, historians have insisted that the terms *South* and *Confederacy* should not be used interchangeably. Richard Current, in *Lincoln's Loyalists* (1992), describes the more than one hundred thousand Southerners, three-quarters of them from the mountains, who either joined the Union army outright or stayed home and undermined the Confederacy from behind the battle lines. Joseph T. Glatthaar has shown how the migration of half a million blacks, from Southern slaves to Northern soldiers and laborers, played a major role in the outcome of the war. Glatthaar concludes, "Free and slave, [blacks] tipped the balance of power squarely in favor of the North."[7] Other historians have argued that the common people of the South never wholeheartedly supported the war, and that their support fell off drastically once it became clear how much they were expected to sacrifice in what they increasingly considered "a rich man's war and a poor man's fight." William W. Freehling sums up the work of recent social historians by stating the case bluntly: "Half of the Slave South's population favored the enemy or favored no one."[8]

Some military historians have clearly lost patience with the growing accumulation of social analysis about why the Confederacy lost the war. In one such discussion, historian Thomas Connelly proclaimed irritably, "Dammit, they lost on the battlefield."[9] And that is certainly true, as far as it goes. But how many battles might have gone differently if the South had been able to draw more fully on its human and material resources? (Or if the North had not begun drawing more and more heavily on Southern resources?) What if Lee's outnumbered armies at Second Bull Run and Chancellorsville had not just been able to drive the Federal armies back but to annihilate them? What if western commanders had had one or two extra corps available at the battles of Shiloh or Stones River, battles in which Southern armies were strong enough to drive their enemies to the edge of destruction, but not strong enough to force them over that edge? Perhaps most important, could Grant have sustained the staggering losses of his eleven-month overland campaign of 1864–65 without the constant influx of replacement soldiers, more than one hundred thousand of them black Southerners?

Of course, it has been cogently argued that several pivotal battles, especially in the West, were lost because of critical lapses in military leadership. But the North certainly had its share of military blunders and blunderers (the B team of Banks, Burnside, and Butler comes readily to mind). The North seemed better able to absorb military disasters because of its ever-increasing advantage in numbers.

One might state the case in terms of simple arithmetic. Apart from its industrial and military advantages, the North began the war with a population of about twenty-one million. The South began with a population of about nine million, 40 percent of it black. To win the war, the North was obliged to conquer the South, not only its vast territory and its armies, but also the will of its people to resist. In the common military wisdom of the time, attackers should enjoy at least a two-to-one advantage, if not a three-to-one advantage, in order to even have a chance of overcoming prepared defenses. In terms of overall population, the North had its two-to-one advantage, but that raw ratio certainly left a great deal of room for doubt. The North never mobilized more than half its men of military age, and it had perhaps as many as three hundred thousand draft evaders and deserters during the war.[10]

But the subtractions on the Southern side would seem to have been much more decisive. Every Southerner who worked or fought for the North must be counted twice, one extra man, or woman, for the Federals, one fewer for the Confederates. The largest single subtraction would be the half million slaves who crossed into the North, of whom more than two hundred thousand bore arms against their former masters. Then come more than one hundred thousand white Southerners, mostly from the mountains. More difficult to tabulate, but certainly deserving consideration, were those who refused to serve, who deserted the army, or who actively resisted government officials on the home front. Some of these latter dissidents might also be counted twice, since they themselves did not serve, and they also tied down large numbers of other Southerners as home guards, civilian marshals, or conscription officers who might otherwise have been available for duty on the battlefront.

In the long run, these subtractions were more than the Confederacy could afford. Southerners today can take pride in their attempted "Second Revolution," remembering well the gallantry, military finesse, perseverance, and resiliency of the Confederate soldiers and civilians through four long years of sacrifice, hardship, privation and long-odds battles. But as the preceding chapters suggest, the Lost Cause may ultimately have been lost because there were just too many Southerners who, for a variety of reasons, were not fully committed, or not at all committed, to the cause.

Yet this book is not about victors or vanquished but about individual lives. Fortunate are they who live in times when one's allegiances are all aligned, when country, state, community, and family all speak with one voice. But when the times are out of joint, as they most certainly were in the years 1861–1865, individuals are forced to choose from among a host of competing loyalties. And out of their choices emerge their stories, their own understandings of that elusive term *freedom*. Regardless of one's own values, sympathies, or heritage, these human stories fascinate and illuminate, and they continue to cast new light on the meaning of the American story.

NOTES

Full bibliographic information can be found in the Bibliography

Introduction

1. Dodge, *Battle of Atlanta*, 114.
2. Current, *Loyalists*, 133, 197.
3. Pressly, *Americans Interpret Their Civil War*, 81.
4. Foote, *Fort Sumter to Perryville*, 58–59.
5. Donald, "Died of Democracy," 86.
6. Ford, "James Louis Petigru," 182.
7. Quarles, *Negro in the Civil War*, xiv.
8. Current, *Loyalists*, 133, 197.
9. Tatum, *Disloyalty in the Confederacy*; Current, *Loyalists*.
10. See Dyer, *Secret Yankees*.
11. See Degler, *The Other South*.

Chapter 1: A Clash of Values in the Antebellum South

1. The exchange of toasts: Cole, *Presidency of Andrew Jackson*, 61; Bowers, *Party Battles of the Jackson Period*, 102–3.
2. Berkin, *A Brilliant Solution*, 16.
3. Ibid., 15–16; Stampp, "The Concept of a Perpetual Union," 3, notes that article 13 asserts that "the Union shall be perpetual." This comes close to contradicting the first three articles of the document, which stress a league of friendship among the states. The evidence provided by Berkin shows that, in practice, it was the first three articles that set the tone for the 1780s, not article 13.
4. Ellis, *Union at Risk*, 48.
5. Ibid., 78.
6. Ibid.
7. Responses of Southern states to nullification: Ames, *State Documents on Federal Relations*, quoted in Degler, *Other South*, 104–5.
8. Ellis, *Union at Risk*, 83.
9. Ibid., 133, 159.
10. Ibid., 91.

11. Ibid., 79.

12. Freehling, *Secessionists at Bay*, 17–18.

13. Ibid., 18; Freehling, "The Divided South," 133, 137.

14. Freehling, *Secessionists at Bay*, 4.

15. Basler, *Collected Works of Abraham Lincoln*, 4:146; Catton, *Coming Fury*, 113.

16. Degler, *Other South*, 18–20.

17. Lerner, *Grimké Sisters*, 18.

18. Ceplair, *Public Years of Sarah and Angelina Grimké*, 333, 336.

19. Ibid., xvi.

20. Lerner, *Grimké Sisters*, 127–28.

21. Ceplair, *Public Years of Sarah and Angelina Grimké*, 26.

22. Ibid., 28–29.

23. Lerner, *Grimké Sisters*, 8.

24. Degler, *Other South*, 21.

25. Freehling, *Secessionists at Bay*, 159.

26. Ibid., 158.

27. Childs, *McDonogh*, 69.

28. Ibid., 84.

29. Ibid., 70.

30. Ibid., 87.

31. Ibid., 144–45.

32. Degler, *Other South*, 46.

Chapter 2: Crossover Soldiers and Their Battles

1. Berkin, *Solution*, 18.

2. McPherson, *For Cause and Comrades*, 15.

3. Davis, *Gray Fox*, 16–17.

4. Robertson, *Stonewall Brigade*, 146.

5. Lewis, *Farragut*, 11.

6. Cleaves, *Rock of Chickamauga*, 5–6.

7. Tucker, "Thomas," 29.

8. Cleaves, *Rock of Chickamauga*, 63.

9. Ibid., 65.

10. Ibid., 69.

11. Ibid., 71.

12. Van Horne, *George H. Thomas*, 16.

13. Cleaves, *Rock of Chickamauga*, 73.

14. Tucker, "Thomas," 35. Van Horne quotes the rumored remark as, "He is a Virginian; let him wait" (*George H. Thomas*, 56).

15. Van Horne, *George H. Thomas*, 87.

16. Ibid., 88.

17. Cozzens, *No Better Place to Die*, 19.

18. Tucker, "Thomas," 33.

19. Catton, *Never Call Retreat*, 47.

20. Van Horne, *George H. Thomas*, 96.

21. Cleaves, *Rock of Chickamauga*, 182.

22. Tucker, "Thomas," 31.

23. Catton, *Terrible Swift Sword*, 63–64.

24. Current, *Loyalists*, 133, 197.

Chapter 3: West Virginia: The State That Seceded from the Confederacy

1. Davis, *Rise and Fall of the Confederate Government*, 2:306, quoted in Riccards, "Lincoln and the Political Question," 566.

2. Freehling, *Secessionists at Bay*, 7.

3. Ibid., 165.

4. Drake, *History of Appalachia*, 51.

5. Freehling, *Secessionists at Bay*, 165.

6. Ibid., 170.

7. Ibid., 173.

8. Rice, *West Virginia*, 113.

9. Ibid., 113.

10. Current, *Loyalists*, 6–7.

11. Riccards, "Lincoln and the Political Question," 533; Ambler, *Francis H. Pierpont*, 94.

12. Lee, *Recollections and Papers*, 51, quoted in Catton, *Terrible Swift Sword*, 52.

13. Current, *Loyalists*, 6–7.

14. Oates, *With Malice Toward None*, 103.

15. Donald, *Lincoln's Herndon*, 52.

16. Oates, *With Malice Toward None*, 103.

17. Ibid., 115.

18. Current, *Loyalists*, 11.

19. Ibid.

20. Ibid., 13.

21. Guelzo, *Lincoln*, 430.

22. Oates, *With Malice Toward None*, 416.

23. Current, *Lincoln Nobody Knows*, 277.

24. Current, *Loyalists*, 18.

25. Lowe, "Francis Harrison Pierpont," 35.

26. Ambler, *Francis H. Pierpont*, 84.

27. Ibid., 91.
28. Riccards, "Lincoln and the Political Question," 7.
29. Ibid., 5.
30. Ibid., 6.
31. Ibid., 554–56.
32. Ibid., 557.
33. Ibid.
34. Current, *Loyalists*, 23.
35. Lowe, "Francis Harrison Pierpont," 45.

Chapter 4: Tennessee Tories

1. Current, *Loyalists*, 15.
2. Drake, *History of Appalachia*, 62–63.
3. Coulter, *Brownlow*, 157.
4. Ibid., 147.
5. Ibid., 157.
6. Ibid., 149.
7. Patton, *Unionism and Reconstruction in Tennessee*, 24–25.
8. Coulter, *Brownlow*, 150.
9. Connelly, *Civil War Tennessee*, 8.
10. Bryan, "Tories Amidst Rebels," 5.
11. Current, *Loyalists*, 29.
12. Ibid., 31.
13. Humphrey, *That Damned Brownlow*, 233.
14. Current, *Loyalists*, 33.
15. Fisher, *War at Every Door*, 54.
16. Coulter, *Brownlow*, 170.
17. Current, *Loyalists*, 18.
18. Fisher, *War at Every Door*, 58; Coulter, *Brownlow*, 174.
19. Patton, *Unionism and Reconstruction in Tennessee*, 61.
20. Kelly, "Brownlow, Part 1," 33.
21. Ibid., 26.
22. McKenzie, *One South or Many?* 74.
23. Kelly, "Brownlow, Part 1," 35.
24. Ibid., 27.
25. Ash, *Secessionists and Other Scoundrels*, 3.
26. Patton, *Unionism and Reconstruction in Tennessee*, 76.
27. Kelly, "Brownlow, Part 1," 27.
28. Coulter, *Brownlow*, 91.
29. Ibid., 137.

30. Kelly, "Brownlow, Part 1," 28.

31. Ibid., 29.

32. Ibid.

33. Ibid.

34. Coulter, *Brownlow*, 159; Kelly, "Brownlow, Part 1," 31.

35. Kelly, "Brownlow, Part 1," 34.

36. Patton, *Unionism and Reconstruction in Tennessee*, 56.

37. Coulter, *Brownlow*, 95, 105.

38. Ibid., 95.

39. Ibid., 98.

40. Ibid., 104.

41. Ibid., 102.

42. Ibid.

43. Ibid., 107.

44. McKenzie, *One South or Many?* 79.

45. Coulter, *Brownlow*, 139.

46. Patton, *Unionism and Reconstruction in Tennessee*, 54.

47. Coulter, *Brownlow*, 160, 187.

48. Ibid., 181–82.

49. Humphrey, *That Damned Brownlow*, 238.

50. Coulter, *Brownlow*, 174; Humphrey, *That Damned Brownlow*, 246.

51. Humphrey, *That Damned Brownlow*, 240.

52. Ibid., 241.

53. Coulter, *Brownlow*, 200.

54. Ibid., 201.

55. Humphrey, *That Damned Brownlow*, 255.

56. Ibid., 257.

57. Coulter, *Brownlow*, 181–82; Groce, *Mountain Rebels*, 50.

58. Groce, *Mountain Rebels*, 6.

59. Bryan, "Tories Amidst Rebels," 6.

60. Current, *Loyalists*, 47.

61. Ibid.

62. Ellis, *Thrilling Adventures*, 13.

63. Ibid., 27.

64. Ibid., 360.

65. Ibid., 146.

66. Ibid., 89.

67. Ibid., 67.

68. Ibid., 166, 185–88.

69. Ibid., 249–50.

70. Connelly, *Civil War Tennessee*, 8.
71. Bryan, "Tories Amidst Rebels," 10.
72. Ibid., 20.
73. Ibid.
74. Humphrey, *That Damned Brownlow*, 267.
75. Kelly, "Brownlow, Part 2," 59.
76. Ibid., 172.
77. Hall, "Shelton Laurel Massacre," 20.
78. Ellis, *Thrilling Adventures*, 381–82.
79. Fisher, *War at Every Door*, 98.
80. Ellis, *Thrilling Adventures*, 23.
81. Patton, *Unionism and Reconstruction in Tennessee*, 63.
82. Bryan, "Tories Amidst Rebels," 22.

Chapter 5: Mossbacks, Deserters, and Guerrillas

1. McPherson, *Battle Cry of Freedom*, vii. McPherson observes that both sides professed to be fighting for freedom.
2. Gallagher, *Confederate War*, 31; Escott, *After Secession,* 127. Desertion figures are not exact, as some deserted more than once while others were counted as deserters temporarily, later returning permanently to the ranks.
3. Gallagher, *Confederate War*, 28.
4. Lonn, *Desertion During the Civil War*, 6.
5. Current, *Loyalists*, 8.
6. Groce, *Mountain Rebels*, 90; Fleming, *Civil War and Reconstructionism in Alabama*, 102.
7. Lonn, *Desertion During the Civil War*, 8–9.
8. Ibid., 12–13.
9. Bardolph, "Confederate Dilemma," 67.
10. Wiley, *Plain People of the Confederacy*, viii.
11. Escott, *After Secession*, 95.
12. Ibid., 116.
13. Horst, *Mennonites in the Confederacy*, 15; Wright, *Conscientious Objectors in the Civil War*, 167.
14. Lonn, *Desertion During the Civil War*, 14.
15. Ibid., 29.
16. Ibid.
17. Escott, *After Secession*, 126.
18. Ibid., 127.
19. Lonn, *Desertion During the Civil War*, 124.

20. All of the narrative description on cave dwellers is taken from Dodge, "Cave-Dwellers of the Confederacy," 514–21.

21. See Auman and Scarboro, "Heroes of America in Civil War North Carolina," 327–63; Hamilton, "Heroes of America," 10–19.

22. Fleming, *Civil War and Reconstructionism in Alabama*, 111.

23. Hoole, *Alabama Tories*, 10.

24. Thompson, *"Free State of Winston,"* 19.

25. Ibid., 22.

26. Ibid.

27. Ibid., 23.

28. Ibid., 23–24.

29. Ibid., 25.

30. Ibid., 25–26.

31. Ibid., 20.

32. Fleming, *Civil War and Reconstructionism in Alabama*, 111.

33. Thompson, *"Free State of Winston,"* 9.

34. Ibid., 5–6.

35. Ibid., 3.

36. Ibid.

37. Ibid., 3–4.

38. Hoole, *Alabama Tories*, 11.

39. Thompson, *"Free State of Winston,"* 4.

40. Ibid., 47.

41. Fleming, *Civil War and Reconstructionism in Alabama*, 102.

42. Thompson, *"Free State of Winston,"* 111.

43. Hoole, *Alabama Tories*, 14.

44. Thompson, *"Free State of Winston,"* 52.

45. Hoole, *Alabama Tories*, 6.

46. Thompson, *"Free State of Winston,"* 59–60.

47. Moore, *History of Alabama and Her People*, 430–31, quoted in ibid., 71.

48. Leverett, *Legend of the Free State of Jones*, 3–4.

49. Ibid., 11.

50. Ibid., 87.

51. Ibid., 5–6.

52. Ibid., 6.

53. Bynum, *Free State of Jones*, 48.

54. Leverett, *Legend of the Free State of Jones*, 39.

55. Bynum, *Free State of Jones*, 98.

56. Ibid., 100.

57. Leverett, *Legend of the Free State of Jones*, 56.

58. Bynum, *Free State of Jones*, 101, 104.
59. Leverett, *Legend of the Free State of Jones*, 57.
60. Bynum, *Free State of Jones*, 104.
61. Ibid.
62. Ibid.
63. Ibid., 109, 123.
64. Ibid., 106.
65. Ibid., 105.
66. Ibid., 106.
67. Ibid., 112.
68. Ibid.
69. Ibid., 112–13.
70. Leverett, *Legend of the Free State of Jones*, xii.
71. Castel, "Guerrilla War," 26.
72. Ibid., 36.
73. Bynum, *Free State of Jones*, 98.
74. Ibid., 98–99.
75. Ibid., 96.
76. Ibid., 124.
77. Leverett, *Legend of the Free State of Jones*, 114.
78. Bailey, "Defiant Unionists," 210.
79. Freehling, *South vs. the South*, 4.
80. Tatum, *Disloyalty in the Confederacy*, 49–50.
81. Bailey, "Defiant Unionists," 225.
82. Silverman, "Stars, Bars, and Foreigners," 277.
83. Ibid.
84. Bailey, "In the Far Corner of the Confederacy," 222.
85. Bailey, "Defiant Unionists," 214.
86. Williams, *With the Border Ruffians*, 232.
87. Bailey, "Defiant Unionists," 214.
88. Ibid., 218.
89. *Official Records*, ser. 1, vol. 9, chap. 21, 615.
90. Lonn, *Foreigners in the Confederacy*, 425.

Chapter 6: "The Wolf Has Come": The Battle for Indian Territory

1. Clark, "Opothleyahola and the Creeks During the Civil War," 52.
2. Debo, *Road to Disappearance*, 143.
3. Wood, *American Revolution*, 6.
4. Josephy, *500 Nations*, 213.
5. McLoughlin, *After the Trail of Tears*, 192.

6. Debo, *Road to Disappearance*, 147.

7. Downey, "The Blue, the Gray, and the Red," 9.

8. Bearss, "The Civil War Comes to Indian Territory," 10.

9. Ibid., 15.

10. Josephy, *500 Nations*, 323.

11. Meserve, "Chief," 449.

12. Bearss, "The Civil War Comes to Indian Territory," 27; Clark, "Opothleya-hola and the Creeks During the Civil War," 57.

13. Bearss, "The Civil War Comes to Indian Territory," 28.

14. Ibid., 30.

15. Ibid., 32.

16. Ibid., 35.

17. Ibid., 36.

18. Ibid., 38.

19. Ibid., 39.

20. Ibid.

21. Trickett, "The Civil War in Indian Territory," 66.

22. Meserve, "Chief," 442.

Chapter 7: Southern Slaves Turned Union Soldiers

1. McPherson, *Negro's Civil War*, 236.

2. Ibid., 244.

3. Litwack, *Been in the Storm So Long*, 37.

4. Freehling, *Secessionists at Bay*, 59, 77.

5. Litwack, "Many Thousands Gone," 55.

6. Bowman, *Civil War: Day by Day*, 10.

7. Freehling, *Secessionists at Bay*, 78.

8. Blassingame, *Slave Community*, 206.

9. Ibid., 208.

10. Litwack, *Been in the Storm So Long*, 13–14.

11. Quarles, *Negro in the Civil War*, xiv.

12. McPherson, *Negro's Civil War*, 143.

13. Freehling, *South vs. the South*, 27.

14. Quarles, *Negro in the Civil War*, 58.

15. Ibid., 59–60.

16. Ibid., 60.

17. Ibid.

18. Trudeau, *Like Men of War*, 62.

19. Litwack, *Been in the Storm So Long*, 59.

20. Wiley, *Plain People of the Confederacy*, 74.

21. Quarles, *Negro in the Civil War*, xv.

22. Wiley, *Plain People of the Confederacy*, 86.

23. Freehling, *South vs. the South*, 143; Litwack, *Been in the Storm So Long*, 32.

24. Sutcliffe, *Mighty Rough Times*, 63.

25. Wiley, *Plain People of the Confederacy*, 72.

26. McPherson, *Negro's Civil War*, 150.

27. Ibid., 147.

28. Ibid., 150.

29. Ibid., 152.

30. Quarles, *Negro in the Civil War*, 54–55.

31. Ibid., 27–28.

32. Ibid., 29.

33. Basler, *Collected Works of Abraham Lincoln*, 5:357, 423.

34. McPherson, *Negro's Civil War*, 163.

35. Trudeau, *Like Men of War*, 14.

36. Ibid., 6.

37. Boatner, *Civil War Dictionary*, 859.

38. Quarles, *Negro in the Civil War*, 46.

39. Trudeau, *Like Men of War*, 16.

40. Cornish, *Sable Arm*, 85–86.

41. McPherson, *Negro's Civil War*, 166.

42. Ibid., 167.

43. Ibid., 167–68.

44. Litwack, *Been in the Storm So Long*, 51.

45. Uya, *From Slavery to Public Service*, 20.

46. Quarles, "Abduction of the 'Planter,'" 8.

47. Ibid.

48. Ibid.

49. Uya, *From Slavery to Public Service*, 22–23.

50. Litwack, *Been in the Storm So Long*, 51.

51. Christopher, *Black Americans in Congress*, 42.

52. Uya, *From Slavery to Public Service*, vii.

53. McPherson, *Negro's Civil War*, 169.

54. Ibid., 172.

55. Trudeau, *Like Men of War*, 32.

56. McPherson, *Negro's Civil War*, 194; Litwack, *Been in the Storm So Long*, 98.

57. Davis, *Rebels and Yankees*, 60.

58. McPherson, *Negro's Civil War*, 192.

59. Ibid., 185.

60. Trudeau, *Like Men of War*, 58.

61. Ibid., 47.
62. McPherson, *Negro's Civil War*, 187.
63. Litwack, *Been in the Storm So Long*, 101.
64. Ibid., 99.
65. McPherson, *Negro's Civil War*, 181.
66. Ibid., 222.
67. Ibid., 182.
68. Ibid., 237.
69. Quarles, *Negro in the Civil War*, 199.

Chapter 8: The Distaff Side of Dissent

1. Hoole, *Alabama Tories*, 7.
2. Faust, "Altars of Sacrifice," 180.
3. Rable, "'Missing in Action,'" 135.
4. Faust, "Altars of Sacrifice," 185–87.
5. Rable, *Civil Wars*, 93.
6. Faust, "Altars of Sacrifice," 196; Escott, *After Secession*, 128.
7. Chesnut, *Diary*, 512.
8. Faust, "Altars of Sacrifice," 195.
9. Ibid., 198.
10. Ibid., 199.
11. Ryan, *Yankee Spy in Richmond*, 63.
12. Ibid., 33.
13. Ibid., 37.
14. Ibid., 137.
15. Hesseltine, *Civil War Prisons*, 115.
16. Ryan, *Yankee Spy in Richmond*, 62.
17. Ibid., 62–63.
18. Elizabeth R. Varon questions whether Van Lew ever used the code name Babcock since another Federal spy was already using that name. See Varon, *Southern Lady, Yankee Spy*, 112–13.
19. Ryan, *Yankee Spy in Richmond*, 105.
20. Ibid., 106.
21. Ibid., 20.
22. Varon, *Southern Lady, Yankee Spy*, 153.
23. Ryan, *Yankee Spy in Richmond*, 22.

Conclusion: Who Lost the Cause?

1. Freehling, *South vs. the South*, 57.
2. Pressly, *Americans Interpret Their Civil War*, 67.

3. Current, "God and the Strongest Battalions," 22.

4. McPherson, "American Victory, American Defeat," 22.

5. Potter, "Jefferson Davis and the Political Factors in the Confederate Defeat," 101–2, 112.

6. Coulter, *Confederate States of America*, 566.

7. Glatthaar, "Black Glory, 138.

8. Freehling, *South vs. the South*, 157.

9. Wakelyn, *Confederates Against the Confederacy*, xv.

10. McPherson, "American Victory, American Defeat," 27; Gallagher, *Confederate War*, 31.

BIBLIOGRAPHY

Abel, Annie Heloise. *The American Indian in the Civil War.* 1919. Reprint, Lincoln: University of Nebraska Press, 1992.

Abzug, Robert H. *New Perspectives on Race and Slavery in America.* Lexington: University Press of Kentucky, 1986.

Ambler, Charles H. *Francis H. Pierpont: Union War Governor of Virginia and Father of West Virginia.* Chapel Hill: University of North Carolina Press, 1937.

Anderson, Charles C. *Fighting by Southern Federals.* New York: Neale, 1912.

Ash, Stephen V. *When the Yankees Came: Conflict and Chaos in the Occupied South, 1861–1865.* Chapel Hill: University of North Carolina Press, 1995.

———, ed. *Secessionists and Other Scoundrels: Selections from Parson Brownlow's Book.* Baton Rouge: Louisiana State University Press, 1999.

Auman, William T., and David D. Scarboro. "The Heroes of America in Civil War North Carolina." *North Carolina Historical Review* 58 (1981): 327–63.

Bailey, Ann J. "Defiant Unionists: Militant Germans in Confederate Texas." In *Guerrillas, Unionists, and Violence on the Confederate Home Front.* Edited by Daniel E. Sutherland. Fayetteville: University of Arkansas Press, 1999.

———. "In the Far Corner of the Confederacy: A Question of Conscience for German-Speaking Texans." In *Southern Families at War: Loyalty and Conflict in the Civil War South.* Edited by Catherine Clinton. New York: Oxford University Press, 2000.

Bailey, Fred Arthur. *Class and Tennessee's Confederate Generation.* Chapel Hill: University of North Carolina Press, 1987.

Bardolph, Richard. "Confederate Dilemma: North Carolina Troops and the Desertion Problem." *North Carolina Historical Review* 66 (January–April 1989): 61–86, 179–210.

Basler, Roy, ed. *The Collected Works of Abraham Lincoln.* 9 vols. New Brunswick, NJ: Rutgers University Press, 1953.

Bearss, Edwin C. "The Civil War Comes to Indian Territory, 1861: The Flight of Opothleyoholo." *Journal of the West* 11 (1972): 9–42.

Beringer, Richard, et al. *Why the South Lost the Civil War.* Athens: University of Georgia Press, 1984.

Berkin, Carol. *A Brilliant Solution: Inventing the American Constitution.* New York: Harcourt, 2002.

Blassingame, John W. *The Slave Community: Plantation Life in the Antebellum South.* New York: Oxford University Press, 1979.

Boatner, Mark M., III. *The Civil War Dictionary.* New York: Vintage, 1991.

Boritt, Gabor S., ed. *Why the Civil War Came.* New York: Oxford University Press, 1996.

————, ed. *Why the Confederacy Lost.* New York: Oxford University Press, 1992.

Bowers, Claude G. *The Party Battles of the Jackson Period.* New York: Octagon Books, 1965.

Bowman, John S., ed. *The Civil War: Day by Day.* New York: Barnes and Noble, 1996.

Brandon, William. *The American Heritage Book of Indians.* Edited by Alvin M. Josephy Jr. New York: Bonanza Books, 1982.

Bray, John. "My Escape from Richmond." *Harper's Magazine* (April 1864): 662–65.

Britton, Wiley. *The Union Indian Brigade in the Civil War.* Kansas City, MO: Franklin Hudson, 1922.

Brock, Peter. *Pacifism in the United States from the Colonial Era to the First World War.* Princeton, NJ: Princeton University Press, 1968.

Bryan, Charles F., Jr. "A Gathering of Tories: The East Tennessee Convention of 1861." *Tennessee Historical Quarterly* 39 (1980): 27–48.

————. "Tories Amidst Rebels: Confederate Occupation of East Tennessee." *East Tennessee Historical Society's Publications* 60 (1988): 3–22.

Buenger, Walter L. *Secession and the Union in Texas.* Austin: University of Texas Press, 1984.

Bynum, Victoria E. *The Free State of Jones: Mississippi's Longest Civil War.* Chapel Hill: University of North Carolina Press, 2001.

Castel, Albert. "The Guerrilla War, 1861–1865." *Civil War Times Illustrated* 13 (October 1974): 4–50.

Catton, Bruce. *The Coming Fury.* Garden City, NY: Doubleday, 1961.

————. *Never Call Retreat.* Garden City, NY: Doubleday, 1965.

————. *Terrible Swift Sword.* Garden City, NY: Doubleday, 1963.

Ceplair, Larry, ed. *The Public Years of Sarah and Angelina Grimké: Selected Writings 1835–1839.* New York: Columbia University Press, 1989.

Chesnut, Mary Boykin. *A Diary from Dixie.* Edited by Ben Ames Williams. Boston: Houghton Mifflin, 1949.

Chesson, Michael B. "Harlots or Heroines? A New Look at the Richmond Bread Riot." *Virginia Magazine of History and Biography* 92 (April 1984): 131–75.

Childs, William Talbott. *John McDonogh: His Life and Work.* Baltimore: Meyer and Thalheimer, 1939.

Christopher, Maurine. *Black Americans in Congress*. New York: Crowell, 1976.

Clark, Carter Blue. "Opothleyahola and the Creeks During the Civil War." In *Indian Leaders: Oklahoma's First Statesmen*. Edited by H. Glenn Jordan and Thomas M. Holm. Oklahoma City: Oklahoma Historical Society, 1979.

Cleaves, Freeman. *Rock of Chickamauga: The Life of General George H. Thomas*. Norman: University of Oklahoma Press, 1948.

Clinton, Catherine, ed. *Southern Families at War: Loyalty and Conflict in the Civil War South*. New York: Oxford University Press, 2000.

Cole, Donald B. *The Presidency of Andrew Jackson*. Lawrence: University of Kansas Press, 1993.

Connelly, Thomas L. *Civil War Tennessee: Battles and Leaders*. Knoxville: University of Tennessee Press, 1979.

Cooper, Michael. *From Slave to Civil War Hero: The Life and Times of Robert Smalls*. New York: Lodestar Books, 1994.

Cornish, Dudley Taylor. *The Sable Arm: Negro Troops in the Union Army, 1861–1865*. New York: Longmans, Green and Co., 1956.

Coulter, E. Merton. *The Confederate States of America 1861–1865*. Baton Rouge: Louisiana State University Press, 1950.

———. *William G. Brownlow: Fighting Parson of the Southern Highlands*. Knoxville: University of Tennessee Press, 1971.

Cozzens, Peter. *No Better Place to Die*. Urbana: University of Illinois, 1990.

Crawford, Martin. *Ashe County's Civil War: Community and Society in the Mountain South*. Charlottesville: University Press of Virginia, 2001.

Current, Richard N. "God and the Strongest Battalions." In *Why the North Won the Civil War*. Edited by David H. Donald. Baton Rouge: Louisiana State University Press, 1960.

———. *The Lincoln Nobody Knows*. New York: McGraw-Hill, 1958.

———. *Lincoln's Loyalists: Union Soldiers from the Confederacy*. Boston: Northeastern University Press, 1992.

Curry, Richard O. *A House Divided: A Study in Statehood Politics and the Copperhead Movement in West Virginia*. Pittsburgh: University of Pittsburgh Press, 1964.

Davis, Burke. *Gray Fox: Robert E. Lee and the Civil War*. New York: Random House, 1956.

Davis, William C. *Rebels and Yankees: The Commanders of the Civil War*. London: Chrysalis Books, 2004.

Debo, Angie. *The Road to Disappearance*. Norman: University of Oklahoma Press, 1941.

Degler, Carl N. *The Other South*. New York: Harper & Row, 1974.

Dodge, David. "The Cave-Dwellers of the Confederacy." *Atlantic Monthly* (1891): 514–21.

Dodge, Grenville. *The Battle of Atlanta, and Other Campaigns.* Council Bluffs, IA: Monarch Printing Company, 1910.

Donald, David H. "Died of Democracy." In *Why the North Won the Civil War.* Edited by David H. Donald. Baton Rouge: Louisiana State Press, 1960.

———. *Lincoln's Herndon.* New York: Da Capo, 1989.

Doran, Michael F. "Population Statistics of Nineteenth Century Indian Territory." *Chronicles of Oklahoma* 53 (1975): 492–515.

Downey, Fairfax. "The Blue, the Gray, and the Red: Indians in the War." *Civil War Times Illustrated* 1, no. 4 (1962): 7–9, 28–30.

Drake, Richard B. *A History of Appalachia.* Lexington: University Press of Kentucky, 2001.

Dyer, Thomas G. *Secret Yankees: The Union Circle in Confederate Atlanta.* Baltimore: Johns Hopkins University Press, 1999.

Ellis, Daniel. *The Thrilling Adventures of Daniel Ellis: The Great Union Guide of East Tennessee for a Period of Nearly Four Years During the Great Southern Rebellion.* New York: Harper, 1867.

Ellis, Richard E. *The Union at Risk: Jacksonian Democracy, States' Rights, and the Nullification Crisis.* New York: Oxford University Press, 1987.

Escott, Paul. *After Secession: Jefferson Davis and the Failure of Confederate Nationalism.* Baton Rouge: Louisiana State University Press, 1978.

Faust, Drew Gilpin. "Altars of Sacrifice: Confederate Women and the Narratives of War." In *Divided Houses: Gender and the Civil War.* Edited by Catherine Clinton and Nina Silber. New York: Oxford University Press, 1992.

Fisher, Noel C. *War at Every Door: Partisan Politics and Guerrilla Violence in East Tennessee, 1860–1869.* Chapel Hill: University of North Carolina Press, 1997.

Fleming, Walter L. *Civil War and Reconstruction in Alabama.* New York: Peter Smith, 1949.

Foner, Eric. "The South's Inner Civil War." *American Heritage* 40 (1989): 47–56.

Foote, Shelby. *The Civil War: A Narrative.* Vol. 1, *Fort Sumter to Perryville.* New York: Random House, 1958.

Ford, Lacy. "James Louis Petrigu: The Last South Carolina Federalist." In *Intellectual Life in Antebellum Charleston.* Edited by Michael O'Brien and David Moltke-Hansen. Knoxville: University of Tennessee Press, 1986.

Franks, Kenny A. "Operations Against Opothleyahola, 1861." *Military History of Texas and the Southwest* 10 (1972): 187–96.

———. *Stand Watie and the Agony of the Cherokee Nation.* Memphis: Memphis State University Press, 1979.

Freehling, William W. "The Divided South, Democracy's Limitations, and the Causes of the Peculiarly North American Civil War." In *Why the Civil War Came.* Edited by Gabor S. Boritt. New York: Oxford University Press, 1996.

———. *The Road to Disunion*. Vol. 1, *Secessionists at Bay, 1776–1854*. New York: Oxford University Press, 1990.

———. *The South vs. the South: How Anti-Confederate Southerners Shaped the Course of the Civil War*. New York: Oxford University Press, 2001.

Gaines, W. Craig. *The Confederate Cherokees: John Drew's Regiment of Mounted Rifles*. Baton Rouge: Louisiana State University Press, 1989.

Gallagher, Gary W. *The Confederate War*. Cambridge, MA: Harvard University Press, 1997.

Glatthaar, Joseph T. "Black Glory: The African-American Role in Union Victory." In *Why the Confederacy Lost*. Edited by Gabor S. Boritt. New York: Oxford University Press, 1992.

———. *Forged in Battle: The Civil War Alliance of Black Soldiers and White Officers*. Baton Rouge: Louisiana State University Press, 2000.

Glazier, Willard W. *The Capture, the Prison Pen, and the Escape*. Hartford, CT: Goodwin, 1867.

Grimsley, Mark. *The Hard Hand of War: Union Military Policy Towards Southern Civilians, 1861–1865*. New York: Cambridge University Press, 1995.

Groce, W. Todd. *Mountain Rebels: East Tennessee Confederates and the Civil War, 1860–1870*. Knoxville: University of Tennessee Press, 1999.

Guelzo, Allen C. *Abraham Lincoln: Redeemer President*. Michigan: Eerdmans, 1999.

Hall, James O. "The Shelton Laurel Massacre: Murder in the North Caroline Mountains." *Blue and Gray Magazine* 8 (1991): 20–26.

Hamilton, Joseph. "The Heroes of America." *Publications of the Southern History Association*. 40 (1907): 10–19.

Hauptman, Laurence M. *Between Two Fires: American Indians in the Civil War*. New York: Free Press, 1995.

Hearn, Chester G. *Admiral David Glasgow Farragut: The Civil War Years*. Annapolis: U.S. Naval Institute Press, 1998.

Hesseltine, William Best. *Civil War Prisons: A Study in War Psychology*. New York: Ungar, 1964.

Hoole, William Stanley. *Alabama Tories: The First Alabama Cavalry, U.S.A, 1862–1865*. Tuscaloosa, AL: Confederate Publishing, 1960.

Horst, Samuel. *Mennonites in the Confederacy: A Study in Civil War Pacifism*. Scottsdale, PA: Herald Press, 1967.

Horton, James Oliver, and Lois E. Horton. *Slavery and the Making of America*. New York: Oxford University Press, 2005.

Humphrey, Steve. *That Damned Brownlow*. Boone, NC: Appalachian , 1978.

Inscoe, John C., and Gordon B. McKinney. *The Heart of Confederate Appalachia: Western North Carolina in the Civil War*. Chapel Hill: University of North Carolina Press, 2000.

————, and Robert C. Kenzer, eds. *Enemies of the Country: New Perspectives on Unionists in the Civil War South*. Athens: University of Georgia Press, 2001.

Jordan, Terry G. *German Seed in Texas Soil: Immigrant Farmers in Nineteenth-Century Texas*. Austin: University of Texas Press, 1966.

Josephy, Alvin M., Jr. *500 Nations: An Illustrated History of North American Indians*. New York: Knopf, 1994.

Kelly, James C. "William Gannaway Brownlow, Part 1." *Tennessee Historical Quarterly* 43 (Spring 1984): 25–43.

————. "William Gannaway Brownlow, Part 2." *Tennessee Historical Quarterly* 43 (Summer 1984): 155–72.

Kendall, Lane Carter. "John McDonogh—Slaveowner." *Louisiana Historical Quarterly* 16 (1932): 125–34.

Kruman, Marc C. *Parties and Politics in North Carolina, 1836–1865*. Baton Rouge: Louisiana State University Press, 1983.

Lerner, Gerda. *The Grimké Sisters from South Carolina*. New York: Schocken, 1967.

Leverett, Rudy H. *Legend of the Free State of Jones*. Jackson: University Press of Mississippi, 1984.

Lewis, Charles Lee. *David Glasgow Farragut: Admiral in the Making*. Annapolis: U.S. Naval Institute Press, 1941.

————. *David Glasgow Farragut: Our First Admiral*. Annapolis: U.S. Naval Institute Press, 1943.

Litwack, Leon F. *Been in the Storm So Long: The Aftermath of Slavery*. New York: Random House, 1980.

————. "Many Thousands Gone: Black Southerners and the Confederacy." In *The Old South in the Crucible of War*. Edited by Harry P. Owens and James J. Cooke. Jackson: University Press of Mississippi, 1983.

Lonn, Ella. *Desertion During the Civil War*. 1928. Reprint, Gloucester, MA: Peter Smith, 1966.

————. *Foreigners in the Confederacy*. Gloucester, MA: Peter Smith, 1965.

Lowe, Richard G. "Francis Harrison Pierpont: Wartime Unionist, Reconstruction Moderate." In *The Governors of Virginia 1860–1878*. Edited by Edward Younger. Charlottesville: University Press of Virginia, 1982.

Marten, James. *Texas Divided: Loyalty and Dissent in the Lone Star State, 1856–1874*. Lexington: University Press of Kentucky, 1990.

McCaslin, Richard B. *Tainted Breeze: The Great Hanging at Gainesville, Texas, 1862*. Baton Rouge: Louisiana State University, 1994.

McKenzie, Robert Tracy. *One South or Many? Plantation Belt and Upcountry in Civil War–Era Tennessee*. New York: Cambridge University Press, 1994.

McLoughlin, William G. *After the Trail of Tears: The Cherokees' Struggle for Sovereignty, 1839–1880*. Chapel Hill: University of North Carolina Press, 1993.

McPherson, James M. "American Victory, American Defeat." In *Why the Confederacy Lost*. Edited by Gabor S. Boritt. New York: Oxford University Press, 1992.

———. *Battle Cry of Freedom: The Civil War Era*. New York: Ballantine, 1988.

———. *For Cause and Comrades: Why Men Fought in the Civil War*. New York: Oxford University Press, 1997.

———. *The Negro's Civil War: How American Negroes Felt and Acted During the War for the Union*. New York: Pantheon Books, 1965.

———, and William J. Cooper, eds. *Writing the Civil War: The Quest to Understand*. Columbia: University of South Carolina Press, 1998.

Meserve, John Bartlett. "Chief Opothleyahola." *Chronicles of Oklahoma* 9 (December 1931): 441–50.

Montgomery, Goode. "Alleged Secession of Jones County." *Publications of the Mississippi Historical Society* 8 (1904): 13–22.

Moore, Albert B. *Conscription and Conflict in the Confederacy*. New York: Macmillan, 1924.

Moran, Frank E. "My Escape from Libby Prison." *Century Illustrated Monthly Magazine* (March 1888): 770–90.

Noe, Kenneth W., and Shannon H. Wilson, eds. *The Civil War in Appalachia: Collected Essays*. Knoxville: University of Tennessee Press, 1997.

Oates, Stephen B. *With Malice Toward None: The Life of Abraham Lincoln*. New York: Harper and Row, 1994.

Osher, David, and Peter Wallenstein. "Why the Confederacy Lost: A Review Essay." *Maryland Historical Magazine* 88 (1993): 95–108.

Owens, Harry P., and James J. Cooke, eds. *The Old South in the Crucible of War*. Jackson: University Press of Mississippi, 1983.

Paludan, Phillip Shaw. *Victims: A True Story of the Civil War*. Knoxville: University of Tennessee Press, 1981.

Parker, Sandra V. *Richmond's Civil War Prisons*. Lynchburg, VA: Howard, 1990.

Patton, James Welch. *Unionism and Reconstruction in Tennessee, 1860–1869*. 1934. Reprint, Gloucester, MA: Peter Smith, 1966.

Potter, David M. "Jefferson Davis and the Political Factors in the Confederate Defeat." In *Why the North Won the Civil War*. Edited by David H. Donald. Baton Rouge: Louisiana State University Press, 1960.

Pressly, Thomas J. *Americans Interpret Their Civil War*. New York: Free Press, 1962.

Quarles, Benjamin. "The Abduction of the 'Planter.'" *Civil War History* 4 (1958): 5–10.

———. *The Negro in the Civil War*. 1953. Reprint, New York: Da Capo Press, 1988.

Rable, George C. *Civil Wars: Women and the Crisis of Southern Nationalism*. Chicago: University of Illinois Press, 1989.

———. "'Missing in Action': Women of the Confederacy." In *Divided Houses: Gen-*

der and the Civil War. Edited by Catherine Clinton and Nina Silber. New York: Oxford University Press, 1992.

Rampp, Larry C., and Donald L. Rampp. *The Civil War in Indian Territory*. Austin: University of Texas Press, 1975.

Raper, Horace W. "William W. Holden and the Peace Movement in North Carolina." *North Carolina Historical Review* 31 (1954): 493–516.

Riccards, Michael P. "Lincoln and the Political Question: The Creation of the State of West Virginia." *Presidential Studies Quarterly* 27, no. 3 (Summer 1997): 549–65.

Rice, Otis K. *West Virginia: A History*. Lexington: University Press of Kentucky, 1985.

Robertson, James I., Jr. "Negro Soldiers in the Civil War." *Civil War Times Illustrated* 7, no. 6 (1968): 21–32.

———. *The Stonewall Brigade*. Baton Rouge: Louisiana State University Press, 1963.

Ryan, David D., ed. *A Yankee Spy in Richmond: The Civil War Diary of "Crazy Bet" Van Lew*. Mechanicsburg, PA: Stackpole, 1996.

Sansom, John W. *Battle of Nueces River in Kinney County, Texas, August 10th, 1862*. San Antonio: n.p., 1905.

Silverman, Jason H. "Stars, Bars, and Foreigners: The Immigrant and the Making of the Confederacy." *Journal of Confederate History* 1, no. 2 (Fall 1988): 265–85.

Stampp, Kenneth M. *The Imperiled Union: Essays on the Background of the Civil War*. New York: Oxford University Press, 1980.

Sutcliffe, Andrea, ed. *Mighty Rough Times, I Tell You: Personal Accounts of Slavery in Tennessee*. Winston-Salem, NC: Blair, 2000.

Sutherland, Daniel E., ed. *Guerrillas, Unionists, and Violence on the Confederate Home Front*. Fayetteville: University of Arkansas Press, 1999.

Tatum, Georgia Lee. *Disloyalty in the Confederacy*. 1934. Reprint, Lincoln: University of Nebraska Press, 1999.

Thompson, Wesley S. *"The Free State of Winston": A History of Winston County, Alabama*. Winfield, AL: Pareil Press, 1968.

Trickett, Dean. "The Civil War in Indian Territory, 1862." *Chronicles of Oklahoma* 19, no. 1 (March 1941): 61–77.

Trudeau, Noah Andre. *Like Men of War: Black Troops in the Civil War, 1862–1865*. Boston: Little, Brown and Co, 1998.

Tucker, Glenn. "George H. Thomas: A Personality Profile." *Civil War Times Illustrated* 5 (April 1966): 28–37.

U.S. War Department. *The War of the Rebellion: A Compilation of the Official Records of the Union and Confederate Armies*. 128 vols. Washington, DC: Government Printing Office, 1880–1901.

Uya, Okon Edet. *From Slavery to Public Service: Robert Smalls, 1839–1915*. New York: Oxford University Press, 1971.

Van Horne, Thomas. *The Life of Major-General George H. Thomas*. New York: Scribner, 1882.

Varon, Elizabeth R. *Southern Lady, Yankee Spy: The True Story of Elizabeth Van Lew, A Union Agent in the Heart of the Confederacy*. New York: Oxford University Press, 2003.

Wakelyn, Jon L. *Confederates Against the Confederacy: Essays on Leadership and Loyalty*. Westport, CN: Praeger, 2002.

Wallenstein, Peter. "'Helping to Save the Union': The Social Origins, Wartime Experiences and Military Impact of White Union Troops in East Tennessee." In *The Civil War in Appalachia: Collected Essays*. Edited by Kenneth W. Noe and Shannon H. Wilson Knoxville: University of Tennessee Press, 1997.

Wiley, Bell Irvin. *The Plain People of the Confederacy*. 1943. Reprint, Chicago: Quadrangle Books, 1963.

Williams, R. H. *With the Border Ruffians: Memories of the Far West, 1852–1868*. Edited by E. H. Williams. 1907. Reprint, Lincoln: University of Nebraska Press, 1982.

Wood, Gordon S. *The American Revolution: A History*. New York: Modern Library, 2002.

Wright, Edward Needles. *Conscientious Objectors in the Civil War*. 1931. Reprint, New York: Barnes, 1961.

INDEX

Index